COMPARATIVE PHYSICAL EDUCATION AND SPORT VOLUME 5

Edited by

Eric F. Broom, PhD
University of British Columbia

Roy Clumpner, PhD
Western Washington University

Brian Pendleton, PhD
Vancouver Community College

Carol A. Pooley
Dalhousie University

Human Kinetics Books
Champaign, Illinois

Library of Congress Cataloging-in-Publication Data

International Seminar on Comparative Physical Education
    and Sport (5th : 1986 : University of British Columbia)
    Comparative physical education and sport, volume 5.

    "Proceedings of the Fifth International Seminar on
Comparative Physical Education and Sport, held May 22–31,
1986, at the University of British Columbia, Vancouver,
British Columbia, Canada"—T.p. verso.
    Bibliography: p.
    1. Physical education and training—Congresses.
2. Sports—Congresses. 3. Physical fitness—Congresses.
I. Broom, Eric F. II. Title.
GV205.I623   1986   613.7   87-37821
ISBN 0-87322-124-9

Developmental Editor: Jan Progen, EdD
Production Director: Ernie Noa
Projects Manager: Lezli Harris
Assistant Editor: Phaedra Hise
Copy Editor: Peter Nelson
Proofreader: Laurie McGee
Typesetter: Sonnie Bowman
Text Design: Keith Blomberg
Text Layout: Gordon Cohen
Printed By: Braun-Brumfield, Inc.

ISBN: 0-87322-124-9

Printed in the United States of America

10 9 8 7 6 5 4 3 2 1

Human Kinetics Books
A Division of Human Kinetics Publishers, Inc.
Box 5076, Champaign, IL 61820
1-800-DIAL-HKP
1-800-334-3665 (in Illinois)

Contents

Contributors

Ian H. Andrews
7349 Coronado Drive
Burnaby, BC
Canada V5A 1P9

Richard S. Baka, PhD
Footscray Inst. of Technology
Dept. of Physical Education
P.O. Box 64, Footscray
Victoria, Australia

Gerald V. Barrell
University of Southampton
Marlbrook, Julian Close
Chilworth Southampton
England

Janice A. Beran
Iowa State University
Dept. of Physical Education and
  Leisure Studies
Ames, IA 50011

Edelfrid Buggel, PhD
Staatssekretariat Fur Kirperkultur
  und Sport
1080 Berlin
MohrenstraBe 6
German Democratic Republic

Timothy J.L. Chandler, PhD
Syracuse University
Dept. of Health and Physical Education
820 Comstock Avenue
Syracuse, NY 13244-5040

Xiong Douyin
National Research Institute of Sport
  Science
1 Tiyuguan Road
Beijing, China

Patrick J. Duffy
Thomond College of Education
Castletroy
Limerick, Ireland

Ren Hai
University of Alberta
Dept. of Physical Education and Sport
  Sciences
Edmonton, AB
Canada T6G 2H9

Herbert Haag, PhD
Institut for Sport und
  Sportwissenschaften
Universitat Kiel
OlshausenstraBe 40
2300 Kiel
Federal Republic of Germany

Ken Hardman
University of Manchester
Centre for Physical Education
Oxford Road
Manchester M13 9PL
England

Pawel Kudlorz, PhD
Akademia Wychowania Fizycznego
ul. Wiejska 1
80-336 Gdansk
Poland

Anthony Mallalieu
St. Peter's School, Oldham
Lancs, England

Donna R. Marburger, PhD
University of Wyoming
2315 Springcreek
Laramie, WY 82070

Peter C. McIntosh, PhD
12 Windmill Drive
Leatherhead
Surrey, KT22 8PW
England

Gordon L. Opel
University of Montana
Missoula, MT 59812

Victor E. Peppard
University of South Florida
Division of Language
Tampa, FL 33620

John C. Pooley, PhD
Dalhousie University
School of Recreation, Physical and
  Health Education
Halifax, NS
Canada B3H 3J5

James Riordan, PhD
University of Bradford
The Modern Languages Centre
Bradford, West Yorkshire BD7 1DP
England

Eric D. Saunders, PhD
Ulster University
56 Mullachmore Park
Greenisland, Co. Antrim
Northern Ireland, UK

Joy Standeven, DPhil
Brighton Polytechnic
Chelsea School of Human Movement
Trevin Towers, Gaudick Road
Eastbourne, BN20 7SP
East Sussex, England

Peter Wilfred Sutcliffe
Sports Council
North West Region
Astley House
Quay Street
Manchester M3 4AE
England

Barry Watkin, DL.D.
University of Wollongong
Faculty of Education
New South Wales
Australia

Earle F. Zeigler
Thames Hall
The University of Western Ontario
London, ON
Canada N6A 3K7

Klaus Zieschang, PhD
Universitat Bayreuth
OpernstraBe 22
Postfach 3008
D-8580 Bayreuth
Federal Republic of Germany

Zofia Zukowska, PhD
Dyrektor
Academy of Physical Education
ul. Marymoncka 34
Warszawa, Poland

Presenters

Abderrahim Baria
Universite de Montreal
Department d'Education Physique
Montreal, PQ
Canada H3C 3J1

David Bean, PhD
University of Calgary
Faculty of Physical Education
Calgary, AB
Canada T2N 1N4

Louis W. Burgener, PhD
Retired Professor
Gesellschaftsstr. 81
CH 3012 Berne
Switzerland

Richard Cashman, PhD
School of History
University of New South Wales
P.O. Box 1, Kensington
Australia 2033

Nicole Chevalier, PhD
Universite du Quebec a Montreal
Department de Kinanthropologie
Montreal, PQ
Canada H3C 3P8

Elizabeth Clowes
University of British Columbia
School of Physical Education
Richmond, BC
Canada V7C 4J5

Arnold W. Flath, PhD
Oregon State University
1730 NW 29th
Corvallis, OR 97331

Frank H. Fu, PhD
The Chinese University of Hong Kong
Physical Education Unit
Shatin, Hong Kong

Barbara Humberstone
Southampton University
Department of Physical Education
The University, Highfield
Southampton, Hauts
England SO9 5NH

Bruce Kidd, PhD
University of Toronto
School of Physical and Health
  Education
Toronto, ON
Canada M5S 1A1

George A. Moore, EdD
Vancouver Community College,
  Langara Campus
Vancouver, BC
Canada V5Y 2Z6

Honey W. Nashman, PhD
George Washington University
School of Education and Human
  Development
Washington, DC 20052

Gordon A. Olafson, PhD
University of Windsor
Faculty of Human Kinetics
Windsor, ON
Canada N9B 3P4

João C.J. Piccoli, PhD
Federal University of Pelotas
Department of Physical Education
Rio Grande del sur
Brazil

Willy Pieter, PhD
University of Oregon
Department of PEHMS
Eugene, OR 97403

Alan F. Rustage
Essex University
The Sports Centre
Physical Recreation Department
Wivenhoe Park
Colchester, Essex
England

Luther C. Schwich, PhD
University of West Florida
Department of Health, Leisure, and
  Sports
4455 Yarmouth Place
Pensacola, FL 32514

Darwin M. Semotuik, PhD
University of Western Ontario
Faculty of Physical Education
London, ON
Canada NGA 3K7

Paulette Shafranski, PhD
California State University–Northridge
Department of Physical Education and
  Athletics
Northridge, CA 91330

Gary D. Sinclair, PhD
University of British Columbia
School of Physical Education and
  Recreation
6081 University Boulevard
Vancouver, BC
Canada V6T 1W5

Howard Stidwill, PhD
416 Third Street West
Cornwall, ON
Canada K6J 2P8

William F. Stier, Jr, PhD
State University of New York College at
  Brockport
Physical Education and Sport
Brockport, NY 14420

Dale P. Toohey, PhD
California State University, Long Beach
Department of Physical Education
1250 Bellflower Blvd.
Long Beach, CA 90840

Peter J. Treadwell
South Glamorgan Institute of Higher
  Education
Cyncoed, Cardiff CF2 6XD
S. Wales, UK

Ralph C. Wilcox, PhD
Hofstra University
Department of Health, Physical
  Education, and Recreation
Hempstead, NY 11550

Preface

The Fifth International Symposium on Comparative Physical Education and Sport was held May 26–31, 1986, at the University of British Columbia, Vancouver, Canada. It was attended by 92 delegates from 15 countries: Australia, Brazil, Canada, People's Republic of China, England, Federal Republic of Germany, Portugal, Switzerland, United States of America, and Wales. Of the six populated continents, only Africa was not represented. The members of the Steering Committee were gratified by the wide representation and were particularly pleased to welcome for the first time delegates from the German Democratic Republic and the People's Republic of China.

The Scientific Committee received some 70 abstracts, and 53 papers were accepted for presentation at the Symposium. Subsequently, the Editorial Committee reviewed all papers for publication in the proceedings. Funding limitations prohibited the publication of all papers, and for this we offer sincere apologies. A list of presenters for the papers not reproduced is contained in this volume.

The international Society on Comparative Physical Education and Sport (ISCPES) was pleased to receive best wishes for a successful Symposium from Dr. August Kirsch, President of the International Council of Sport Science and Physical Education (ICSSPE).

During the Symposium, ISCPES's Distinguished Service Awards were presented to Peter C. McIntosh (England) and Uriel Simri (Israel). C. Lynn Vendien Scholarships were awarded to Margo Gee (Canada) and Anthony Mallalieu (England).

Acknowledgments

The International Society on Comparative Physical Education and Sport (ISCPES) wishes to extend its appreciation to the members of the 1986 ISCPES Scientific Committee—Eric F. Broom, University of British Columbia; Roy Clumpner, Western Washington University; and Brian Pendleton, Vancouver Community College—for the rigorous review and selection of abstracts of papers presented at the Symposium. The ISCPES is also grateful to these three and Carol Pooley, Dalhousie University, for the editing of all manuscripts appearing in this publication.

The Society wishes to express its appreciation to the School of Physical Education and Recreation, University of British Columbia, for its cooperation in the organization of the Symposium; and to Timothy J. L. Chandler, Syracuse University, and Ralph C. Wilcox, Hofstra University, for their evaluation of the Symposium program.

The Symposium Steering Committee also wishes to thank the government of Canada (Sport Canada), the Government of British Columbia, the British Council, the University of British Columbia Alumni Association, the Strathcona Trust Fund, and commercial sponsors for their generous support.

PART I

Keynote Addresses

President's Address

The Use and Abuse of Comparative Physical Education and Sport

John C. Pooley

Bad dreams and persistent relatives always keep turning up. Sometimes we learn from their recurrence. I hope the latter is true in this instance, for I seem to keep turning up to comment about method, theory, and, indirectly, scholarship and their interrelationship. However, when Eric Broom, Brian Pendleton, and Roy Clumpner began to review the abstracts for this symposium, they were "amazed how misunderstood our field is" and wrote that "comparison is frequently missing." They believed a definitional paper would therefore be valuable.

In preparing for this address I have looked through the journals we have published and the proceedings from the first two seminars at Wingate and Halifax. Unfortunately, I was not able to review the Minneapolis and Malente Proceedings (though both are to be published this year). I note that my participation in each of these seminars dealt at least in part with method or the status of research. The subjects remain important, however, and following a further suggestion from Eric Broom, I will again address them.

Newcomers to the field of comparative study in a variety of fields will note the continuing debate over methodology in the literature. For example, in comparative education, various methods have been advanced by comparative educators, ranging from the formally structured social science approaches of Holmes, Bereday, Noah, and Eckstein, to the (usually) less formal historical or philosophical approach practiced by Lauwreys, Hans, and Kandel.

A similar debate can also be found in comparative physical education and sport literature. In the *Proceedings from the Second International Seminar on Comparative Physical Education and Sport* (1982), Fu advocated a standardized method of conducting comparative research, whereas Simri stated that many comparative studies actually neglect comparison; Haag claimed that very few comparative studies were truly comparative. Other hybrids are applied to data; there appear frequent references in papers

3

and book reviews and occasional entire papers devoted to methods. The variety of approaches put forward today reflects the progress of methodological considerations in the field of comparative study. This is neither surprising nor unwelcome; other fields engage in the same dialogue. It is precisely this wide variety of approaches in use that is the focus of much debate. Consequently, methodology is dynamic and has become more scientific (meaning that research has become more organized and less biased, more scholarly and less shallow) and more varied.

A critical term for us is *comparative*. Whereas all sciences rely on comparison to advance research and develop theories that, in turn, are tested by subsequent studies, only studies that use data, or address events or issues, from two or more locations are "comparative" in the context of our interest. *Data* refers to elements of, or entire, systems of physical education and sport.

Often, comparativists are eager to determine more about physical education and sport with intent to improve their own practices. How may this occur? Diffusion in sport occurs informally and formally: *informally* through international contests and the bureaucracies that arrange them, through reporting and the analysis of the results by the media, and through international visits by individual clubs; and by such more *formal* means as articles published in national and international sport journals, through research published in scholarly journals, and through papers presented at international symposia.

Diffusion is less possible for physical education except through individual visits, formal papers in scholarly journals, and conferences and symposia. The formal mode brings us here.

This paper examines the considerations important in conducting comparative studies in the field of physical education and sport. A review of the current state of the art is followed by an outline of major methodological issues. Then follow some strategies for improving comparative research and a statement about the scope for comparative research in sport and physical education.

Comparative Physical Education and Sport: The State of the Art

The field of comparative education can be seen as a forerunner to the field of comparative physical education and sport, given its size and the longer time it has been operating. Consequently, certain characteristics have been inherited, including debates concerning methodology, and it seems reasonable to compare these two fields.

The education journals *Comparative Education* and *Comparative Education Review* (British and American journals, respectively) and the journal *Comparative Physical Education and Sport* were examined from the perspective of the methodological approach of each article: social science; historical-philosophical; "area" or "topic" studies that were called "comparative studies"; and miscellaneous studies (studies combining two or more of these approaches, or ones that simply could not be labeled). Percentages of use of the different methodological approaches are shown in Figure 1.

The largest percentage of social science studies was found in *Comparative Physical Education and Sport*. Contributors to *Comparative Education* favored the historical-philosophical method. *Comparative Education Review* was similar to the former in using a social science approach; the historical-philosophical approach was also used, albeit to a lesser extent than the British publication. The small number of contributors in the *Comparative Physical Education and Sport* group offers a unique opportunity for close collaboration between peers, compared to the larger education group. Joint research is more manageable, and methodology can be more easily monitored.

A second finding is the relatively small number of area or topic studies found in all three journals. Whereas a single country, area, or topic study

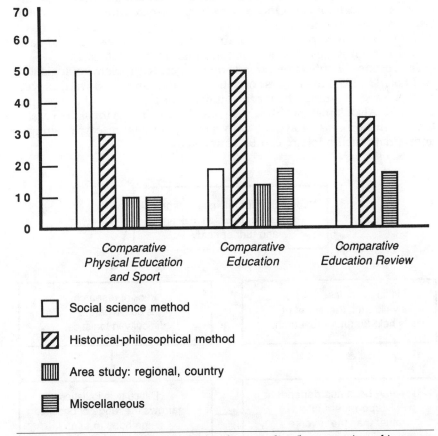

Figure 1. Comparison of methodological approaches (by percent) used in papers found in selected journals of education and physical education and sport (1980-85). *Note.* Selections of book reviews, methodology, and informational sections were excluded.

offers a valid source of information, this approach (not, of course, comparative) is losing ground, probably in part due to the current debate about the need for comparative data.

In the comparative methodology in physical education and sport, there appear to be at least four general weaknesses. In fact, these problems are somewhat cyclical, as illustrated in Figure 2. First, there appears to be an absence of *critical* research, meaning that there are few studies that address current problems and issues in physical education and sport systems and that can be put to practical use in helping to solve problems. Anthony (1982) has pointed out that "if we can show that comparative strategy really helps planners to solve problems and sports administrators to handle their budgets more wisely, the comparative movement will find more bases in higher education and more power to its elbow" (p. 19). Therefore, researchers should consider current issues important in systems and should provide alternative solutions for administrators, politicians, and practitioners. One way to focus research topics on current issues is to ask journal editors to identify themes for specific editions of a journal and invite papers that address them. In this way, a solid base of research on issues, themes, or concepts can be established.

The absence of critical research is due in part to problems of logistics. As I noted in 1981, the process of data collection can be awkward as well as expensive to arrange between countries, or regions, and the people involved. Also, it may not always be possible to arrange for skilled assistance in this process. However, with careful planning, research using an appropriate methodology can be completed.

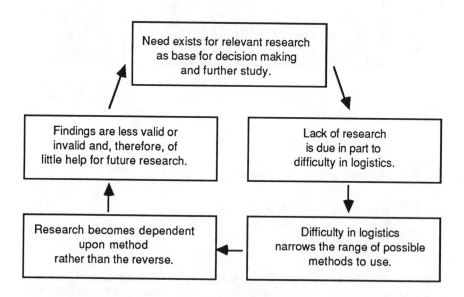

Figure 2. Problems in conducting research in comparative studies in physical education and sport.

Furthermore, perhaps it is the current concern over methodology that leads many authors to seem to be more concerned with "fitting a method" than with choosing an appropriate topic. There appears to be a rather narrow view of methodology: that one must choose one or another approach and complete one's study using only that approach. Instead, authors should be sure of the relevance of their topics and be prepared to apply sound principles of research—including the most appropriate methodology—for that topic.

Finally, related to the need for relevant research, there needs to be more detailed data analysis. That is, not only should the results be presented, they should also be analyzed and interpreted. Details of findings need to be "teased out," so that the answers that the paper seeks to find can be easily understood. In other words, the data analysis should lead to some kind of prediction or statement that can distinguish why the paper was undertaken and how it can contribute to change. A good example of such an analysis can be found in the 1983 paper by DeMartini.

Having read most of the journal papers, there is no question that many strain the imagination, let alone the realism of comparisons. Many authors seem blissfully ignorant of the fundamental notion of comparison, which is that a minimum of *two* phenomena be compared in some way. If we are to keep allowing a single phenomenon to form the basis for description and explanation, we ought to include the term *international* in journal titles.

Methods

Whereas the concept of *sport* needs defining in a general sense, it seems less important to agree on its scope for the purpose of members of this society. The same is true for our understanding of the meaning of the term *physical education*, although this is much easier to define, being the physical activities formally taught or informally practiced in educational institutions. No matter whether sport and physical education are narrowly or broadly defined, each must be defined as specifically as possible in any given study, so that others may interpret the results or conclusions of the study in a meaningful way. Such a practice contributes to our assessment of research; it is either systematic and scholarly, or haphazard and imprecise.

It is very important that—whatever type of methodology is chosen, whether social science, historical, or pedagogical models—the method of analysis must use comparative data. This assumes that at least two units, systems, regions, states, organizations, or institutions are compared. As Farrell has asserted that "there is no such thing as comparative methodology. There are comparative data to which a variety of analytical tools may be applied" (1979, p. 5).

As defined in the *Oxford International Dictionary, comparison* is the bringing together of two or more things for the purpose of noting their similarities and differences. Given this definition, *comparative study* could be defined as the *examination* of two or more phenomena for the purpose of noting their similarities and differences. "Properly done," Noah has said, "comparative study can help us understand better our past, locate ourselves more exactly in the present, and discern a little more clearly what our (educational) future might be" (1984, p. 551).

It has been suggested that three fundamental questions could be considered necessary for undertaking any truly comparative study, regardless of approach. The researcher should address such questions as how two or more phenomena are the same or different, under what conditions they are the same or different, and why they are the same or different.

In a field that is becoming more social-science-oriented, it is perhaps helpful to hear how Shaw (1979) has distinguished the social science approach from the historical-philosophical approach. She has stated that the scientific method creates a hypothesis that is essentially based on theory and seeks to find an explanation. The point of difference is in the use of observation and experimentation to find an explanation, as opposed to the reliance upon a case study, or ethnocentric, approach often found in the historical-philosophical methods. In the field of physical education and sport, two studies that could be compared are those by Beran (1982), and by Jones and Pooley (1982), because they are examples of the different approaches: historical-philosophical and social science, respectively.

The extreme historical approach holds that each system is unique and can therefore be studied only as an individual case. The extreme social science approach, though, holds that research is of little use unless it is empirically based, subjected to sophisticated statistical techniques, and has wide-ranging applications. One implies no order in society and in persons' actions and behaviors; the other implies considerable order. The latter is more likely to lead to theories; the former is less likely. An approach between the two probably would strike a reasonable balance.

Farrell's definition of comparative education may be useful. He claims that "comparative education attempts to study a class of phenomena, usually called *education*, which seek . . . to explain the complex web of interrelationships which can be observed within . . . and between educational systems and other kinds of systems" (1979, p. 5). Farrell's definition is suitable as a basis of understanding, substituting the term *physical education and sport* for *education*.

When the discipline of comparative education was founded in the early 1800s, one of the primary reasons for undertaking such study was not only to learn about other systems of education but also to learn *from* these other systems (Yates, 1984). As comparative education progressed, simple methods of observation led to biases and misrepresentations of other countries and their systems (Bennett, Howell, & Simri, 1983). Later, though, the methods of comparison have become increasingly complicated. It is now deemed necessary to take certain specific considerations into account when doing a comparative research project (Eckstein, 1982).

One of the factors leading to misrepresenting an area being studied is the size of the population from which data are being collected. In order to represent an area or region faithfully, this population must be sizable

(Haag, 1982). That is, it must be large and varied enough to be truly representative of the people of that region. For example, in his article on physical education teachers and professional training programs in Norway, Sweden, and Denmark, Polidoro (1977) used only one institute in each country to represent the entire country. Obviously, this institute may differ in size, affiliation, and representativeness from another in the same country. In such instances, the author should be more explicit.

Size of population is just one factor that must be carefully considered. Race, religious beliefs, and cultural traditions found in the particular society or societies being studied are also important representational factors. It is in regard to these factors that data collection can be a very complicated process. It becomes necessary, then, to take into consideration subtle, as well as obvious, differences between societies or regions.

Confusion increases with a language barrier. If it is very easy to be misled among different English-speaking nations or regions, it is increasingly complicated when studying a country or region where a different language is spoken. It is necessary to be careful in translating the meanings of terms and expressions.

Such care should be extended to religious and cultural values, and also societal behavior patterns. There may be a tendency to assume that what exists at home, exists abroad. Thus, it is necessary to verify one's assumptions (Levine, 1985).

In the light of these factors, the practice of comparative study is difficult. Shortcomings in one's work may exist. Recognizing and accounting for these shortcomings is most important. By one's so doing, the study becomes more credible, and the shortcomings seem less potent. One practices abuse when drawing incorrect conclusions from data or arguing a case for the development of X in country Y on the basis of haphazardly collected, shallow evidence. As Noah has added, there is a danger in trying to find an "easy solution abroad for complex problems at home" (1984, p. 551).

A persistent question in comparative research is whether it is possible to make comparisons based on dissimilar groups, societies, or ideologies. It would seem to be easier if units were fundamentally more alike, because one would not have to account for differences (or similarities) on the basis of inherently diverse fundamental characteristics. For example, it would appear to be "safer" to compare elements of sport in Canada and Australia—given their comparable sizes, climatic extremes, population distributions, political affiliations, past immigration policies and language—rather than two dissimilar nation states, such as the Soviet Union and Japan. Indeed, it *is*! However, because sport *is* compared—both in structure and especially in the outcome of competition—between dissimilar states, one should not avoid comparison, but should take great care in accounting for differences and still learn from this experience.

Once data have been collected with such care, how may they be applied? Should it be quantified or qualified? Howe (1985) has provided a clear explanation of the two different approaches. Whereas the techniques

of participant observation, simple observation, interviewing, or questionnaire may be the same in both quantitative or qualitative studies, a difference occurs in analyzing these results. In simple terms, a qualitative
analysis describes in *words* the outcome of the results, whereas a quantitative analysis describes the same outcome in *numbers*. Further, Howe
claims that words can provide a rich and meaningful explanation "of
processes occurring in the context of everyday life." However, Howe also
admits that words can be "imprecise, ambiguous, or open to multiple
interpretation" (p. 219).

In light of Howe's comments, one should consider the value of both
quantification and qualification, and perhaps realize that it is not always
necessary to limit oneself to one or the other technique. Some years ago
(Pooley, 1979), having recognized the "polar tendencies" involved in
doing so, I believed there was a tendency to ignore the unique social qualities of a region in favor of presenting an objective quantitative analysis.
Likewise, there is a tendency to ignore existing evidence that may be
found in statistical trends and may either further support or refute one's
subjective analysis. Thus, it seems important to consider the value of each
technique.

Somewhat similar to these polar tendencies is the question of whether
to rely on empirical data or theory. Beamish (1982) has asked that the
researcher observe the relationships that exist not only both within and
between individuals and groups but also in facts and theory in a given
study; the researcher can draw his or her own interpretations from these
relationships. He claims it is dangerous to assume that a few facts are
the complete truth just because some theory should be found to support
them, especially in areas that are unfamiliar. Similarly, Silvennonen (1982,
p. 305) has stressed the need to observe theory as well as facts in order
to get an "inside understanding" of the culture being studied.

We might combine these methods; indeed, they are interrelated and
must be considered together. There is a danger in relying solely on theory
found in others' research, because these findings may be inaccurate or
out of date. There is also danger in relying on one's own empirical data,
because such results may have certain shortcomings. Therefore, it is most
beneficial to combine empirical data and theory, using them together,
to more strongly support or refute a particular hypothesis.

How does one decide on the best methodological approach? Should
it be a historical approach or a social science approach? Should the choice
be one method or the other? The article "Comparative Education in
China," by Jing and Zhou (1985), offers interesting comments in answer
to some of these questions in studying a relatively new system of education still in its developing stages. In this respect, the authors note the
huge need for comparative education techniques in their country. They
express strong opinions about the value of the various approaches currently being debated, the benefits and strengths of each method depending on the topic under study. Perhaps in our more developed comparative
education systems it would be wise to listen to these words; that is, we
should be aware of the values and the disadvantages of any particular

methodological approach and be willing to accommodate the strengths of each in our own work, when appropriate. In this way, we do not have to be limited by exclusive reliance on one approach.

Strategies for Improving Comparative Research

It would be interesting to determine why and how scholars become interested in comparative physical education and sport, as demonstrated either by their teaching of comparative courses or involvement in research. Having a lively interest in people and events throughout the world—whether generally, or specifically to sport and physical education or related concepts—is a natural and worthy beginning, but it is not enough to give license to either teach or conduct research in the comparative area. Those who contribute to the growth of our field need to be introduced to examples of good comparative research and then, using such research, learn strategies for comparisons.

Because it is unlikely that there is a sufficient number of scholars interested in comparative methodology in separate universities or even separate countries (a sample of our members' backgrounds would suggest this), why not consider offering a two-day course on comparative methodology and research prior to our next seminar in 1988? The first day could be devoted to an examination of existing models and theories related to the domains of social science, history, and pedagogy (the three major interests of our members); the second day could be devoted to an examination of different methodological approaches, with advantages and disadvantages illustrated.

There are other ways to learn about methods and theories in our field. One is collaborating with a colleague in another country and sharing literature (whether others' or our own). Another way is working on a joint enterprise wherein each study partner contributes to different stages of a single research enterprise, initially in topic agreement, then on theoretical and procedural approaches on data collection, and finally on data analysis and discussion. Other variations of learning from others are obviously possible with some imagination and initiative. The realization of our directory of scholars could be the first step to joint enterprises.

Another would be to spend a sabbatical or a leave with a colleague—during which time a joint piece of research could be attempted—or at an exchange where data can be collected and compared with data earlier or subsequently collected in one's own environment. For those fortunate enough to have graduate students, yet another way to collaborate would be through students' research, either by sending them to complete data collection elsewhere under the guidance of others or by using them as "collectors" connected with one's own research.

A more indirect way to encourage comparative study is to combine the group approach with a journal issue. Let me explain. A small number of interested scholars could be approached to take part in a piece of research based on an agreed-upon question and data collection strategy.

Independent papers could be submitted for publication, thereby safe-guarding the needs of individuals to publish. The scholar(s) who either volunteered or were invited by the editor to formulate the research would analyze the data from respective regions or countries and contribute to the comparative analysis and conclusions. This is a simple, but practical, way to complete comparative research.

As indicated, a variation could be used for our next seminar, with several presentations made in a joint session. The first would address the issue under study and set the scene for research. Then would follow two or three reports of independent data, which would be followed by a comparison of the data, whether cross-national or otherwise. There are several advantages: Such a study would be truly comparative; researchers' costs would be minimal; ideas in this process would be shared; and such an approach is undoubtedly heuristic, that is, it could easily lead to further joint efforts. Finally, for those who have never attempted comparative studies but who are interested in trying, a less formidable way to become involved is through the replication of an existing study.

A serious problem facing potential scholars in our field is the unavailability of graduate schools offering either master's or doctoral programs. Whereas master's students can be accommodated in various institutions in Europe and North America, many are accommodated only due to the interests and energies of just one professor (sometimes two). I am unaware of any comparative work in physical education and sport at the doctoral level, although general comparative education is available at a few institutions. I suspect many people offer comparative courses by inclination, self-training, and subsequent experience, rather than as a result of unique qualifications. I also feel obliged to comment that in an era of reduced budgets, increased specialization, and limited opportunities for faculty growth, the list of elective comparative courses may diminish.

Scope for Comparative Research in Sport and Physical Education

The subject matter of our domain (sport and physical education) has been addressed earlier, and the need for broad definitions of these concepts has been acknowledged. The point I now make is that all propositions using these concepts require comparative treatment (cross-national, cross-cultural, cross-regional, and so on) if we are to fully understand and benefit from a knowledge of what others have, are doing, or are about to do. As in education, so, too, in physical education; as in lifestyle, so, too, in sport—we exist in an increasingly smaller world and, therefore, must be aware of others around us (the best way to understand this phenomenon is by visiting a small island for a short period; within days it becomes "smaller").

When considering sport in particular, and especially elite sport, it is practiced and conceptualized only by comparisons based on regional, cultural, and ideological differences. Therefore, comparisons must be made (cross-nationally or otherwise) if we are to understand the range of possibilities for physical education and sport and, in particular, to find ways to improve our own systems and practices. For example, the current curse of football (soccer) hooliganism can best be explained in cross-national comparison, rather than in studying only a single country. In finding ways to control violence in one country, it would be short-sighted not to examine the ways other countries accommodate fans.

There is a variety of pertinent and persistent issues in physical education and sport from which comparativists can choose. For example, what are the educational merits of compulsory, compared to elective, physical education throughout high school? What are the different effects of concentrating upon intramural, rather than interscholastic, sport in schools on subsequent physical activity levels throughout adulthood? How *can* either competitive program ensure the student's continuing involvement in sport after leaving school, assuming this is considered a desirable objective? How can elements of successful national sport models be implemented by other nations, states, or other definable geographic or political regions within nations? Can international competition in sport contribute to increased cohesion between countries or larger configurations of nations, or does it create more tension? More specifically, which elements improve harmony; which, conflict?

These macro questions can be matched with equally pertinent micro studies, some of which may be significant in their own right or may contribute to larger macro issues. For example, a study of two high schools representing different political, social, or geographical groups can provide clues for more broadly based groups. Similarly, an examination of the types and extent of sport offerings in two communities in the same state, province, or country can reveal valuable insights for more extensive studies using larger configurations of groups, as well as being valid and useful in their own right. I recently visited a high school in Tasmania in which there was no interscholastic sport. It was on the north coast and was surrounded by more traditional schools that competed against each other and other schools elsewhere in the state. It would be revealing to determine what effect, if any, this omission had on sport and physical activity practices of the school population during and after school and whether there was an impact on school spirit and academic work.

Using another tack, it requires little detective work to reveal serious physical education and sport problems in discrimination, morality, and elitism. These and other problems are waiting to be investigated.

The rich sources of data available in our field must be exploited. Data banks on sport are available; information retrieval systems have become very sophisticated; opportunities for collaboration are increasingly possible, resulting from the proliferation of national and international meetings; and there is an increase in the number of journals and texts that, in whole or part, are devoted to comparative studies. The way ahead looks promising.

In discussing current issues in comparative physical education and sport, one further issue arises: the scope of the field. It is apparent that research interests encompass three major groups of scholars: sociologists, historians, and pedagogists (the physical sciences are not included). This fact is supported by reviewing the 1978, 1980, and 1982 international seminars. Although the seminar in 1982 included papers from the physical sciences, they did not receive an overwhelmingly enthusiastic response.

In summary, when considering the scope of our field, members' interests are the best guide. Because social scientists, historians, and pedagogists have almost exclusively represented the membership since Wingate in 1978, such foci ought to prevail until, or unless, members' interests change. Consequently, it would seem reasonable that the editor of our journal and the program committee of our next seminar continue to be guided by members' interests and that, should a researcher outside these domains submit an article for publication or presentation, it be rejected. Naturally, if interests of members change, then also ought the research published and papers delivered change in focus. The focus of interest is therefore naturally, rather than artificially, circumscribed.

Conclusions

One of Noah's remarks seems appropriate for closing: "With all its problems, comparative study is a most desirable way of approaching an understanding of (physical) education and sport. The challenge is to do it in ways that are valid, persuasive, practically usable, and, above all, enlightening" (1984, p. 561). Certainly the field of comparative physical education and sport, still in its developing stages, has in it some dedicated and talented comparative researchers. Judging from our activities since 1978, our field will continue to grow and benefit physical education and sport in many societies. One last point: Apart from extending the quantity and quality of research in our own journal, our visibility and status would increase immeasurably if members published comparative papers in journals representing the parent disciplines.

We have an important task ahead. The institutions of sport and physical education exist in other institutions and systems both within and between countries. It seems incredibly parochial and, therefore, limiting in the extreme if future teachers, coaches, administrators, and officials being formally educated in tertiary institutions are denied the benefit of cross-national and cross-cultural insights. It is our responsibility to provide these insights.

Acknowledgment

My thanks to one of my students, Sandy Gillis, for help in preparing this manuscript.

References

Anthony, D. (1982). Current issues and trends in comparative physical education and sport. *Comparative Physical Education and Sport*, 2(10), 4-20.

Beamish, R. (1982). A critical examination of epistemological limitations to the positivist approach to comparative sport study. In J.C. Pooley & C.A. Pooley (Eds.), *Proceedings from the Second International Seminar on Comparative Physical Education and Sport* (pp. 131-162). Halifax, NS: Dalhousie University

Bennett, B., Howell, M., & Simri, U. (1983). *Comparative physical education and sport* (2nd ed.). Philadelphia: Lea and Febiger.

Beran, J.A. (1982). Primary school physical education in the Philippines and Nigeria. In J.C. Pooley & C.A. Pooley (Eds.), *Proceedings from the Second International Seminar on Comparative Physical Education and Sport* (pp. 163-171). Halifax, NS: Dalhousie University.

DeMartini, J.R. (1983). Sociologists working in applied settings. *Sociological Perspectives*, **26**, 341-351.

Eckstein, M. (1982). Comparative methodology from the perspective of comparative education. In J.C. Pooley & C.A. Pooley (Eds.), *Proceedings from the Second International Seminar on Comparative Physical Education and Sport* (pp. 375-394). Halifax, NS: Dalhousie University.

Farrell, J.P. (1979, February). The necessity of comparison in the study of education: The salience of science and the problems of comparability. *Comparative Education Review*, pp. 3-16.

Haag, H. (1982). Research methodology in sport science: Implications for the comparative research approach. In J.C. Pooley & C.A. Pooley (Eds.), *Proceedings from the Second International Seminar on Comparative Physical Education and Sport* (pp. 89-110). Halifax, NS: Dalhousie University.

Howe, C.Z. (1985). Possibilities for using a qualitative research approach in the sociological study of leisure. *Journal of Leisure Research*, **17**, 212-224.

Jing, S.B., & Zhou, N.Z. (1985). Comparative education in China. *Comparative Education Review*, **29**, 240-250.

Jones, G., & Pooley, J.C. (1982). Cheating in sport: A comparison of attitudes toward cheating of Canadian and British rugby players. In M.L. Krotee & E.M. Jaeger, (Eds.), *Proceedings from the Third International Seminar on Comparative Physical Education and Sport* (pp. 335-345). Champaign, IL: Human Kinetics.

Levine, R. (1985, December). It wasn't the time of my life. *Discover*, pp. 66-67.

Noah, H.J. (1984). The use and abuse of comparative education. *Comparative Education Review*, **28**, 550-562.

Polidoro, J.R. (1977). Professional preparation programs of physical education teachers in Norway, Sweden, and Denmark. *Research Quarterly*, **48**, 640-646.

Pooley, J.C. (1979). Quantitative and qualitative analysis in comparative physical education and sport. In U. Simri (Ed.), *Comparative Physical Education and Sport: Proceedings from an International Seminar* (pp. 83-93). Netanya, Israel: Wingate Institute for Physical Education and Sport.

Pooley, J.C. (1981). Comparative physical education and sport: Background, problems, and prospects. *Comparative Physical Education and Sport,* 1(6), 4-13.

Pooley, J.C., & Pooley, C.A. (Eds.) (1982). *Proceedings from the Second International Seminar on Comparative Physical Education and Sport* (p. 507). Halifax, NS: Dalhousie University.

Shaw, S. (1979). The scientific approach to comparative sport and physical education. In R. Howell, M.L. Howell, D.P. Toohey, & D.M. Toohey (Eds.), *Methodology in comparative physical education and sport* (pp. 166-188). Champaign, IL: Stipes.

Silvennonen, M. (1982). Some views of the development of qualitative research methodology in the comparative study of physical education and sport. In J.C. Pooley & C.A. Pooley (Eds.), *Proceedings from the Second International Seminar on Comparative Physical Education and Sport* (pp. 305-322). Halifax, NS: Dalhousie University.

Simri, U. (Ed.) (1979). *Comparative Physical Education and Sport: Proceedings of an International Seminar* (pp. 228). Netanya, Israel: Wingate Institute for Physical Education and Sport.

Yates, B.A. (1984). Comparative education and the third world: The nineteenth century revisited. *Comparative Education Review,* 28, 533-549.

University of British Columbia Alumni Association Lecture
Politics and Sport: Uniformity and Diversity

Peter C. McIntosh

The argument of my address today is that the growth of international sport has been accompanied by standardization of practice and structure within nations and between nations, that important features of this standardization are political influence and political control, and that the diversity of structure and practice that still remains is under threat.

First, I want to limit my use of the term *politics*. Politics, in a general sense, is about power: who has it, how it is obtained, and how it is exercised. Every social organization has a power structure: It is possible to study and analyze the politics of the family, the church, industry, or, of course, sport. Aristotle, however, originally used the term with reference to the *polis*, or city-state, that he knew, then the repository of ultimate power. *Political* in this sense means almost the same as *governmental*. Today there are few, if any, city-states such as Aristotle analyzed, but governments as repositories of ultimate power there certainly are. In this address I shall use the terms *politics* and *political* in the narrow Aristotelian sense.

Ancient Precedents

The city-states of Aristotle's time fostered drama, religion, athletics, and political activity. Archeological remains show a striking similarity at different sites in Olympia, Athens, Epidaurus, Nemea, Aargos, Delphi, and elsewhere between theaters, temples, and athletic stadia. The stadia are all approximately 200 meters long, and the athletic contests were standardized. The Greeks were under no illusion that politics and sport were separate. Indeed, at Athens, Alcibiades claimed that his victories in the Olympic chariot races in 416 B.C. entitled him to political appointment as one of the generals in the military expedition against Syracuse. He was appointed. The expedition was a disaster, from which you may draw what conclusions you like.

When Philip of Macedon conquered the city-states and his son Alexander the Great extended his empire to the River Indus, Greek stadia and their standardized athletic program were spread throughout the eastern Mediterranean region. The government of the Roman Empire perpetuated the Olympic and other Games for more than 2 centuries in the East; while in the Western empire, the Flavian Amphitheater—or Colosseum— constructed at Rome in A.D. 80, was replicated on a smaller scale in many other cities.

The collapse of the Roman Empire, with its municipal system, and the rise of a feudal system, largely tribal in character, gave rise to games and sports of great variety throughout Europe. Only the sports of ruling aristocracy, such as the martial sports, the tournament, fencing, and the game of royal tennis, were standardized.

Government of Modern Sport

It was in the 19th century that the standardization of modern sports within nations and, later, between nations took place. At first this process excited neither the interest nor the intervention of governments. This intervention came later. Table 1 shows the dates when governing bodies of selected sports were established in different countries. It seems that a certain level of industrialization, together with the development of railways and a communications system, were prerequisites. Britain was ahead in organizing and standardizing sports, but not by many years.

Although international governing bodies or federations were generally not established until the 20th century, there was a measure of international standardization through the influence of the governing body in the country from which the game or sport was exported. Two codes of football were exported from Britain in the late 19th century: the handling game of rugby to countries where Britons went to live and to dominate—Australia, South Africa, New Zealand, and Canada; and the kicking game of soccer to

Table 1   Dates of Foundation of National Sports Associations

Sport	Germany	U.S.A.	Sweden	Britain	Canada
Association football	1900	—	1904	1863	1880
Swimming	1887	1878	1904	1869	1894
Cycling	1884	1880	1900	1878	1880
Rowing	1883	1872	1904	1879	1880
Skating	1888	1888	1904	1879	1878
Athletics	1898	1888	1895	1880	1884
Lawn tennis	1902	1881	1906	1886	1894
Skiing	1904	1904	1908	1903	1921

countries where Britons went to trade in Europe and South America, or to exploit the native population without taking up permanent residence, as in Africa and Asia. In the United States, and later in Canada, the British game was soon modified to become a peculiarly North American game.

Many other games and sports came from Britain and were similarly standardized from there. Table 2 shows the dates at which some of these sports were formally organized under governing bodies. The Football Association (1863) was the first significant modern sports association with a democratic electoral constitution. Earlier bodies, such as the Jockey Club, were private, exclusive, and self-appointing bodies that exercised authority over their sports through the social prestige of their members.

It is of interest that when de Coubertin, who was a confessed Anglophile, set up the International Olympic Committee, he chose as his model not the new democratic associations but the constitutions of the older, aristocratic, self-appointed clubs. He specified the organizing body of the Henley Royal Regatta as his model. The International Sports Federations followed the electoral systems of the national associations.

Table 2 The Organization of Sport in Great Britain

Sport	Earliest national organization	Date
Horse racing	Jockey Club	c. 1750
Golf	Royal and Ancient Golf Club	1754
Cricket	Marylebone Cricket Club	1788
Mountaineering	Alpine Club	1857
Association football	Football Association	1863
Swimming	Amateur Metropolitan Swimming Association	1869
Rugby football	Rugby Football Union	1871
Sailing	Yacht Racing Association	1875
Cycling	Bicyclists' Union	1878
Skating	National Skating Association	1879
Rowing	Metropolitan Rowing Association	1879
Boxing	Amateur Boxing Association	1879
Athletics	Amateur Athletic Association	1880
	Amateur Athletic Club	1866
Hockey	Hockey Association	1886
Lawn tennis	Lawn Tennis Association	1888
Badminton	Badminton Association	1895
Fencing	Amateur Fencing Association	1898

Early Years of International Sports

The International Olympic Committee (IOC) was set up in Paris in 1894 to organize Olympic Games. There had been Games that had called themselves Olympic in Sweden, in Britain, and elsewhere, but they never commanded extensive support even in their own countries and were certainly not international in character. The IOC from the beginning aimed at international status and an international athletic festival for which, of course, standardization of sport within participating countries was essential. The enterprise nearly foundered at the outset, but succeeded because de Coubertin obtained the support of the Greek government. The prime minister was opposed to holding the Games in Athens, but de Coubertin used his contact with the Crown Prince and the King to overcome political opposition and then to secure the support of the succeeding prime minister.

Two problems beset the Olympic Movement in its early years. The first was the question of amateurism. The international congress at the Sorbonne in 1894 from which the IOC sprung had been summoned to reach agreement on what or who was an amateur sportsman. It was only partially successful. The concept of amateurism in sport was derived from the British class system of the 19th century. The system was imperfectly understood elsewhere and was not fully accepted as a uniform basis for sport even in Britain. Whatever definition of amateurism was devised by the IOC, and later by the international federations of sport, the different interpretations in different countries effectively prevented standardization for nearly a century.

In 1976 the IOC abandoned the term *amateur*, but hoped to retain the ideal of sport for sport's sake by means of its rule 26 on eligibility. Different sports and different national governing bodies still frustrated a uniform application of the rule on eligibility. Although the government of the U.S.S.R. gave way on cash payments to athletes and discontinued them when it joined the IAAF in 1947 and the Olympic Movement in 1951, state support of elite athletes continued and was never a secret. Since then many other countries and their national Olympic committees (NOCs) have moved in the same direction.

The second problem, the national identity of competitors, did attract the interest of governments, unlike the first problem. The identity problem arose in preparations for the Olympic Games of 1908. Briefly, the question was whether the constituent parts of the great empires of Germany, Austria-Hungary, and Britain should be allowed to enter separate teams. Germany raised no objection to the British Dominions entering their own teams, but the United States did object. The storm broke in 1912. A number of NOCs had been set up in countries that were not politically independent. Bohemia (Czechoslovakia) and Hungary were part of the Austro-Hungarian Empire; Finland was a province of Russia, and so was Poland; Ireland was part of the United Kingdom. A number of ad hoc decisions were taken amid a flurry of diplomatic activity, which resulted in some curious incidents, such as the hoisting of the Russian flag alongside the flag of Finland for a victory ceremony. It was the only time that the Russian flag was hoisted.

The underlying principle that de Coubertin tried to apply was that "sports geography" had an undeniable existence and was quite distinct from "political geography" (1977, p. 562). The principle was not always accepted. Finland was struck off the list of Olympic nations in 1914, but returned in 1920 (Olympic Review 1976). The IOC has tried to apply sports geography at variance with political geography to the organization of the Olympic Games on a number of occasions since 1912, notably in dealing with the problem of two Germanies and the problem of two Chinas.

Two Germanies

At the end of World War II, Germany was divided into four zones of occupation; before long the three zones occupied by Britain, France, and the United States became the Federal Republic of Germany, and the Russian zone became the German Democratic Republic. Germany was not invited to take part in the Olympic Games of 1948, on the ground that there was no National Olympic Committee to invite. In 1949 the Federal Republic set up such a Committee, which was recognized by the IOC in 1950. The Democratic Republic set up its Committee in 1951, but the Federal Republic's Committee claimed to represent all Germans, including those in the "Soviet-occupied zone."

The IOC refused either to adopt the political stand of NATO and recognize only the Republic or to accept the Democratic Republic as an independent state. Instead, the IOC tried to apply sports geography and create one nation, or at least one national team. After initial success, the Democratic Republic withdrew, and only athletes from the Federal Republic took part in the Olympic Games at Helsinki in 1952.

In the Games of 1956 and 1960, however, a unified team from both Germanies participated and the president of the IOC said in a speech:

Another example of an important victory for sport over politics has been the united German team that has now appeared on four different occasions at the Olympic Games in 1956 and in 1960. . . . The spectacle of East and West German athletes in the same uniform marching behind the same leaders and the same flag is an inspiration under present political conditions and a great service to all the German people who wish for a united people. (Brundage, cited in Guttmann, 1984)

This statement amounts to a hope that political geography could be induced through sport to conform to sports geography.

The hope evaporated in 1964, though, when the IAAF recognized two Germanies and allowed both to compete in the European Championships in 1966. In the Olympic Games of 1968, two separate teams competed, but under the same flag and using the same anthem. By 1972 sports geography had completely given way to political geography.

Two Chinas

In 1949 civil war in China ended with Communists under Mao Tse-tung in control of the mainland and nationalists under Chiang Kai-shek in Taiwan. Each government claimed jurisdiction over the whole of China, and each territory had its own NOC claiming to represent all Chinese citizens. The IOC refused to recognize either NOC but permitted athletes from anywhere in China to compete in the Olympic Games in Helsinki. Forty-one athletes arrived 10 days late from People's Republic on the mainland, but none competed.

Preceding the Olympic Games in 1956 at Melbourne, there was a vitriolic correspondence between the president of the IOC and the NOC of the People's Republic, which was demanding the exclusion and expulsion of Taiwan's NOC. It ended with the withdrawal of the People's Republic from the IOC and also from many international sports federations.

The Taiwanese took part in the Olympic Games in 1960 at Rome under the name *Taiwan*, instead of *Republic of China*. At this time the president of the IOC stated that the IOC did not deal with governments and that NOCs represented geographical areas in which they operate "about which there can be no dispute" (Brundage, cited in Guttmann, 1984). Guttmann (1984) has pointed out that this had ceased to be a very helpful distinction, because the IOC dealt only with geographical areas that had governments. In 1976 the name of the Taiwanese team was again in dispute, now between the IOC and the Canadian government. The government won, and the Taiwanese did not compete.

In 1976, too, the IOC had another opportunity to assert the supremacy of sports geography when a Guyanan athlete, whose NOC had withdrawn from the Olympic Games under political pressure, applied for entry as a stateless individual. His application was rejected, and sports geography was thus further discredited as a viable alternative to political geography.

The problem of two Koreas is curiously different in that governments are trying to persuade the IOC to reorganize the Olympic Games of 1988 according to sports geography, rather than political geography. In January 1986 the issue was still in doubt.

Two Irelands

There are very few examples of sports geography superseding political geography, but one does exist in a most unlikely area, where international dissension is bitter and political dispute is carried on with violence and terror. The Irish Rugby Football Union (RFU) has jurisdiction over the whole island—both the autonomous Republic of Ireland and Northern Ireland, which is a province of the United Kingdom. Furthermore, the Union has four branches; its northern branch, Ulster, incorporates areas both inside and outside the political province of Ulster, or Northern Ireland. The clubs of the RFU and the Union itself embrace both Protestants and Catholics; the RFU has successfully resisted attempts by the IRA to divide it along sectarian lines. Whether the organization of rugby football in Ireland is an exception that proves the rule or provides a model for imitation in the future are questions that deserve further study.

Governments and Nongovernmental Organizations

The interest and intervention of governments in international sport has increased greatly since de Coubertin enlisted the support of the Greek government in his revival of the Olympic Games. The British government set a precedent in 1926 when it entered a Royal Air Force team flying Royal Air Force planes in the Schneider Cup Air Race and won.

The Olympic Games in 1936 in Berlin and the events leading up to them afforded the German government an opportunity to use international sport to promote its policies, its image, and its ideology. Mandell (1971) assessed the successes and failures of the German government in exploiting the Games for political purposes. Hitler was forced to make some concessions on the composition of the German Olympic Committee and on his anti-Semitic campaign. The Nazi myth of Nordic superiority was destroyed by the performances of Jesse Owens and other blacks. However, Germany won more medals than any other nation, and the prestige of the German government and nation was enhanced more than it was damaged.

After World War II, governments had their own international organization in the form of the United Nations and its agencies. From 1952 one of these agencies, UNESCO, began to take an interest in sport and physical education. Its activities and studies at first concerned education and mass sport, but in 1975 UNESCO called a worldwide conference of ministers of sport, which set up a permanent committee of 30 member states to promote physical education and sport. This body had an obvious appeal to the third world that the IOC did not have. Every member state had one vote. In the Olympic Movement, on the other hand, there were more than 100 NOCs, but by no means did all of them have members on the IOC, comprising only 80 members. Furthermore, some nations that had hosted the Olympic Games had two members on the IOC, so that the nonrepresentation of new recruits to the Olympic Movement was considerable.

There came a suggestion that UNESCO should take over the organization of the Olympic Games. The IOC then embraced the International Sports Federations and National Olympic Committees in the Tripartite Commission to consult and advise on the future of the Olympic Movement. It also increased its own membership and enlarged its Executive Committee. In some alarm the president of the IOC agreed to meet the director-general of UNESCO and address a meeting in 1977. This began a dialogue that has continued. The threat of complete political takeover has receded. The Tripartite Commission has become the Commission for the Olympic Movement and includes a representative of the active athletes for whom the Olympic Games are held. This is as far as its democratization has gone.

Autonomy of the IOC and NOCs

The IOC was set up as an autonomous body independent of governments, but has had difficulty in remaining so. One of de Coubertin's aims for the Olympic Movement was that it should promote international good-will and a more peaceful world. These were political aims attainable only by influencing governments. It would have been naive to suppose that interaction would have been in one direction only. The political independence of the IOC and of many NOCs was always at risk. The Olympic rules stated that for a National Olympic Committee to be recognized, it had to be autonomous and must resist, among other things, all political pressure.

As the desire to compete in the Olympic Games spread around the world, it reached countries where, because of the underdevelopment of sport or because of the ideologies in operation, only government action could establish an Olympic Committee. Some Latin American governments regularly appointed the presidents of their NOCs. When the Russians applied for recognition in 1947 they expected to appoint their own members of the IOC itself; they were told that this was contrary to IOC rules. Precisely how Konstantin Andrianov and Aleksei Romanov were nominated is not clear. They could not be regarded as delegates of the IOC to the Soviet Union in the same way that other members of the IOC were supposed to represent the IOC in their countries.

Block voting along predictable lines now took place. According to Guttmann (1984), Avery Brundage, president of the IOC, complained of this subservience to politics but accepted it as the price to be paid for the universalism of the Olympic Movement.

NOCs were even more politicized than the IOC. In February 1980 it was still possible for the IOC to vote unanimously to continue for arrangements for the Olympic Games in Moscow, despite strong pressure from the U.S. government to abandon them. However, when the time came for NOCs to decide whether to compete in Moscow, many of those whose IOC members had in February voted to support the Games, succumbed to their governments' pressure—orchestrated by the government of the U.S.—and declined to go. The British Olympic Committee, drawing upon a long tradition of self-government in sport, successfully resisted government pressure to withdraw and sent a large team to the Games. The keenness with which governments of Western nations tried to use international sport to achieve political objectives external to sport surprised many observers, and the capacity of NGOs for independent political action was seen to be small. The boycott of the Olympic Games in capitalist countries in 1980 was followed by the boycott of the Olympic Games in 1984 by NOCs in socialist countries.

Variety in NOC Constitutions

In view of the almost universal inability of NOCs to resist political pressure, the variety of constitutions that the IOC allows is ultimately of little consequence, but should be noted because it reveals great differences in the quantity and quality of influence that sports people themselves have in their own countries. The Olympic Charter stipulates that however an NOC is constituted, the representatives of the Olympic Sports must be the voting majority. The British Olympic Committee consists of the 26 representatives of Olympic Sports together with the Honorary Officers and two members of the IOC—33 in all. The Canadian Olympic Committee (COC) is incorporated within the Canadian Olympic Association, which has 225-250 individual members in four categories, with members representing Olympic Sports having a majority. The Association elects the COC Board of Directors, and the Board elects an Executive Committee of 11. At each stage the representatives of Olympic Sports are ensured of a majority, but many more people have a voice in Olympic affairs in Canada than in Britain. The NOC of New Zealand corresponds closely to that of Britain; the NOC of the United States resembles that of Canada.

Rich and Poor in the Olympic Movement

The most significant differences between NOCs are seen in the results that they achieve, especially when these results are related to the economic wealth of the countries. One hundred forty NOCs took part in the Olympic Games of 1984: 685 medals were awarded to 46 NOCs; 94 teams returned home without a medal. Table 3 shows the medal-winning countries and their gross national products (GNPs). Of those that won 3 or more medals, all but 2 had GNPs of more than U.S. $1,100, while 7 out of the 11 that won 20 or more medals had GNPs of more than U.S. $11,000.

Table 4 shows the GNPs of the countries that sent competitors but won no medals. It is clear from these two tables, without statistical analysis, that a high GNP is no guarantee of success in the Olympic Games, but that success is much less probable without a high GNP.

The number of medals won by the U.S. would not have been so great had many of the socialist countries not withdrawn. Socialist countries did not have as high a GNP as most of those in the top ten, but they would have been in the U.S. $1,000+ group.

Table 4 also shows that countries with a GNP as low as U.S. $80 were able to send competitors. This was because the IOC paid the expenses of four competitors and two officials from any NOC that applied for grant aid. Table 5 shows that the money came from television fees, and most of this money came from the U.S. The rich of America thus helped to make the Olympic Games accessible to the poor, but they could not redress day-to-day poverty and even starvation, or the lack of facilities and opportunities for sport that are the lot of more than half the population of the world.

Table 3   Gross National Products of the 1984 Olympic Games Medal Winners

NOC	Medals	GNP ($U.S./cap)
U.S.A.	176	12,820
F.R.Germany (West)	59	13,450
Romania	51	2,540
Canada	44	11,400
Great Britain	37	9,110
Italy	33	6,960
China	31	300
Japan	31	10,080
France	26	12,190
Australia	24	11,080
Sweden	21	14,870
Korea	19	1,700
Yugoslavia	19	2,790
Finland	12	10,680
Holland	11	11,790
New Zealand	11	7,700
Brazil	9	2,220
Switzerland	8	17,430
Mexico	7	2,250
Denmark	6	13,120
Spain	5	5,640
Belgium	5	11,920
Portugal	3	2,520
Jamaica	3	1,180
Kenya	3	420
Norway	3	14,060
Austria	3	10,210
Morocco	2	860
Venezuela	2	4,220
Nigeria	2	870
Egypt	2	650
Greece	2	4,420
Taipei	2	NA

(Cont.)

Table 3 (Cont.)

NOC	Medals	GNP ($U.S./cap)
Puerto Rico	1	1,910
Algeria	1	2,140
Ivory Coast	1	1,200
Ireland	1	5,230
Zambia	1	600
Turkey	1	1,540
Cameroon	1	880
Thailand	1	770
Pakistan	1	350
Iceland	1	12,860
Syria	1	1,570
Peru	1	1,170
Colombia	1	1,380

Note. 46 NOCs won one or more medals; 94 NOCs won no medals. Data from "Roll of Honour," 1984, *Olympic Review,* and from *International Yearbook and Statesman's Who's Who,* 1983/84.

Table 4 Gross National Products of the 1984 Olympic Games Non-medal Winners

NOC	GNP ($U.S./cap)[a]	NOC	GNP ($U.S./cap)
Qatar	27,720	Papua New Guinea	840
United Arab Emirates	24,660	Philippines	790
Kuwait	20,900	Swaziland	760
Luxembourg	15,910	Dominican Republic	750
Bermuda	12,910	Guyana	720
Saudi Arabia	12,600	Solomon Islands	640
Bahrain	8,960	Honduras	600
Virgin Islands	7,010	Bolivia	600
Oman	5,920	Lesotho	540
Trinidad and Tobago	5,670	Tonga	530
Singapore	5,240	Indonesia	530
Israel	5,160	Liberia	520

(Cont.)

Table 4 (Cont.)

NOC	GNP ($U.S./cap)[a]	NOC	GNP ($U.S./cap)
Hong Kong	5,100	Djibouti	480
Neth. Antilles	4,540	Mauritania	460
Gabon	3,810	Yemen	460
Cyprus	3,740	Senegal	430
Bahamas	3,640	Ghana	400
Malaysia	3,600	Togo	380
Malta	3,600	Sudan	380
Barbados	3,500	West Samoa	370
Surinam	3,030	Gambia	370
Uruguay	2,820	Mozambique	360
Cayman Islands	2,730	Niger	330
Chile	2,560	Madagascar	330
Argentina	2,560	Sierra Leone	320
Brit. Virgin Islands	2,100	Benin	320
Fiji	2,000	Central Africa	320
Panama	1,910	Haiti	300
Seychelles	1,800	Guinea	300
Iraq	1,740	Sri Lanka	300
Paraguay	1,630	Tanzania	280
Jordan	1,620	Somalia	280
Antigua	1,550	India	260
Costa Rica	1,430	Rwanda	250
Tunisia	1,420	Uganda	220
Ecuador	1,180	Zaire	210
Guatamala	1,140	Malawi	200
Congo	1,110	Mali	190
Belize	1,080	Eq. Guinea	180
Botswana	1,010	Nepal	150
Zimbabwe	870	Bangladesh	140
Nicaragua	860	Chad	110
Grenada	850	Bhutan	80

Note.   Data from ''Roll of Honour,'' 1984, *Olympic Review,* and from *International Yearbook and Statesman's Who's Who,* 1983/84.
[a]GNP not available for Andorra, Liechtenstein, Monaco, San Marino, Burma, El Salvador, Lebanon, and Mauritius.

Table 5   Finance of the Olympic Movement From Television Fees in 1984

Region (broadcaster)	Payment $U.S. (million)	Hours transmitted
U.S. (ABC)	225.0	187
Europe (EBU)	19.8	380 +
Japan	18.5	235
Australia	10.6	310
Canada	3.0	220
Warsaw Pact (OIRT)	3.0	?
Latin America (OTI)	2.1	200
New Zealand	0.5	210
Philippines	0.4	100
Africa (UNRTA)	0.2	?
	283.1	

Ritual and Competition

There is one further point to be made about uniformity and diversity in the Olympic Movement. Levi-Strauss (1966) has pointed out that in games, the ritual is conjunctive and the competition is disjunctive. The rituals of the Olympic Games—especially the opening and closing ceremonies, with their displays of national flags, emblems, and costumes—unite the athletes and spectators as friendly members of a family of nations. Although governments are not overtly taking part, the flags and emblems (other than the Olympic emblems) are political symbols that the Olympic Congress in Baden-Baden in 1981 was very unwilling to abandon. Even the victory rituals are conjunctive rather than disjunctive. The races and contests, however, are disjunctive, with political rivalries and antagonisms ready to erupt, as was demonstrated in the womens' 3,000-meter race in 1984. To what extent the Levi-Strauss thesis applies to other international sporting events and world championships has yet to be investigated.

Commercial Uniformity

Commerce is one of the nongovernmental unifying forces that have proved themselves able to cross both national and ideological frontiers. The trademark on the vest of the Russian athlete shown in the IOC's

Olympic Movement (1984) is significant. For the Olympic Games in Moscow, more than 1,000 non-Russian firms were official suppliers or sponsors. Among these firms were France's Adidas and Thompson CSF, Switzerland's Swiss Timing, Finland's Nokia, Italy's Olivetti, and Denmark's Storno as well as business enterprises within COMECON (McIntosh, 1983; Novikov, 1981). Neither currency restrictions nor objections to capitalist enterprise were allowed to hinder the commercial development of the Olympic Games. In 1985 the IOC itself was using a commercial firm, International Sport and Leisure, to market the Olympic emblem of five linked rings throughout the world. Commercial pressure is already rivaling political pressure upon NGOs and is tending toward monopoly and uniformity.

"Mass Sport" and "Sport for All": Structures

Since 1945 many governments have developed policies to promote mass sport and sport for all. The political organizations that have been established to develop and implement these policies are much more varied than the governmental NOCs, which are principally concerned with elite sport.

First, there are government ministries and departments of sport, such as the U.S.S.R. All Union Physical Culture Council (established in 1930), which in 1968 became the All Union Committee on Physical Culture and Sport attached to the Council of Ministers. The Committee's resolutions on sport are binding on all ministries and public organizations. Similar committees were set up in each of the 15 Soviet republics (Riordan, 1976).

Second, there are nongovernmental federations of national bodies of sport that are granted funds by governments and enjoy a great measure of independence in promoting both the interests of their member clubs and the recreation of the population at large. Sweden has such an NGO; Figure 1 shows how an elected assembly distributes and administers funds provided by central and local government.

Third are quasi-nongovernmental organizations (QUANGOs). Great Britain has a federation of national governing bodies not unlike that in Sweden, but the government does not use it to implement policy or distribute money. Instead, the government has set up a sports council with a chairman and 26 members, all appointed by the government, and an administrative staff of 550 to develop policies for both mass sport and elite sport and to spend an annual grant—£30 million in 1985. The extent to which the sports council has freedom to carry on the day-to-day organization of sport without direction or intervention by the government depends upon the view of the Minister of Sport on his role at any one time.

A variation of this structure is for a sports council to be advisory and not executive, as it was when first established in Britain and still is in New Zealand. In Britain, however, the Minister of Sport was chairman and attended all meetings, whereas in New Zealand the Minister appoints a chairman and does not usually attend meetings himself. In the latter

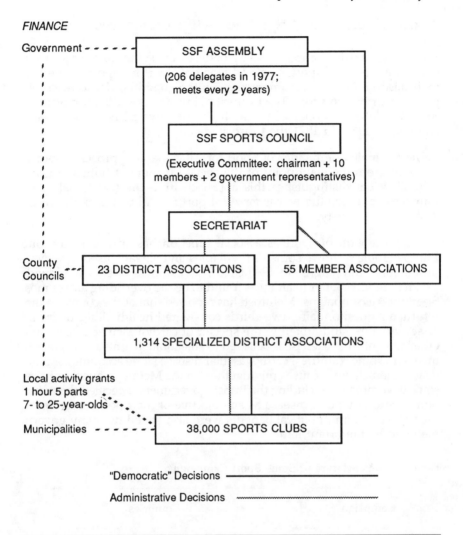

FINANCE

Government ⎯ ⎯ ⎯ ⎯ ⎯   SSF ASSEMBLY

(206 delegates in 1977;
meets every 2 years)

SSF SPORTS COUNCIL

(Executive Committee: chairman + 10
members + 2 government representatives)

SECRETARIAT

County
Councils ⎯ ⎯ ⎯   23 DISTRICT ASSOCIATIONS   55 MEMBER ASSOCIATIONS

1,314 SPECIALIZED DISTRICT ASSOCIATIONS

Local activity grants
1 hour 5 parts
7- to 25-year-olds

Municipalities ⎯ ⎯ ⎯ ⎯ ⎯ ⎯   38,000 SPORTS CLUBS

"Democratic" Decisions ⎯⎯⎯⎯⎯⎯⎯⎯

Administrative Decisions   ⎯⎯⎯⎯⎯⎯⎯⎯

Figure 1.   Organization of sport in Sweden.

case, the advice of the council to government is mediated through bureaucrats; the emphasis, if not the content, may be changed in the process.

Fourth are NGOs of different sizes and different constitutions promoting sport locally, regionally, and nationally, but uncoordinated by a government. This is the situation in the U.S., where the President's Council on Physical Fitness has no funds to distribute and performs merely an advisory and exhortatory function.

"Mass Sport" and "Sport for All": Objectives

Sports organizations and governing bodies were set up to cater for well-defined interests of sportsmen and women. Sport for sport's sake was their raison d'être. Governments have intervened in order to reach objectives extrinsic to sport. The Council of Europe used the term *Sport for All* to describe the policy of promoting mass physical recreation that it adopted in 1966. In 1971 the Council stated,

> The originality of the idea of Sport for All is that it approaches sport mainly from the standpoint of the social functions it fulfills or can fulfill. What distinguishes this approach from the traditional one toward sport are the words *for All*. Sport for All concerns the role of sport in society.

The promotion of sport as a social function has spread far beyond Europe. Table 6 shows some of the names and slogans used in various promotional campaigns. In 1980 UNESCO commissioned a worldwide progress report. Better health was found to be the overriding aim of most Sport for All campaigns. McIntosh has reported that of the countries that returned a questionnaire, two-thirds considered health either their first or second aim. Undoubtedly, the specter of cardiovascular disease and other ailments that exercise is believed to ameliorate haunts many governments. In some countries, cardiovascular disease alone accounts for more deaths than all other causes put together. In the McIntosh questionnaire, some governments, including the British government, specified the reduction of coronary heart disease as an objective of their policies for sport. Mental, social, and political benefits were also stated by many governments to be important aims.

Table 6 Nomenclature of Some Sport Campaigns

Campaign	Countries
TRIM	Norway, Sweden, Denmark, Netherlands
TRIMM	Federal Republic of Germany
Sport for All	United Kingdom, Colombia
Physical Fitness and Sports	United States
Come Alive	New Zealand
Life Be in It	Australia
Kuntourheilu	Finland
Deportes Para Todos	Spain, Brazil

In assessing the success of governments' policies in achieving the aims and objectives that they have set, it is certainly possible to measure the increase or decrease in participation in sport, if only approximately. It is impossible, however, to say how far extrinsic social and political aims have been realized. As far as health is concerned, longevity and mortality rates are crude indices of health. Table 7 shows that in selected Western European countries, mortality rates have decreased in a 12-year period while Sport for All campaigns were being conducted. However, Table 8 shows that deaths from ischemic heart disease, which was a specific target of the British and other governments, have increased. Factors other than exercise—such as smoking and diet—affect heart disease, and , certainly, no causal relationship between exercise and health can be deduced from these statistics. They do indicate, however, that the problem of heart disease is more acute than it was before Sport for All campaigns were initiated.

Table 7 General Mortality Rates

Country	1969 (%)	1981 (%)
England and Wales	11.9	11.7
France	11.4	10.3
F.R.Germany	12.2	11.7
Netherlands	8.4	8.1

Note. From World Health Organization, (1972, 1983).

Table 8 Deaths From Ischemic Heart Disease

Country	1969 Deaths Total	1969 Deaths Per 100,000 population	1981 Deaths Total	1981 Deaths Per 100,000 population
England and Wales	139,428	285.6	155,196	302.9
Scotland	17,823	334.1	18,633	360.6
France	39,992	79.5	50,571	94.2
F.R.Germany	103,739	170.5	132,086	214.2
Netherlands	22,096	171.6	25,056	175.8

Note. From World Health Organization, (1972, 1983).

Similarly, other social aims, such as reduction of juvenile crime, violence, and vandalism and the enhancement of moral values—all of which have been stated as aims of Sport for All by one government or another—do not appear to the ordinary observer to have been achieved in the last 10 or 20 years.

The wonder is that both governments and NGOs continue to promote sport for the extrinsic benefits and effects, rather than for sport's intrinsic satisfaction. There have been some instances of the spontaneous eruptions of sport for sport's sake. One of the fastest growing sports of the last 10 years, jogging, coupled with marathon racing, owes little to either governments or existing governing bodies of sport. The London Marathon was started by two Olympic medal winners in the steeplechase as a private enterprise and in 1986 had 80,000 applicants for 17,000 places. Improved health is a bonus in the eyes of many joggers, but enjoyment and a sense of well-being is the dominant reason for participating for most of them.

Conclusions

I have, in this address, indicated some of the forces that have been operating to produce uniformity both in elite sport and in mass sport, or "sport for all." The trend to uniformity has been manifested in the social objectives, the structures, and the programs of sport. The most powerful influence has been political, that is to say, the policies of governments both within their own countries and internationally. Paradoxically, however, it has been governments that have threatened the unity that they themselves originally produced, as the history of sporting boycotts has shown. NGOs are recognizing more and more clearly that only governments can solve the problems that governments have created. In July 1985, the president of the IOC, in his opening address to the 90th session of the IOC, stated that he was turning to the United Nations Organization to protect the Olympic Games and launched the idea of a UN resolution that would "invite member nations"—that is, governments—"to contribute to the organization and staging of the Games" (Samaranch, 1985).

The trend to uniformity in the world of sport continues. It has important cultural, social, and political consequences for us all. The trend and its consequences, therefore, deserve the most careful study by members of the International Society on Comparative Physical Education and Sport.

References

Coubertin, P. de. (1977). Olympic memoirs XIII. *Olympic Review*, 119.

Council of Europe. (1971). *Planning the future VIII.*

Council of Europe. (1971). *Conclusions and prospects* CCC/EES 2.5-6, 22. Strasbourg.

Guttmann, A. (1984). *The games must go on*. New York: Columbia University Press.

International Olympic Committee. (1984). *The Olympic movement*. Lausanne, Switzerland: Author.

International Yearbook and Statesman's Who's Who (pp. 13-18). 1983/84. East Grinstead, West Sussex: Thomas Skinner Directories.

Levi-Strauss, C. (1966). *The savage mind*. London: Wiedenfeld and Nicholson.

Mandell, R. (1971). *The Nazi Olympics*. New York.

McIntosh, P.C. (1981). *Sport for All programmes throughout the world*. Cologne, West Germany: ICSSPE/UNESCO.

McIntosh, P.C. (1983). *Importation of sports equipment*. Cologne, West Germany: ICSSPE/UNESCO.

McIntosh, P.C., & Charlton, V. (1985). *The impact of sport for all policies 1966-1984 and a way forward*. Study 26. London: The Sports Council.

Novikov, I.T. (1981). *Report of the Olympiad 80 Organizing Committee to Olympic Congress 1981*. Lausanne, Switzerland: International Olympic Committee.

Olympic Review. (1976). 103/104. Lausanne, Switzerland: International Olympic Committee.

Riordan, J. (1976). Sport in Soviet society. *Stadion II, 1*. Cologne, West Germany: E.J. Brill.

Roll of honour. (1984). *Olympic Review*, **203**, 630-710.

Samaranch, J.A. (1985). *Speech to 90th Session IOC in Berlin 1985*. Lausanne, Switzerland: International Olympic Committee.

World Health Organization. (1972). *WHO world health statistics*. Geneva: Author.

World Health Organization. (1983). *WHO world health statistics*. Geneva: Author.

The Development of Sport in the German Democratic Republic: 1950–1985

Edelfrid Buggel

Permit me to introduce my country to you. The German Democratic Republic (G.D.R.)—situated in Central Europe—is some 110,000 square kilometers in total area, corresponding to 100th place in world standing; has some 16.7 million people, which ranks about 40th; ranks about 10th in industrial production; and has maintained its place among the three leading sports nations of the world for the last 15 years.

The development of G.D.R. sport since the 1950s has been termed a "sports miracle." However, athletic results at international level are not based on miracles but, rather, on a complex of developmental factors, seven of which I will present. These factors could, however, become effective in their complexity as well as in detail only because from the very beginning, the objective and subjective laws, capacities, and conditions that have been central to the antifascist-democratic society, and also later to the socialist society, have been utilized purposefully, continuously, and optimally during the historical period concerned on the basis of Marxist-Leninist philosophy and guided by the Socialist Unity Party (SED).

The Status of Physical Education and Sports in the G.D.R.

Physical Education and sports enjoy status as a relevant field of study in the G.D.R. It is well known that the Constitution, laws, and other official decrees in a country are of high political importance for the society as well as for every individual's life. We, therefore, keep the fact highly relevant that physical education and sports have been defined in all the fundamental documents of party and government, mass organizations (trade unions, youth, and women's organizations) up to the Constitution of the G.D.R. In the Constitution of the G.D.R., we find the following—
In Article 18:

Physical culture, sport, and active outdoor recreation, being elements of socialist culture, shall serve the all-around physical and mental development of citizens.

In Article 25:

All citizens shall have the right to participate in cultural activities. Under the conditions of the technological revolution and mounting intellectual demands, these are assuming growing importance. State and society shall encourage the participation of citizens in cultural activities, physical culture, and sport, in order to aid the comprehensive development of socialist personality traits and to ensure an increasing satisfaction of cultural interests and needs.

In addition to the Constitution, the "Youth Act of the G.D.R.," issued in 1950, and the "Labour Code of the G.D.R." are especially important for the development of physical culture and sport. In section 35 of the Youth Act, we read that

The readiness and initiative of younger people . . . to go in for sports shall be supported by officials of state and economy, by teachers and educators. Activities designed to promote physical culture and sport shall be included in annual and factory plans and in collective agreements of companies.

In Section 223 of the Labour Code, heads of factories or institutions shall be committed to support the constitutional right of G.D.R. citizens to participate in physical education and sports morally and materially. In other words, these laws, decrees, and decisions have been defined as being *managerial obligations*; they are *rights for the citizens*. Thereby a wide individual range has been offered for an enjoyable, zestful participation in sports that provides for increasingly high levels of health and performances.

Examples of these policies include these:

- Construction and maintenance of sports facilities are financed by the state budget or by factories, communities, and townships. Expenditures are shown in Figure 1.
- Sport facilities increased from 35.6 to 132.4 square meters from 1957 to 1985 (see Table 1).
- The admission to sports facilities is free of charge.
- The provision of sports equipment for obligatory physical education lessons, as for the organized practice and competitive activities, is free of charge.
- Six percent of a factory's profit is allocated to sports, culture, and recreation.
- There is free travel or travel at reduced fares when public transport is used by sport teams.
- There is paid time off for short periods for voluntary sports officials, referees, and umpires.
- Public health and insurance cover all people who take part in sports at an organized level (sports accidents are considered equivalent to working ones, medical treatment is free of charge, and insurance sickness pay corresponds to full net earnings for up to 78 weeks).

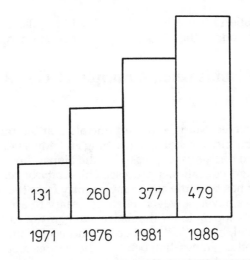

Figure 1.   Public spending (state budget) for sports facilities (in million marks).

Table 1   Sport Facilities

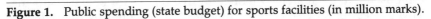

Facility	1955	1970	1985
Stadiums	150	312	330
Sports grounds	900	924	1,368
Sports halls and gyms	1,127	3,614	5,728
Indoor swimming pools	41	96	200
Swimming facilities	474	574	695
Ski-jumping hills	230	371	332
Field houses and hostels for athletes	595	1,306	1,668

From the very beginning of the G.D.R.'s existence, physical education and sports have not been on the social "outskirts." Quite the contrary! They have developed equivalently and closely intertwined with other societal fields, for example, education, health, culture, and working and living conditions for more than 30 years.

Springing from that societal objective basis, there was not only established a strong need for athletic activity according to individual wishes and opportunities in all the population's strata, but there was also formed a high public reputation and attitude toward all ways and means of sport engagements. These included preschool physical education, compulsory physical education lessons in general schooling, college university level sport, sport periods in the services, Sport for All, and top-class athletics.

Unity: The Fundamental Principle of G.D.R. State and Sport Policy

All laws and decrees start from the principle that the human being and his or her all-around, harmonious teaching and education are the centers of all issues and decisions, expressed in the biopsychosocial unity of the instructional and educational process. This unity of school, mass, and top-class sport has been the aim in my country from the very beginning. Several decades have, however, been necessary to achieve the present level of optimal cooperation with relative autonomy of each of these areas. On the one hand, every field has become more specialized and differentiated; on the other, integration between these three areas improved continuously, aiming at an ever more effective service for one's well-being. This process of 35 years' development is represented by many facts.

Physical Education Curriculum

Physical education lessons in kindergartens (which are attended by almost all children in G.D.R. between 3 and 6 years of age), compulsory sport lessons in general 10- or 12-year schools, and such lessons in professional schools, junior or senior colleges, and in universities are programmed according to a uniform, scientifically based state curriculum. The standards reflect societal requirements, age, sex, health status, and other criteria, in the interest of a high level of basic physical training.

Sports Badge Program

The requirements and standards of the Sports Badge Program of the G.D.R. are derived from the previously mentioned criteria, inviting mass participation in voluntary sports activities. The athletic standards of the sports badge program result from a G.D.R.-representative investigation. Specific athletic abilities have been defined from age- and sex-specific differences in performances and attitudes toward certain sports. The basic requirements include endurance runs or hiking, pull-ups or push-ups, triple hop or standing long jump, dodge run, and sport shooting.

Additional requirements for the silver or gold badges are swimming, sprint running, long or high jump, distance throwing or shot put, and one sport of choice. An example of a point score table is shown in Table 2. The standards for bronze, silver, and gold levels have been selected to give every citizen the opportunity to test fitness related to the basic physical abilities—endurance, strength, speed, and mobility—according to the point score table. This is a highly stimulating function for everybody. Since 1981, 4 million citizens—that is, more than 30% of the population—have

Table 2 Scoring Table for Sports Badges (age group V, 35–45 years)

Points	1,000-m run (female) 2,000-m run (male) (min)	Push-ups	Long jump from standing position (m)	Dodge-run (s)	Air-pressure gun shooting at 4 m	Endurance swimming (min)	60-m run (s)	Long jump (m)
Male								
1	no time requirement	15	1.70	15.5	25	10	10.5	3.45
2	10:10	20	2.05	13.8	30	15	9.5	4.00
3	9:00	25	2.25	13.0	35	20	9.0	4.45
Female								
1	no time requirement	5	1.20	17.5	15	10	14.0	2.45
2	6:40	10	1.55	15.5	20	15	11.8	2.90
3	6:00	14	1.75	14.0	30	20	11.0	3.20

Note. Minimum point requirements: bronze, 8 points; silver, 20 points; gold, 26 points.

annually met the requirements for this sports badge. Our aim is to involve all citizens. Figure 2 shows badges awarded since 1957.

These standards and requirements of the state Sports Badge Program are not only the basis for mass sport activities but also for the training programs of younger people and for top-class athletes. No athlete is granted admission to the Children and Youth Spartakiads if he or she has not met the requirements for the gold sports badge.

Social Status of Sport Lessons

The societal status of sport lessons at the 10- or 12-year general high schools has been elevated by making them a main subject; sport marks are equivalent to those in other main subjects. This process was paralleled by a revaluation of the sport teacher, putting him or her on the same level as teachers of science and the humanities.

Committee for Physical Culture and Sports

The organic cooperation between these three areas is guaranteed by a united, coordinated management of physical culture and sport. The Committee for Physical Culture and Sports of the G.D.R., in which all the related ministries and societal organizations are represented by their deputy ministers or vice-presidents, respectively, has been established as a consultative societal organ. Through this body, it became possible to discuss all the basic problems of physical culture and sport and to pass

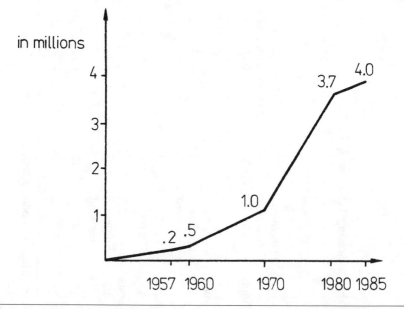

Figure 2.   Sports badges awarded in the G.D.R. since 1957 (in millions).

corresponding recommendations. Each ministry or societal organization then transfers these recommendations to its own realm for discussion. The structure of the Committee for Physical Culture and Sports is shown in Figure 3. The German Gymnastics and Sports Union (DTSB) and the State Secretariat for Physical Culture and Sport of the G.D.R. government carry particular responsibilities.

Implementation of Sport Programs

It is a demanding task to implement the unity of school, mass, and top-class sport in such a small country as the G.D.R., with its pretentious economic and social program. The task requires bringing the demands for complexity or variety into accord with the aspect of concentration. Despite all those promotional activities for the varied athletic interests of our citizens—proven by 36 existing sport associations in the DTSB and 7 in the Society for Sports and Technology (GST), with 64 sports and several hundreds of events—the G.D.R. has had to concentrate upon traditionally, as well as climatically and geographically, conditioned sports

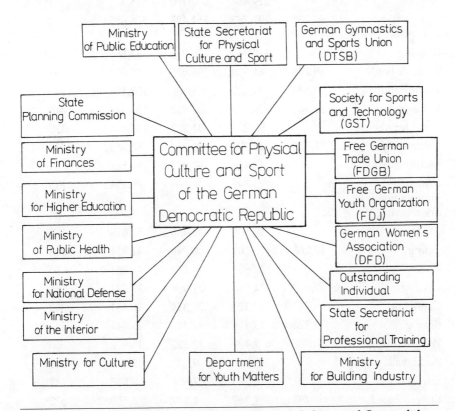

Figure 3. Structure of the Committee for Physical Culture and Sport of the G.D.R.

44 Buggel

and events in relation to its material, technological, and personal resources. Table 3 shows the increase of membership in some selected sport associations since 1951.

This is the reason every sport had a developmental prospective in the G.D.R. from the very beginning. Growing material, financial, and personal requirements make it, however, impossible for all sports to meet the conditions necessary to participate capably in continental or world championships or in Olympic Games. The G.D.R. has therefore withdrawn from some sports on the international level during the past 35 years

Table 3 Membership in Selected Sport Associations

Sport	1951	1965	1977	1985	Increase (%)
Football (soccer)	194,177	365,232	567,451	556,912	187[a]
Angling		219,487	402,100	515,321	135[b]
Gymnastics free exercise	94,631	293,783	354,493	386,685	309[a]
Bowling		110,743	164,213	193,686	75[b]
Track & field	69,248	61,930	183,025	178,867	158[a]
Team handball	71,535	89,672	163,086	155,474	117[a]
Volleyball	21,961	20,653	109,805	120,372	448[a]
Table tennis		50,853	94,283	116,941	130[b]
Swimming	35,375	47,276	88,209	82,563	133[a]
Motor sports		48,426	60,073	81,569	68[b]
Hiking/ mountaineering/ orienteering		23,843	36,608	75,154	215[b]
Judo		19,831	43,468	52,619	165[b]
Skiing	10,266	26,601	36,946	42,914	318[a]
Chess		27,835	36,867	41,751	50[b]
Cycling	7,418	14,946	21,906	27,271	268[a]
Canoeing	6,017	19,121	25,324	26,651	343[a]
Boxing	9,728	13,116	22,112	23,641	143[a]
Weight lifting		2,497	12,522	18,972	660[b]
Basketball		3,996	9,225	13,915	248[b]
Fistball		6,763	7,956	9,913	47[b]
Luge/bobsled	493	1,169	2,747	3,559	622[a]

[a]Membership increase since 1951. [b]Membership increase since 1965.

(e.g., basketball, water polo, alpine skiing, modern pentathlon, field hockey, tennis). These sports are nevertheless cultivated further on a national or mass sport level, and international friendship competitions are also staged.

Because a high level of compulsory school sports are recognized as being a decisive basis for every citizen's health and fitness, the material and personal resources of school sports have been especially concentrated upon during the history of G.D.R. sports. While in 1955, 1,000 halls of more than 180 square meters were at the schools' disposal, there were more than 4,200 of that size in 1985. By 1995 every school will possess its own sport hall. Also, since 1950 a large number of physical education teachers have received their academic professional training. Through these improvements, every child will receive 2 or 3 hours of compulsory physical education lessons weekly during his or her 10 to 12 years of schooling, plus 1 to 3 hours of voluntary athletic activities per week in the school sports club.

Implementing this unity of school, mass, and top-class sports ensures, on the one hand, all-around physical education and instruction for all citizens from childhood to older ages, and lifelong athletic activities in correspondence with their biological status or social situations and their individual interests. It facilitates, on the other hand, not only bringing athletic talents to world-class levels; it also guarantees the reintegration into the preferred mass sport events of those who could not develop their talents or who drop out of top-class athletic talent programs because of medical or other personal reasons.

Unifying Organized and Independent Activities

Engagements in sports should not be left as something automatic, either in mass or top-class sports, whenever that engagement is to be developed in quantitative and qualitative aspects. Lifelong, regular, and effective participation in mass sports, or world-class results in top-class sports, can be achieved, however, only if the individual is convinced of their necessity. He or she must be ready to voluntarily accept the loads and requirements of athletic exercises, practice, and participation in competitions. Also, he or she must bring a high amount of personal independence and conscious cooperation. This is particularly true with top-class athletics.

During the 35 years of G.D.R. sport history, priority has been given to the organized participation in sports under the guidance of a coach, sport teacher, or instructor, and the growth of membership in the sports clubs. Numbers of sports clubs and sports associations in the DTSB are presented in Figure 4 and Table 4. Sport sociological investigations in 1965 and 1977 have significantly demonstrated the increased needs of G.D.R. citizens to participate in a stable exercising or practicing group or team under the guidance of a methodically trained sport instructor. These needs are caused by the attitude that a greater performance bettering and emotional effect could thereby be reached than by doing physical exercises

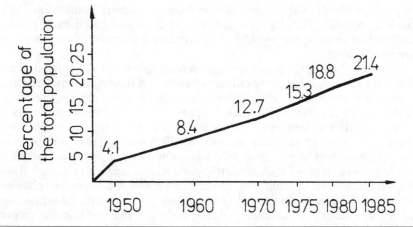

Figure 4. Membership in the German Gymnastics and Sports Union (DTSB) of the G.D.R.

Table 4   Number of Sports Clubs and Sections of the DTSB of the G.D.R.

Year	Clubs	Sections
1950	4,500	19,000
1960	6,013	23,542
1970	7,359	32,352
1975	8,036	35,504
1980	9,274	37,765
1985	10,249	43,749

on one's own. The following are examples of the wide variety of popular contests and competitions provided for mass sport activities:

- The "Strongest Apprentice of the G.D.R." contest (increasing from 25,000 participants in 1971 to 400,000 in 1985)
- 2,788 "Keep-Fit" running activities in 1985 (3,378,347 participants overall in hiking and running events, including 70,000 in the Berlin Peace Run alone)
- The "Table Tennis Tournament of the Thousands" (increasing from 150,000 participants in 1976 to 500,000 in 1985)
- 39,000 sports festivals held in factories, living areas, and holiday resorts (5.5 million participants in 1985)

The criteria of organized activities comprises regularity and continuity. Exercising, practicing, and competitive periods are staged in accordance with scientifically based and practically proven principles. These principles are guidelines, but not dogmas, for the coach, sports teacher, or instructor. They have to be applied according to the actual situation of the sport or practice group concerned in a constructive way.

Continuity is one reason for the successful G.D.R. sports development. There are senior officials and coaches who have done their work already for decades and therefore possess wide experience. However, younger people are also asked to continuously and prospectively prepare themselves to become managerial officials or coaches, thus making possible a smooth transition into the future.

There is an interesting trend that has become visible during the historical development of G.D.R. sports when it comes to the relation between organized athletic activities and autonomous, independent participation in sports. Parallel to the widening and stabilizing engagement in organized sport activities performed under the guidance of a sport teacher or coach, increasing numbers participate in sports with friends or their families (16% in 1965 to 26% in 1978). In addition, the number of adults who exercise on their own is growing (10% in 1965 to 17% in 1978). This evidence of the growing need to participate in sports variably and several times per week throughout the year reflects the organized transfer of knowledge by the schools, sports organizations, and mass media as far as medical, educational, and instructional values are concerned.

One could also speak of an individual method of organized participation, because regularity, standards, and methodical organizational forms have gained more importance. With 43% of the adult G.D.R. population engaged in voluntary sport activities (as was shown by sport sociological studies), we may conclude that the typical sport-liking public opinion results from existing laws, decrees, and regulations as well as from top-class athletic results, and has a strong background in the people's own regular athletic experiences.

Training and Qualifications of Sport Professionals

We hold the number—as well as the quality—of professionally trained and further qualified coaches, physical education teachers, and sport scientists to be another criterion of the results achieved in G.D.R. sports. The system of training and further qualification, which is fully capable at present, had to start from rather poor conditions at the end of the 1940s. At that time some 60 students graduated from five universities as academically trained sport teachers.

Today the eight sport scientific departments (sections) at universities and educational academies bring 500 graduates annually into practice after they have finished a 5-year program with two major subjects. Another 500 receive an accentuated training in physical education subjects during their professional teacher training for classes 1-4. Kindergarten nurses, during their professional training, take a similar program.

The founders of the German Academy for Physical Culture in Leipzig in 1950 opened the opportunity for 4-year academic training of coaches and sport teachers with diplomas, particularly for working in sport organizations. Since 1950 more than 15,000 students have graduated from the DHfK, each one with a guaranteed job under good social conditions—an essential presupposition for solid and creative work.

Paralleling this development, the numbers of honorary instructors, referees and umpires, and officials who were trained at a progressively rising level during the years increased as shown in Figure 5. The following principles have shown their validity in academic or vocational training in the field of physical education and sports:

1. The unity of sport scientific instruction and political education to socialist personalities.
2. The unity of theoretical and practical training as broad basic training and a highly specialized qualification during studies (curriculum of the DHfK).
3. Close cooperation between academic institutions and practice partners (a) to recruit youngsters for sport studies (former top-class athletes and younger people who possess experience as voluntary sport officials or instructors); (b) to select the graduates for their future professional work as teachers, as coaches, in the various managerial levels, in certain groups or territories; and (c) to organize an assistant's period for every graduate for some years.
4. The scientifically most talented individuals may prepare their doctor's theses during a 3-year research study or a scientific

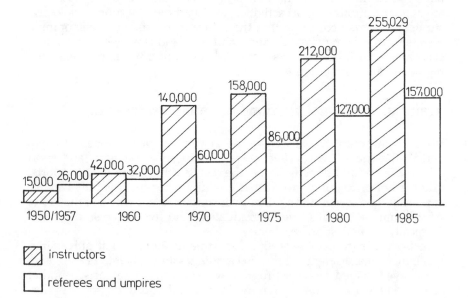

Figure 5. Number of honorary instructors and referees and umpires in the G.D.R.

aspirancy. All nine sport scientific academic institutions of the G.D.R. are entitled to grant the PhD or Dr.habil. The DHfK alone has so far trained the following graduates on the three academic levels: 16,000 sport teachers or coaches with diplomas, 470 doctors, and 55 Doctors habil. The DHfK has at present a staff of some 500 professors, assistant professors, and scientific and technical workers.

5. For about 10 years, further qualification has gained equally high attention as the professional training itself. This results from the concept that sport scientific knowledge becomes outdated after 3 or 4 years because of the extremely dynamic nature of science and technology. Therefore, a further qualification system has been established in the G.D.R. that invites every full-time coach, physical education teacher, scientist, sport physician, and official every 2-4 years to sit in courses for 3-6 weeks. The most qualified and experienced scientists, officials, and coaches give lectures, and panel discussions are held thereafter. Honorary sport officials, instructors, referees, or umpires are informed of the latest findings in their sports or field of responsibility during courses every 2 years.

Science and Research

Scientific research has high priority in the development of physical education and sport. As early as the 1950s, far-reaching laws and decrees were passed to begin theoretically based and pragmatically effective sport scientific research work; this is the basis for the high level at present. During the past decades, the following procedures and attitudes have been established in the G.D.R. and have proven their value:

1. Sport science has developed into a respected, complex scientific discipline. Sport science subdisciplines, like sport sociology, sport history, biomechanics, sport pedagogics, and sport methodology, have experienced an increasing specialization. In addition, there has been a process of integration between these subdisciplines and interdisciplinary cooperation with "neighboring" social sciences, medical sciences, and technological sciences.

2. Points of reference for sport science research activities are the requirements put forward by societal practice. The research projects are selected by the sport scientist together with the sport "practitioner." Research concepts and results have to be justified to the representatives of practice, because research experiments are carried out in close cooperation with the latter.

3. It is obvious that a small country like the G.D.R. has at its disposal only a limited research potential in relation to equipment, people, and finances. We must therefore, concentrate on theoretical and practical projects according to their relevance for advancement or to their actual effects in the fields of school, mass, or top-class sports.

4. Sport science research work is centrally guided and planned in the G.D.R. by the Scientific Council for Physical Culture and Sport. We thereby ensure that the research potential is concentrated upon topics that are relevant to society and that effective cooperation of the researchers can be maintained. However, because any creative research work requires a high level of individual autonomy and generosity, a research order contains the necessary regulations.

Sportsmedicine

A modern system of physical education is unthinkable nowadays in a country without an efficiently working system of sportsmedicine. In the G.D.R., sportsmedicine is a respected clinical discipline and effective system of taking care of athletes. Despite the large difficulties the G.D.R. had to face during its first few years of existence, great attention was given to the development of sportsmedicine from the very beginning.

Meanwhile, it has developed into a respected independent medical and clinical discipline within human medicine's domain. In the early 1950s, there were only 41 sportsmedicine physicians, most of them part-time, whereas at present some 1,300 physicians are members of the Society for Sports Medicine of the G.D.R. They work full or part time in the Sports Medicine Service of the G.D.R. as the sports physicians in sports associations or sports schools, in more than 300 Sports Medical Advisory Centers in the districts and countries distributed all over the territory of the G.D.R., and in academic or research institutions.

The organic integration of sportsmedicine as one field of public health is expressed by the fact that an agreement was reached between the Ministry of Public Health, the DTSB, and the State Secretariat for Physical Culture and Sport, offering checkups and consultations to every citizen free of charge when he or she intends to start sport activities and one or two (depending on the sport) medical checkups annually. Also, therapeutic treatment is available in the case of sport injuries.

Physicians from public health services are also included in activities in school and mass sports. Their particular attention is given to the care of children and adolescents in compulsory or extracurricular sport periods. Age group and top-class athletes are continuously medically supervised throughout the year by sport physicians in order to support their optimal athletic progress and to prevent or minimize sport injuries.

During medical studies, sportsmedicine subjects are taught within each specialization (orthopedics, physiology, pediatrics, etc.). In addition, prominent sportsmedicine specialists offer lectures on specific items to interested medical students. Since 1964 there has been a 4-year further qualification required for one becoming a sportsmedicine specialist.

Recruiting, Selecting, and Promoting Talented Athletes

The development program of sports in the G.D.R. has been termed the *Spartakiad movement*. This follows the traditions of the revolutionary workers' movement that had organized Workers' Olympiads under that heading as early as the 1920s. Since 1965, Children and Youth Spartakiad Games in summer and winter sports are staged in the G.D.R. The main objective of these competitions is to invite ever more young people to take part in sports according to Olympic ideals. Spartakiads are held at various territorial levels, annually in the counties, whereas regional competitions in the 15 districts of the G.D.R. and national Spartakiads are staged alternatively every 2 years.

Preliminary competitions are first organized in all schools. About 90% of all pupils participate in them to determine the best athletes in each age group and sport; these are thereby qualified to enter county Spartakiads. In addition to competitions in the basic sports—track and field, swimming, gymnastics, and team games—the most popular sports in the county concerned are also included—among them table tennis, billiards, tennis, bowling, orienteering, running, angling, and chess.

Conditions for entry are advertised several months in advance, so that all schools can prepare carefully for participation. In track and field, swimming, weightlifting, and speed skating, contestants are required to meet certain qualifying standards; whereas in sports in which tournaments are held, such as football, competition begins early so that only the best school teams are playing each other during the Spartakiad. Contestants who win medals or reach highest rankings at county levels are eligible for participation in Spartakiad competitions at regional or national levels. The growth of the Spartakiad is shown in Table 5.

The Spartakiad Games are jointly sponsored by the German Gymnastics and Sports Union (DTSB), the Free German Youth (FDJ) and its Young Pioneers' branch, and the Ministry of Education (to which all schools are subordinated). They find support from local authorities, nationally owned

Table 5 Entries for the Spartakiad Games (in thousands)

Spartakiad Games	1967	1976	1985
Preliminary competitions for county spartakiads			
Summer	2,500	3,700	3,500
Winter	58	103	70
County spartakiads			
Summer	406	875	997
Winter	14	34	31
District spartakiads			
Summer	58	98	100
Winter	3	5	5

enterprises, trading organizations, and medical centers. Media representatives are also involved; the press, TV, and radio give much space and time in reporting on the competitions.

Children and Youth Spartakiads are a regular feature in societal life and attract the population's widespread interest. For the youngsters taking part, they are an unforgettable experience, not least because of the opening, closing, and victory ceremonies modeled on the Olympics; the large crowds of spectators; and the numerous cultural events staged in conjunction with the Spartakiad. About 90% of all internationally successful athletes won their first medals during Spartakiad competitions.

Children and Youth Sport, comprising all sport events and possessing the Spartakiad competitions as its core, makes it possible that talent can be spotted rather early by the school physical education teacher or the sport club's instructor. These young athletes may enter training centers available in all the 226 counties of the G.D.R., where instructors and coaches who possess higher degrees of qualification are working. The child stays a member of the sports group that enters him for competitions. During county and district Spartakiads, in which coaches of sports clubs take part as observers, the best athletes are selected for membership in sports clubs, provided that they and their parents agree.

Sports clubs have been the "centers of excellence" in the G.D.R. since 1954/55, with at least one of them in every district. Part of these sports clubs are Children and Youth Sports Schools, in which the curriculum of the 10-grade high school is adjusted to practices and competitions. Children enter the Children and Youth Sports School and the sports club at various ages. In gymnastics this is done from the 4th grade on; in weightlifting, only from the 9th grade on.

University entrance qualification (the so-called Abitur) can also be reached at these schools, because general education is as highly respected as athletic performance. This is the reason schooling is also maintained during practice courses. Lessons are given only in small groups, in order to achieve a high level of learning intensity. The duration of schooling can be prolonged for 1 or 2 years, if necessary. Also, top-class athletes are granted additional periods of study during their time at universities or academies.

We attach great importance to an athlete achieving high results in a solid professional training provided during his or her athletic career, guaranteeing social security for him or her. The unity of athletic practice and professional training is implemented throughout the year. All is not without problems, when it comes to making this principle real.

Also, it is consonant with the principle to give priority to the long-term, systematic training structure of the younger athlete, in contrast to the ambitious interests of a coach who may want the athlete to reach high athletic performance too early. We have sometimes argued with a coach that there should be no specific practicing, or not too much of it, before versatile, basic physical training has been implemented sufficiently. Therefore, the principle of versatility has been enforced with the Spartakiad competitions, where not only were the performances of specific events included into Spartakiad victory totals of the lower age groups, but the results from versatility contests were also figured in. In team handball, for example, there is also an athletic "polyathlon" consisting of handball distance throw, 30-m sprint run, and 30-m dodge run (dodging a ball). Canoeists of the age group 14-15 have to run 800 m or 1,500 m and complete an athletic test including bench pressing and an agility run. All participants aged 13-15 in track and field events have to qualify by successfully completing multi-item tests (60-m run, 60-m hurdles, long jump, shot put, 800-m run).

Conclusions

I have tried to present the sport concept of my country during the period from 1950 to 1980 in seven essential aspects and factors. This development was far from being without problems; remarkable difficulties had to be overcome along the way. They were, however, not factors of inhibition, but acted as stimulating forces for change aiming at the developed socialist society in the G.D.R.

Physical education and sports have been integrated into that developmental process as high-standing social categories. By their means and methods, they make sport as widely and highly respected for the sake of society as well as for every individual, and they bring athletic performance to the highest possible level on a world scale.

State and Sport in Developing Societies

"Syty golodnomu ne tovarishch."
("The well fed are no companion to the starving.")
—Russian proverb

James Riordan

Surely no one who witnessed the harrowing TV scenes of famine in Ethiopia will forget the matchstick children, the skeletal men and women, the millions who starved to death. Millions are still starving. Yet Ethiopia is the homeland of Olympic champions Yifter and the late Bikila. It is one of the most successful of all African nations at the Olympic Games. How can a country spend money on sport when so many of its people are dying of hunger?

Ironically, at a time when some in the Western metropolises are casting doubt on Western sports in their competitive and commodified forms—including the Olympics, which are said to have become too big, too nationalistic, too political, and too commercialized—some governments of modernizing societies are among the strongest defenders of the colonial faith in Western sports and the Olympics. This paper sets out to examine some of their reasons and the dilemmas Western sports pose.

Sport and State in Developing Nations

What is a developing society? In very general terms, as Ayi-Bonte (1973) has put it, they are "those countries where efforts are being made to catch up with countries which have already taken a mighty leap forward in industry and commerce, in education, science, and technology." It is possible to distinguish them quantitatively by UN findings concerning gross national product, vital statistics, or urban-rural imbalance. Developing states contain the bulk of the world's people and make up over three-quarters of the world's nations.

We have to consider most Communist states as well, especially those whose recent or present development has rested on an overwhelmingly

illiterate peasant population bearing the standard features of social back-
wardness, like China and the U.S.S.R. (for the U.S.S.R., see Tables 1-3).
The U.S.S.R., it should be stressed, is one of the most developed of the
developing countries. So it is with all Communist states, save Czechoslovakia, the German Democratic Republic, and, possibly, Hungary.

Developing societies are relatively poor, agricultural, and young (in
terms of postcolonial or postrevolutionary development); and mainly
socialist, in respect of their predominant public ownership of the means
of production, central planning, and political ideology.

We in the developed West must realize that almost all our debates on
comparative sport are utterly irrelevant to the great majority of people in
the world whom we see (if we see at all) through our own distorted vision.
Our own unique patterns of Western sport and our debates are no more
than a mirror of our own societies; our sports are neither "natural" nor
necessarily "right" for other peoples. In societies of scarcity—societies
striving to build a new life for mainly illiterate, starving, impoverished
peasant populations—Western commercialized sports, on the one hand,
and the gentlemanly "sport for sport's sake," sport as the private garden
of human activity, on the other, are often looked upon as indecent and
irrelevant to the needs of developing states.

Sport in developing societies is a serious business, with serious functions to perform. It is, accordingly, state controlled, encouraged, and
shaped by specific utilitarian and ideological designs (it is by no means a
matter of fun and games). In its development in many countries of Africa,
Asia, and Latin America, it is associated with hygiene, health, defense,
patriotism, integration, productivity, international recognition—even cultural identity and nation building. Sport, therefore, often has the quite
revolutionary role of being an agent of social change, with the state as
pilot. In any case, after a nation's "liberation," there is rarely a leisure
class around to promote sport for its own disportment.

Nation Building

All developing nations face problems of political stabilization; economic,
social, and cultural progress; and national integration of ethnically diverse
populations. A major problem is that of nation building: the inculcation
of political loyalties to the nation as a whole, transcending the bounds
of kinship, race, language, religion, and geography. As Adefope (1973)
has said of Africa,

> Nations were carved out and created by colonial masters in the 19th
> and early 20th centuries, in some cases so arbitrarily that peoples of
> the same background, culture and origin were either separated or
> brought together with other peoples of completely different origin
> and background. Consequently, one finds that many African nations
> are, even now, still in search of true national identities. (p. 561)

What better than sport to help them find those identities? After all, sport—with its broad relevance to education, health, culture, and politics, and its capacity to mobilize people (predispose them toward change)— may uniquely serve the purpose of nation building and help foster national integration. It reaches and unites wider sections of the population than probably any other social activity. It is easily understood and enjoyed, cutting across social, economic, educational, ethnic, religious, and linguistic barriers. It permits some emotional release (reasonably) safely, it is relatively cheap, and is easily adapted to support educational, health, and social welfare objectives.

Furthermore, it is here that the sports introduced by Westerners may have some advantages over indigenous folk games. The latter, as Adefope has said,

> are linked to festivals which take place annually in the various communities. In some cases some of the sports are linked to religious celebrations or rituals. Indigenous sports have therefore served only as a means of expressing tribal or ethnic identity. Modern sports . . . have served as an important means of expressing national identity. (p. 562)

Western sports however, also have serious drawbacks in their new settings, which will be discussed later.

Integration

Related to nation building is the state-desired aim of integrating a multinational population, often in transition from a rural to urban way of life, into the new nation-state. Many modernizing societies are simply loose confederations of different ethnic groups with diverse colors, languages, traditions, religions, stages of economic growth, and prejudices.

Let us look at the world's three most highly populated nations. The billion people of China consist of at least a dozen distinctly different ethnic groups. The country is divided into 21 provinces and five ethnic autonomous regions. The minorities consist of aborigines (Chuan, Yi, Miao, Manchu, Puyi) and Koreans in the east and Mongols, Turks (Uighurs), and Tibetans in the west.

India's three-quarters of a billion people belong to three major linguistic groups (Hindi, Urdu, and Punjabi account for 46% of the population) and dozens of other groups: Telugu, 10%; Tamil, 8%; Marathi, 8%; Bengali, 8%; Gujarati, 5%; Kanarese, 4.5%; Oriya, 3%; Malayalam, 3%; and Assamese, 1%. In addition, Kashmiri, Sanskrit, and English are spoken.

The U.S.S.R. certainly consists not only of Russia; Russians actually make up just under half the total Soviet population today. The U.S.S.R. is a multinational federation of 286 million people containing more than 100 nationalities. The country is divided into 15 Union Republics—each generally based on a separate ethnic, geographic group—and many other administrative subdivisions. Every weekday, children go to school in as many as 87 different language-schools, and daily newspapers come out in 64 languages.

The governments of all three of these great countries have quite deliberately taken Western sports from town to country and, especially in the case of the U.S.S.R., from the European metropolis to the Asiatic interior. Each nation uses sports to help integrate the diverse peoples into a new unified country, sports promoting a new patriotism that transcends petty national and ethnic affiliations.

Here is an example from Soviet history. In October 1920, shortly after the Russian Revolution of 1917 and even before the Civil War was over, the new Soviet government organized the First Central Asian Olympics in the old Islamic center of Tashkent. This was the first time in history that Uzbeks, Kazakhs, Turkmenians, Kirgiz, and other Muslim peoples, as well as Russians, Ukrainians, and other Europeans, had competed in any sporting event together. As was made clear later by Rodionov (1975), "The integrative functions of sport are vast. This has immense importance for our multinational state. Sports contests, festivals, spartakiads and other forms of sports competitions have played a key part in cementing the friendship of Soviet peoples" (p. 6).

Defense

Insofar as most developing states were born in war and today live under the constant threat of war, terrorism, and subversion, it is hardly surprising that defense is a prime priority, thereby often creating a "militarization" of sport. The role of the military in sport is further heightened by central control of sports development.

In China, the U.S.S.R., and several other Asian and African states, the sports movement was initially the responsibility of the armed forces and even today is frequently dominated by instrumental defense needs and military or paramilitary organizations. Thus, most developing nations have a national fitness program with a bias toward military training, sometimes modeled on the Soviet "Ready for Labor and Defense" system. Thus, in China, as Glassford and Clumpner (1973) have attested, "a major component of physical culture in Chinese schools is the military preparation programme based extensively on the Soviet GTO (national fitness) system. Route marches of ten to 20 kilometres, grenade throwing, dashes, mock and real rifle training form the core of this programme" (p. 8).

All Communist and some nonaligned states have a strong military presence in the sports movement through army and security forces clubs, provide military sinecures for more or less full-time athletes, and, at times, have established direct military supervision over sport and physical education. They are also linked through the Sports Committee of Friendly Armies, set up in Moscow in 1958, then embracing all members of the Warsaw Pact plus China, North Korea, and North Vietnam. Cuba joined in 1969, Somali joined in 1973, and other African states (Ethiopia, Madagascar, Chad, Cameroon) have subsequently joined. (China left in 1960.)

Similarly, the sports club Dinamo, run and financed by the security forces in the various Communist states and often bearing the Soviet name (as in Albania, Bulgaria, East Germany, and Yugoslavia), is the largest sports organization in the Communist nations and links all such clubs in regional international tournaments.

In many developing countries, therefore, particularly in the Communist community, the armed and security forces provide much of the funds and many of the facilities that enable people to take up and pursue a sport, especially full time; the armed forces thereby help to ensure that as many people as possible are physically fit, mentally alert, and possess the qualities (patriotism, willpower, stamina, ingenuity) that are of particular value for military preparedness (not to mention for internal policing against dissidents and deviants). Furthermore, the military organization of sport appears to be an efficient way of deploying scarce resources in the most economical fashion and of using methods of direction that are more effective than those coming from civilian organizations.

Hygiene and Health

Of all the functions of state-run sport in modernizing societies, promoting and maintaining health must take top priority. In many such states, sport comes under the aegis of the health ministry. Inasmuch as Soviet sports development has been based for much of the Soviet period on a population at a comparatively low health level, and because it has served as a model for several other modernizing societies, it is instructive to examine that experience briefly. Of course, postrevolutionary Soviet Russia was not as backward as are some African and Asian nations today, but the country was among the world's poor nations (10 million starved to death in 1921, for example), had recently been a semicolony, and received virtually no aid from outside (see Tables 1 to 3).

When the Bolsheviks took power in October 1917, they acquired a semifeudal empire, 80% of which consisted of peasants and was illiterate, with over 100 different ethnic groups. The country was in a state of war-ruin and chaos. It was a land with an overwhelmingly inclement climate, where disease, epidemics, and starvation were common, and where most people had only a rudimentary knowledge of hygiene. The new rulers well knew it would take a radical economic and social transformation to alter the situation significantly. However, time was short, and able-bodied and disciplined men and women were needed urgently—first for the country's survival, then for its recovery from the ravages of war and revolution, for its industrial and cultural revolution, and for its defense against probable further attacks.

Regular participation in physical exercise, therefore, was to be one means—relatively inexpensive and effective—of improving health standards rapidly and a channel by which to educate people in hygiene, nutrition, and exercise. For this purpose, a new approach to health and recreation was sought. The name given to the new system was *physical culture*. The pre-Revolution and Western concepts of sport and physical

Table 1   Life Expectancy at Birth (in years) in Russia and the U.S.S.R.,
1896–1986

Year	All	Men	Women
1896–97[a]	32	31	33
1926–27[b]	44	42	47
1955–56	66	63	69
1960–61	69	65	73
1965–66	70	66	74
1970–71	70	65	74
1971–72	69	64	74
1981–82	69	63	74
1985–86	70	69	74

Note. From *Narodnoye khozyaistvo SSSR v 1962 godu* [USSR economy in 1962] (p. 493). Moscow: Statistika, 1963. *Narodnoye khozyaistvo SSSR v 1965 godu* [USSR economy in 1965] (p. 603). Moscow: Statistika, 1966. *Strana Sovetov za 50 let* [Land of the Soviets over 50 years] (p. 260). Moscow: Finansy i statistika, 1967. *SSSR v tsifrakh v 1973 godu* [USSR in figures for 1973] (p. 196). Moscow: Finansy i statistika, 1974. *Narodnoye khozyaistvo SSSR v 1986 godu* [USSR economy in 1986] (pp. 497-499). Moscow: Statistika, 1987.

[a]In 50 provinces of European Russia. [b]In the European part of the U.S.S.R.

education were thought to be too narrow to express the far-reaching aims of the cultural (mental and physical) revolution underway. Physical culture was to embrace health, physical education, competitive sport—even civil defense and artistic expression. The acquisition of that culture was said to be an integral process that accompanied a person throughout life.

As Semashko, himself a doctor and the first health commissar (also concurrently chairman of the Supreme Council of Physical Culture), made plain shortly after the Revolution (1928),

> Physical culture in the Soviet understanding of the term is concerned not with record breaking, but with people's physical health. It is an integral part of the cultural revolution and therefore has personal and social hygiene as its major objective, teaching people to use the natural forces of nature—the sun, air and water—the best proletarian doctors. (p. 3)

In other words, physical culture was to be a plank in the health campaign, encouraging people to wash, clean their teeth, to eat and drink sensibly, to employ a rational daily regime of work, rest, and sleep. Hence, Semashko (1926) put forward the slogan of "Physical culture 24 hours a day"—8 hours of work, 8 hours of sleep, and 8 hours of recreation (p. 27).

Table 2   Birth Rates, Death Rates, and Rates of Natural Increase[a] in Russia and the U.S.S.R. in Selected Years, 1913–1982

Year	Birth rate	Death rate	Natural increase[c]
1913[b]	45.5	29.1	16.4
1926	44.0	20.3	23.7
1928	44.3	23.3	21.0
1937	38.7	18.9	19.8
1939	36.5	17.3	19.2
1940	31.2	18.0	13.2
1946	23.8	10.8	13.0
1950	26.7	9.7	17.0
1955	25.7	8.2	17.5
1960	24.9	7.1	17.8
1965	18.4	7.3	11.1
1970	17.4	8.2	9.2
1975	18.1	9.3	8.8
1980	18.3	10.3	8.0
1982	18.9	10.1	8.8

Note. From *Strana Sovetov za 50 let* [Land of the Soviets over 50 years] (p. 257). Moscow: Finansy i statistika, 1967. *Narodnoye khozyaistvo SSSR v 1972 godu* [USSR economy in 1972] (p. 46). Moscow: Statistika, 1973. *SSSR v tsifrakh v 1973 godu* [USSR in figures for 1973] (p. 18). Moscow: Finansy i statistika, 1974. *Narodnoye khozyaistvo SSSR v 1983 godu* [USSR economy in 1983] (p. 30). Moscow: Statistika, 1984.

[a]Per thousand of population. [b]In present territory. [c]Birth rate minus death rate.

Furthermore, the country was in the grip of a typhoid epidemic and had long suffered from such near-epidemic diseases as cholera, leprosy, tuberculosis, and venereal disease. It suffered, according to Semashko (1928), from "dreadfully backward sanitary conditions, the ignorance and nonobservance of rules for personal and public hygiene, leading to mass epidemics of social diseases such as syphilis, trachoma, scabies, and other skin infections" (p. 6). Physical culture, therefore, was to help combat serious diseases and epidemics. The therapeutic value of regular exercise, for example, was widely advertised in the intermittent anti-TB campaign of the late 1920s.

However, physical culture was not confined to improving only physical health; it was regarded as important in combating what the leaders defined as antisocial behavior in town and country. They reasoned that if young people could be persuaded to take up sport and engage in regular

Table 3 Long-Term Comparison of Russian/Soviet and United States
GNP

Year	Population (millions) Russia[a]/ U.S.S.R.	U.S.A.	GNP per capita (1975 dollars) Russia/ U.S.S.R.	U.S.A.	Soviet-U.S.A. ratio (%)	Official Soviet calculation of Soviet-U.S.A. ratio (%)
1913	157.9	97.2	600	2,500	24	—
1928	151.1	120.5	629	2,931	21	—
1940	195.1	132.1	904	3,182	28	—
1950	180.1	152.3	1,213	4,315	28	31
1960	214.3	180.7	1,838	4,993	37	58
1965	230.9	194.3	2,182	5,882	37	59
1970	242.8	204.9	2,722	6,523	42	>65
1975	254.5	213.6	3,088	6,972	44	—
1977	—	—	—	—	60	—
1982	—	—	—	—	—	67

Note. From *Narodnoye khozyaistvo SSSR 1922–1982* [USSR economy 1922–1982] (p. 91). Moscow: Statistika, 1983. "Soviet Economic Growth. Achievements Under Handicaps" by H. Block. In *Soviet Economy in a New Perspective* (p. 268), 1976, Washington: Joint Economic Committee of the United States Congress. "U.S. and U.S.S.R. Comparisons of GNP" by I. Edwards et al. In *Soviet Economy in a Time of Change. Vol. 1* (p. 370), 1979, Washington: Joint Economic Committee of the United States Congress.

[a]Population for 1913, boundaries of Imperial Russia; for 1928, those of the interwar U.S.S.R.; from 1940, postwar boundaries.

exercise, they might develop healthy bodies *and* minds. As Landar (1972) has written, the Ukrainian Communist Party issued a resolution in 1926 expressing the hope that "physical culture would become the vehicle of the new life . . . a means of isolating young people from the baneful influence of the street, homemade alcohol, and prostitution" (p. 14). The role assigned physical culture in the countryside was even more ambitious: It was

> to play a big part in the campaign against drunkenness and uncouth behaviour by attracting village youth to more sensible and cultured activities. . . . In the campaign to transform the village, physical culture is to be a vehicle of the new way of life in all measures undertaken by the authorities—in the fight against religion and natural calamities. (p. 15)

In 1985, the name of sport was still being invoked to combat alcoholism and religion, as new monographs by Nekrasov (1985), Stepovoi (1984), and Lisitsyn (1985) have attested.

Physical culture, then, stood for "clean living," progress, good health, and rationality. It has been regarded by the authorities as one of the most suitable and effective instruments for implementing their social policies, as well as for social control implicit in the program. It was to be the "handmaiden of Soviet medicine." Also, according to Semashko's oft-repeated dictum (1928), "there can be no physical culture without medical supervision." This was to "symbolize the bond between medicine and Soviet physical culture" (p. 8).

As industrialization got underway at the end of the 1920s, physical exercise also became an adjunct, as was everything else, of the Five-Year Plan. At all workplaces throughout the country, regimes of therapeutic gymnastics were introduced with the intention of boosting productivity, cutting down absenteeism due to sickness and injury, reducing fatigue, and spreading hygienic habits among the millions of new workers who had just previously inhabited bug-infested wooden huts in the villages.

There is no space to go into much greater detail about the development of health-related sport in the U.S.S.R. Suffice it to say that the nation has come a long way in its 71 years: from educating peasants in the virtues of washing and cleaning their teeth; preaching the virtues of *mens sana in corpore sano* (a healthy mind in a healthy body) to illiterate and starving people, from nomadic Kazakhs to maritime Inuits, from Siberian tribes to Muslim peoples in Soviet Central Asia, from the Slavs to the Caucasians; and dealing with epidemiology, hygiene, and nutrition—to providing the foundation of the country's progressing to becoming the world's most successful all-around sporting nation. It is, regretfully, the latter aspect that has taken the West's attention—not the former ones, which are of far more relevance to modernizing nations everywhere.

Social Policies

There are many facets of social policy relevant to sport that concern developing countries. Some have been touched upon above (combating crime, particularly juvenile delinquency; combating alcoholism and prostitution; attracting young people away from religion, especially all-embracing faiths like Islam that impinge upon large segments of social life).

Another aspect of the use of sport for social purposes is the concern that it can make some contribution to the social emancipation of women. The international example of women's increasing sports participation and success, particularly by nonwhites, can affect women in developing countries in which women have traditionally been discouraged (or banned) from pursuing a sport.

A strong motivation here may be the desire by government leaders for national recognition through international sporting success. Thus, contact with more "enlightened" nations in the sporting arena is having its effect. As the Nigerian Anyanwu (1980) has said,

Despite the social or cultural sanctions against women's participation in sports, Nigerian women have made a remarkable breakthrough in participation which hitherto was the exclusive preserve of men. . . . This change can be attributed to the impact of cultural contact between Nigerian traditional culture and that of the Western world. (p. 92)

Under the influence of the American women's example, Chinese women have taken up weightlifting. In May 1985, as Wubin has reported, "140 musclewomen in 23 teams from various parts of the country participated in the Jinan tournament" (1985, p. 6).

The impact of women's sport is even greater—though emancipation far more protracted and painful—in communities in which, by law or convention, women have been excluded from public life and discouraged from baring face, arms, and legs in public. In fact, some multiethnic communities have quite deliberately used sport to break down prejudice and gain a measure of emancipation for women. This has been a conscious policy in Communist nations with sizable Muslim populations, such as Albania, the U.S.S.R., and Afghanistan. In a reference to women of Soviet Central Asia (bordering on Iran, Turkey, and Afghanistan), Davletshina (1976) has asserted that "sport has become an effective and visible means of combating religious prejudice and reactionary tradition; it has helped to eradicate the spiritual oppression of women and to establish a new way of life" (p. 62). It is a sobering thought that had the grandmothers of such Soviet Union gymnasts as Nelli Kim or Elvira Saadi appeared in public clad only in a leotard as girls, they would almost certainly have been stoned to death, as Sviridov (1963) illustrates from just such murders in Uzbekistan in the 1920s—and as would happen to women today in some fundamentalist Islamic societies.

Even in non-Muslim societies, sport has been used as a means of liberation. For example, when PASOK, the Greek Socialist Party, came to power, it launched a huge campaign to encourage female participation in physical culture. In the first year alone, 180,000 women novices took part—and this in a country where the Orthodox Church had excommunicated the entire staff of the Academia Gymnastica 10 years ago for permitting a public female gymnastic display.

Significantly, it was 1980 before a black woman athlete ever won an Olympic field event—Cuba's Maria Colon, in the javelin throw. Also, in 1984 two women athletes from India and Morocco were the first women from their respective countries to reach Olympic track finals, the latter winning a gold medal.

Change can be painfully slow. However, inasmuch as women's sport attainments are reflecting, reinforcing, and even *precipitating* processes of social change in the role and status of women, this clearly offers exciting prospects for the future of women in both developing and developed societies.

International Recognition

For young countries trying to establish themselves in the world as nations to be respected—even recognized—sport may uniquely offer the opportunity to take the limelight in the full glare of world publicity. This is particularly salient to those nations confronted by bullying, humiliation, boycott, and subversion from big powers in economic, military, political, and other areas. As Fidel Castro (1974) has said of imperialist states, in regard to Latin America, "Imperialism has tried to humiliate Latin American countries, has tried to instill an inferiority complex in them; that is part of the imperialists' ideology to present themselves as superior. And they have used sport for that purpose" (p. 288). In that context, therefore, Castro (1976) sees Cuban Olympic success as "a sporting, psychological, patriotic, and revolutionary victory" (p. 12).

This puts particular responsibility on athletes from developing nations, in that they are seen by politicians as encouraging a sense of pride in their team, nationality, or country—even in their political system. The patriotic pride generated by sports success, especially against the world's strongest nations, further helps to integrate ethnically diverse societies. In a survey of top athletes of Central Africa, Barushimana and Maximenko (1978) of Ruanda found that "the strongest motive in the participation of an African in sport is national prestige, that is the striving to bring fame and renown to his country and thus enhance its international prestige." In his survey, as many as 90% of top African athletes put that factor as the first of their motives for engagement in sport (p. 40).

Where other channels have been closed, success in sport would seem to have helped such countries as Cuba, China, the U.S.S.R., and many other states of the developing world attain a measure of recognition and prestige internationally. Sport is unique in that, for virtually all modernizing societies, including the U.S.S.R. and China, it is the *only* medium in which they have been able to take on and beat the economically advanced nations. This echoes the point made by the West Indian C.L.R. James (1963) about the huge satisfaction felt by the West Indies in beating England at the old colonial masters' game of cricket.

For the Communist states, this sports success takes on added importance in view of what they see as the battle of the two ideologies for influence over the rest of the world. As Balashov (1973) has put it, "The mounting impact of socialist sport on the world sports movement is one of the best and most comprehensible means of explaining to people throughout the world the advantages that socialism has over the capitalist system" (p. 3). Castro (1974) looks forward to the day when Cuba can prove the superiority of its national sport, baseball, over that of U.S. baseball: "One day, when the Yankees accept peaceful coexistence with our country, we shall beat them at baseball too and then the advantages of revolutionary over capitalist sport will be demonstrated" (p. 290).

Despite some sporting setbacks, there is ample evidence to show that the economically advanced Communist states have gone a long way to achieving their target of world supremacy, especially in the Olympic Games.

Problems in the Development of Sport

Despite (or even because of) state control of sport, a number of problems exist in the development of sport in developing countries. Sport movements can be expensive and oriented toward an elite group of performers.

As Ayi-Bonte (1973) of Ghana has written of the dilemma his country faces, "In our efforts to keep our name among sports-loving nations of the world, we are often torn between giving instruction to the talented few or the skilled performer and giving instruction in the basic fundamentals to as many as possible" (p. 580).

Sport can also be manipulated for political, business, and personally corrupt purposes. The legacy of colonialism has also meant that many sports are suited to a socially differentiated society (golf, tennis, horse-riding). From his examination of the social background of Indian athletes, Sohi (1981) discovered that

> in terms of the traditional caste system, most of the athletes came from higher castes. And in view of the emerging class system, most belong to the middle class. . . . There is sufficient evidence that there is a social hierarchy of sports which follows the status hierarchy in stratification. (p. 59)

Moreover, the inherent values of inherited sport may run counter to strong, existing values. In discussing Olympic sports, the West German sports scholar Eichberg (1984) has pointed out that they are

> by no means universal, but rather a specific result of social development in the framework of European and Western societies of the last 200 years. The configurations of Western sports correspond to the patterns of Western industrial capitalist societies (as well as those of the East European state economic systems following them). (p. 98)

Such patterns are by no means "natural" or desirable for developing countries. Also, they have led to excesses in world sport that bother many developing nations, as well as many of us in the West: the aggression and brutality of elite sport, the chemical manipulation of athletes, the professional training of children who are unable to defend their rights and interests, the construction of highly specialized top sports facilities that are too expensive for most modernizing nations, and so on.

Such problems are, of course, not confined to developing countries; they affect traditionally disadvantaged groups in Western societies, such as women and ethnic minorities. The problem women face is whether to play sports on male terms, using the competitive power structures of patriarchal capitalism; whether to try to adapt the sports and their accompanying structures to their own needs; or whether to reject them altogether. The central questions Margaret Talbot (1984) has posed for women are: "Whose game should women play? According to whose rules? The contest should be assessed according to whose criteria?" (p. 1). She argues for a "redefinition of sport *and* women which does not make them a gender contradiction in terms" (p. 13).

Moreover, ethnic minorities in Western countries have, within their own countries, problems of disadvantage similar to those of developing nations. The many studies of black baseball players in the U.S., native

Indian runners in Canada, and West Indian cricketers in England have demonstrated this well.

What Sort of Sport?

The issue at stake is whether sports in newly independent states should grow out of indigenous national traditions, should be superimposed by colonial and neocolonial pressures, or should arise from some mixture of the two. This is not a simple issue for nations seeking a cultural identity. After all, in many of them, the Western-imposed sports have taken hold in the popular consciousness and do seem to play a part in crossing ethnic boundaries that more people-specific indigenous sports do not, as previously discussed.

It has to be recalled that Western values were introduced into Africa and Asia through European administrators, military officers, missionaries and merchants, between the 18th and 19th centuries. As the Nigerian Adedeji (1979) has written, "They demonstrated in many ways that the black people were mere savages, with neither value system nor real culture"—this despite the fact that "the values created by Nigerians over the years in music and dance, songs and stories, sports and games, sculpture and paintings are great and remarkable" (p. 63).

Out of the ensuing conflict between indigenous and Western sports and values through the years, "Western values became dominant over indigenous values." Despite this erosion, Nigerians soon

> discovered the double standard which was entrenched in the newly-adopted value system. For there was one form of "universal Christian values" for the Blacks and another form for the Whites. European clubs hardly accepted Nigerians to play games with them. (p. 65)

All the same, the sports remain—some taken over by the new elite, some modified and purged of their commercial and socially and sexually exclusive character (e.g., into amateur boxing, rather than professional, in all Communist states). As the Cuban Garcia Bango (1973) has said, "It was essentially necessary to eradicate the traditional concept of sport and its discriminatory and exclusive character, as well as its misuse for commercial purposes" (p. 385). Some Western sports, moreover, are promoted in pristine form for the reasons mentioned above, particularly for international prestige.

In some developing states, however, attempts are being made to rehabilitate folk games that rely more on group solidarity and fun, on their own national cultural traditions. Such is the case with the Northern Games, involving the indigenous peoples of North America; the Games of the Peoples of the North in northeastern Siberia; and in the folk game festivals of several African and Asian countries.

Likewise, China staged its first Minority People's Folk Games in Beijing between 8 September and 20 October in 1985; it attracted some 3,000 participants from 30 ethnic groups, competing in 7 sports and taking part in 27 display games covering 4 age groups. As Zhao Chongqi (1986) has reported, "The festival was a gala occasion and a grand review of interesting and colorful folk games that have evolved from daily life and work activities. It contributed to research into traditional games and the culture of minority peoples" (p. 34).

Libyan Bedouin games and Chinese Wushu; Indonesian martial arts and rattan ball games; Inuit contests and drum dances in Greenland and Canada; a whole host of folk games in the U.S.S.R., including Uzbek Kyzz-kuu chasing games on horseback, Russian lapta and gorodki ball games, and various folk wrestling styles (from Georgian chidaoba to Yakut hapsagai sash wrestling and Moldavian trynta)—these are just some examples of folk games from the four continents. In Western Europe, too—in Belgium, Denmark, Holland, and Portugal—the interest in folk games is awakening anew.

All these initiatives toward a new pattern of recreation are, as Eichberg has written, developing "in the context of social and national criticism of international neocolonial dominance in sport and industrial capitalism" (p. 101).

Elsewhere, as other writers have noted, the two cultural patterns are enjoying a side-by-side existence. In Brazil, as Augusto (1969) has written, indigenous sports are practiced alongside Western sports. In Ethiopia, as noted by Sazima (1969), traditional games are likewise promoted equally with Western sports.

Some Western sports have become fully integrated into local communities at all levels, their original values adapted to serve the new milieus. The sports now seem even more at home there than they do in their land of origin. This appears to be true of cricket in the West Indies and soccer in Brazil. A similar adaptation/emasculation has occurred, of course, in the opposite direction: such sports as polo and lacrosse, for example, have been taken from the colonies into the metropolises and turned into sports that are often now socially and sexually exclusive.

On the whole, though, Western sports and local games often provide an unstable mixture, and it is a long haul to revive folk games. The corrosive effect of Western sports and values is hard to withstand, especially because traditional games emerged from and reflected a preindustrial, patriarchal, and ritualistic pattern of life. Also, Westerners have tended to treat traditional games with contempt. As Adedeji (1979) writes of folk games in Nigeria,

> Young people's belief in them has been shaken and undermined. Their self respect has also been destroyed. Western values have also devalued the human resources of Nigerian youth; the greatest value they had to develop, they refused to accept together with their culture. (p. 68)

To some people, especially the younger generation, in developing nations, Western sport, like Western dress, represents progress, civilization, a means of international communion, and a path to fame. It is a problem faced by folk dancing against the appeal of disco music, folk song against rock and roll, folk drama against soap opera. The dilemma is tersely stated in "Unmask the Enemy," an editorial of the *Third World Liberator* (1986), published in Malaysia:

> First World control, exploitation and Third World dependence is sub-limated in the realm of culture. The pervasive influence of the Western mass media can be seen from the fact that 90 percent of the news articles, radio broadcasts, films and TV programmes worldwide come from the US, Japan or a handful of European countries.

> *Dallas* is shown to TV viewers from Egypt to Manila. *Rambo* is played to packed audiences from Lebanon to Brazil. Coca-cola has become the "real thing" among Third World youth and Western pop music blares from loudspeakers in shopping complexes and discos every-where. Through the mass media the transnational companies have effected the transnationalisation of the culture of the "developed" world. The twin processes of Westoxication and cultural alienation are complete. In its place we find a generation, a whole society, which has lost its cultural moorings, its pride and integrity, aping what is at best a bastardised lifestyle, at worst a poor parody of the original.

> In the process this Westoxication breeds cultural inferiority among our peoples and we lose confidence in ourselves—becoming alien people in our own societies who are ashamed of our roots, our origins. This form of cultural domination is insidiously destroying us.

> For a generation of young people who grew up without the cultural experience, or ever suffered the brutalising aspects of colonisation, for this new generation, the enemy is unseen, as it colonises the hearts and the mind. (pp. 1–2)

However, in searching for a new pattern of sport that is rooted in alternative concepts of life, of the body, of everyday practice, we must beware of harking back to some remote romantic age of folk sport, roman-ticizing about indigenous sports as if they are neither brutal, nor patri-archal, nor tied to ritualistic behavior that is no longer in step with the popular mood. It has to be recalled that the gradual demise of traditional communal activities in Britain in the 18th and early 19th centuries was a reflecting of the "gentling" of society, an assertion of the family as against the community, a movement in attitude by which the old sports were seen as primitive relics of a bygone age. In some sense, developing societies may be going through a similar process, and traditional games will only survive or revive if they have genuine roots in the contemporary community.

Conclusions

To Westerners accustomed to notions of sport as the garden of human activities—and often a private garden at that—of sport for sport's sake; of sport for profit; and of sport for professional entertainment measured in both millions of dollars and centimeters, grams, and split seconds, sport in developing states comes as an exciting revelation. In economies of scarcity, a massive social force like sport cannot be excused responsibility, cannot be allowed to be merely a means of escape (important as that sometimes is). Furthermore, while it may sometimes be proper to defend the freedom of sport (say, from bureaucratic state manipulation), let us be careful not to give it a status more important than life itself.

Precisely because sport is potentially such an immense social force, it is far too important to be permitted to develop haphazardly or be left to the whim of private clubs, businessmen, circus promoters, and rich foreigners—as it was in virtually each developing country before its national liberation and regeneration.

The state control and planning of sport in such modernizing communities as Cuba, Nicaragua, China, the Soviet Union, and even Ethiopia may well have more relevance to developing nations than does our Western experience of sports development. That said, it is equally clear that Western sports and organization do have an important role to play in Africa, Asia, and Latin America—though it has to be a responsible one, and this can only happen when we in the First World stop trying to make Third World sport merely an appendage of our own system. As the *Third World Liberator* has put it,

> Today Third World education is a mere appendage to the First World. It has culturally enslaved us to serve their needs. The very fact that it has created self-seeking careerists who often emigrate to the West to sell their skills to the highest bidder, with no sense of any social commitment to their people and their society only goes to show how little the Western education model has benefited us. It has not helped us to understand our societies and our problems better. It has not brought about a transformation of our peoples and our societies and the creation of more just, equal and humane individuals. (p. 4)

The fact that sport is germane to developing countries and to their social change would seem beyond dispute. What *kind* of sport, however, is a matter for debate—perhaps a mixture of indigenous games and Western sports modified and adapted to suit local conditions and national culture? Yet without state support to promote and protect a nation's cultural identity, the latter can trample upon the young shoots of the former—or even emasculate and package them up for mass consumption and profit, as has happened with some popular games and pastimes in Western societies (e.g., darts, snooker, bowls—even fun runs—in Britain).

One thing is certain: Far from being a luxury, *sport—or, better still, physical culture—in modernizing societies is an absolute necessity.*

Acknowledgment

I would like to acknowledge my gratitude to Dennis Brailsford, Bruce Kidd, Peter McIntosh, and Margaret Talbot for their valuable comments on, and contributions to, this paper.

References

Adedeji, J.A. (1979). Social and cultural conflict in sport and games in developing societies. *International Review of Sport Sociology*, **14**, 60-69.

Adefope, H.E.O. (1973). The role of sport in the creation of national identity and its contribution to the search for understanding between different communities and cultures. In Ommo Grupe (Ed.), *Sport in the modern world* (pp. 560-567). New York: Springer Verlag.

Anyanwu, S.U. (1980). Issues in and patterns of women's participation in sports in Nigeria. *International Review of Sport Sociology*, **15**, 87-95.

Augusto, M. (1969). Physical education in Brazil. *Physical Education Around the World*, **monograph 3**, 20-27.

Ayi-Bonte, S.G. (1973). Sports instruction in developing countries. In Ommo Grupe (Ed.), *Sport in the modern world* (pp. 575-581). New York: Springer Verlag.

Balashov, V.S. (1973). Sotsialistichesky sport [Socialist sport]. *Sport v SSSR* [Sport in the USSR], **6**, 2-4.

Barushimana, A., & Maximenko, A.M. (1978). Attitudes towards sporting activity of top-class athletes in Central Africa. *International Review of Sport Sociology*, **13**, 39-49.

Castro, F. (1974). In S. Castanes (Ed.), *Fidel: Sobre el deporte* (pp. 287-298). Havana: El Deporto.

Castro, F. (1976). *El Deporto*, **3**, 1-13.

Chongqi, Z. (1986). Minority people's sports meet. *China Sports*, **3**, 33-35.

Davletshina. R. (1976). Sport i zhenshchiny [Sport and women]. *Teoriya i praktika fizicheskoi kultury* [Theory and practice of physical culture], **3**, 60-64.

Eichberg, H. (1984). Olympic sport: Neocolonisation and alternatives. *International Review for Sport Sociology*, **19**, 98-108.

Garcia-Bango, J. (1973). The Cuban revolution: Experiences in the development of physical culture, sports and recreation. In Ommo Grupe (Ed.), *Sport in the modern world* (pp. 385-388). New York: Springer Verlag.

Glassford, G., & Clumpner, R. (1973). Physical culture inside the People's Republic of China. *Physical Education Around the World*, **monograph 6**, 7-18.

James, C.L.R. (1963). *Beyond a boundary*. London: Hutchinson.

Landar, A.M. (1972). Fizicheskaya kultura: Sostavnaya chast kulturnoi revolyutsii na Ukraine [Physical culture: A component part of the Ukraine's cultural revolution]. *Teoriya i praktika fizicheskoi kultury* [Theory and practice of physical culture], **12**, 10-22.

Lisitsyn, B.A. (1985). *Sport i religioznye organizatsii* [Sport and religious organizations]. Moscow: Fizkultura i sport.

Nekrasov, V.P. (1985). Fizicheskaya kultura protiv pyanstva [Physical culture against drunkenness]. *Teoriya i praktika fizicheskoi kultury* [Theory and practice of physical culture], **7**, 37-39.

Rodionov, B.B. (1975). Sport i integratsiya [Sport and integration]. *Teoriya i praktika fizicheskoi kultury* [Theory and practice of physical culture], **9**, 5-10.

Sazima, D. (1969). Physical education in Ethiopia. *Physical Education Around the World*, **monograph 3**, 52-53.

Semashko, N. (1926). *Puti sovetskoi fizkultury* [Paths of Soviet culture]. Moscow: Fizkultura i sport.

Semashko, N. (1928). Desyatiletie sovetskoi meditsiny i fizicheskaya kultura [A decade of Soviet medicine and physical culture]. *Teoriya i praktika fizicheskoi kultury* [Theory and practice in physical culture], **5**, 1-9.

Sohi, A.S. (1981). Social status of Indian elite sportsmen in terms of social stratification and mobility. *International Review of Sport Sociology*, **16**, 58-67.

Stepovoi, P.S. (1984). *Sport. Politika. Ideologiya* [Sport. Politics. Ideology.]. Moscow: Fizkultura i sport.

Sviridov, G. (1963). *Jackson ostayotsya v Rossii* [Jackson stays in Russia]. Moscow: Fizkultura i sport.

Talbot, M. (1984, July). *Women and sport: A gender contradiction in terms?* Paper presented at the International Conference of the Leisure Studies Association, Falmer, Sussex, England.

Unmask the enemy. (1986). *Third World Liberator*, **1**, 1-4.

Wubin, Z. (1985). A rising sport in China. *China Sports*, **9**, 5-7.

PART II

Sport

The Design of Marathon Studies for Comparative Purposes

Gerald V. Barrell
David Holt
Jill M. MacKean

For many sports, there exists no comprehensive list of participants; however, researchers seek to study participants, their characteristics, and their performances. We here describe the design of a study of marathon runners, but the general principles also apply with greater or lesser force to other sports and activities.

In marathon running, samples are often obtained by selecting from those who take part in particular events; in fact, it is common for competitors from a single event to be used. A major objective is often to describe the characteristics of participants and to relate these to the population from which the runners originate. Thus, the fact that the participation rate is five times as high for one subgroup compared to another is of direct interest.

A second common objective is a direct comparison between subgroups, such as regarding the average hours spent training each week by two age groups. Here the comparison is internal to the sample data in the sense that general population information is not required. The sampled competitors from the two subgroups must be representative of their subgroup. Other analyses, such as regression analysis, fall within this category of analyses internal to the study data.

A third objective is the comparison with other studies from different regions or points in time. In comparative studies it is essential to understand the link between each sample and the population from which it was drawn, because one would want to know whether observed differences could be accounted for by differences in the structure of the populations being compared.

A basic problem, which is particularly true for studies that sample competitors in one event only, is relating the sample obtained to all competitors in any area. Events have greater appeal for those who live locally and yet attract some (perhaps better) participants from greater distances.

It is not clear in what sense the participants in any event are a sample from any larger population of runners. In addition, even for would-be competitors within the locality, those who actually compete are unrepresentative of all marathon runners. There is an overrepresentation of those who compete more often and a corresponding underrepresentation of those who compete less often.

To illustrate, suppose that there are 4,600 marathon runners living in an area. Their weekly training mileages and relative frequency of competition are given in Table 1. The relative frequency of competition shown means that those in the third category compete twice as often as those in the first. At an event the overrepresentation of those frequent competitors results in an average training mileage of 37.2 miles, compared with the true population average for the 4,600 runners of 31.4 miles.

In addition, if the event attracted heavy trainers from farther afield, there would be a further bias if the actual competitors at any event were taken to represent competitors in general. Comparisons between subgroups could also be affected. The difficulty extends to regional or historical comparisons, because the extent to which those who take part in a particular marathon are representative of all runners in the area is unknown. Apparent differences may simply reflect the unrepresentativeness of the sample and differences in the frequency of competition, rather than real differences between the regions or years. In Table 1, for example, if the relative frequencies of competition had been (1, 1, 2, 2, 2), the population average would still have been 31.4 miles but the competitors' average would be reduced to 33.6 miles.

Wessex Marathon Study

In a recent study of marathon runners, a design was used that, to a large extent, permitted the impact of these various factors to be explored. In 1984 a study was conducted of marathon runners living in the Wessex

Table 1 Comparison of Weekly Training Mileage and Relative Frequency of Competition

Weekly training mileage	Relative frequency of competition	Number of runners
10	1	350
15	1	640
25	2	1,900
45	3	1,260
60	4	450

region of England, where there has been an increase in both marathon and half-marathon events, from one event in 1981 to 26 events (13 marathons and 13 half-marathons) in 1984. The number of entries has also grown substantially. The target population was taken to be Wessex residents who had completed at least one marathon in 1984. This definition excluded marathon runners who did not complete a marathon during the year, such as those who were prevented through illness or injury; however, the use of a calendar year as the reference period excluded only the chronically sick or injured. The remaining weakness in the definition was the exclusion of people who had prepared for a marathon and had entered or even started, but who failed to *complete* any marathon in 1984. A separate study was undertaken to obtain information on this group.

We use the data from this study to evaluate various alternative designs that might have been used. No list of marathon runners existed in 1984, and the only practical approach was to base the study on a comprehensive list of events that could easily be compiled. Four approaches were possible; the first was to base the study on a single marathon event. A number of studies have adopted this approach, but this was quickly rejected on the grounds that the participants would likely not accurately represent the target population.

The second alternative was to select a larger sample of marathon events within the region and to select all or a sample of the competitors at each selected event. This overcomes some of the deficiencies of basing the sample on a single event. The selection would be biased toward the runners who compete more often, but all samples have this problem, which can be overcome by reweighting techniques. The most likely flaw is the fact that any marathon runner who does not compete in a marathon within the region cannot be included in the sample. Estimates of the number of marathon runners, in total or in specific subgroups of interest, would be downward biased, as would the corresponding participation rates for population subgroups.

The third alternative design was to include in the sampling frame not just marathons within the region but also marathons outside the region (but close enough to attract Wessex residents). We term this larger list the *extended sampling frame*. We emphasize that the target population was still Wessex residents. Any runner selected who subsequently proved to live outside Wessex would be rejected from the sample (as were such runners selected from marathons held within the region). The problem with this alternative is that there is no natural limit to the extra marathons to be included. To greatly extend the sampling frame is unrealistic, because distant events require selecting large numbers of competitors for only a small number of Wessex residents.

The fourth alternative approach was to extend the sampling frame by including half-marathon events. This is a valid design, even if we study only those who complete a full marathon, but there is a cost. For the previous alternatives, we could identify Wessex residents by their addresses without contacting them and know that each had completed a full marathon. For half-marathon competitors, we would be unable to tell, until we contacted them, whether they had also completed a full marathon elsewhere in 1984. The benefit was that all Wessex marathon runners were available to be selected, so long as they had completed a full or half-marathon in the sampling frame used. Also, a sample could be selected of both full and half-marathon runners, and estimates could be made for full or half-marathon runners separately or together.

The study design adopted was using an extended sampling frame of marathon and half-marathon events. A two-stage design was used. At the first stage the events were stratified into full and half-marathons, and also into large and small events, on the basis of the estimated number of competitors from Wessex. A simple random sample of events was selected from each stratum (14 events in all). For the second stage, the results from each selected event were used to stratify competitors into four time strata (with different boundaries for full and half-marathons), and a simple random sample of competitors was chosen from each time stratum. Addresses for the sample were obtained from entry forms. In total, a sample of 1,637 Wessex competitors was chosen, although this was reduced to 1,470 after the duplications arising from selecting the same runner at different events had been identified.

The achieved sample, like all samples from competitors at events, was biased toward the frequent competitor and needed to be reweighted during analysis to compensate for this. No contact was made with respondents until the end of 1984. In this way, a complete competition history for the year—in particular, the number of completed marathons and half-marathons that were in the extended sampling frame—could be obtained from each respondent; this is an essential requirement for reweighting during subsequent analysis. A mail questionnaire was sent to each selected runner with a follow-up letter for nonrespondents. Finally, a small team of interviewers made personal contact with persistent nonrespondents, resulting in an overall response rate of 93%.

Results

We may estimate the number of marathon runners in Wessex and subdivide these into those who ran a marathon within Wessex; those who did not, but who ran a marathon in the extended frame; and those whose only full marathons were too distant from Wessex to be included in the extended frame. The estimates are downward biased, due to people who ran in marathons distant from Wessex and who completed no half-marathons in the sampling frame. It is our feeling that these are few, but we have no direct evidence of this.

We note from Table 2 that an estimated 334 marathon runners (22.2% of the Wessex total) competed only in full marathons that were too distant from Wessex to be included in the sampling frame. Had we not included a sample of half-marathons, this group could not have been identified, and estimates based on marathon events only would have been severely biased. The London Marathon (18,000 runners) probably accounts for a substantial proportion of these additional marathon runners, but

Table 2 Estimated Number of Wessex Marathon Runners, by Location of Marathon

	Location of marathon	Number of runners
Local	Within Wessex	1,103
	Not within Wessex, but on the extended list	67
Distant	Completed a half-marathon on the extended sampling frame	334
Total		1,504

to have included the London Marathon in the sampling frame would have required a substantial sampling operation in order to identify Wessex residents. The impact of the half-marathon sample on the estimated number of marathon runners, and therefore on participation rates, is substantial.

Equally important, the impact varies for different age groups, social classes, and so forth, as Table 3 reveals.

We see from Table 3 that whereas 22.2% of Wessex marathon runners competed only at a distance from Wessex, this value is 43.6% for women. Also the "distant" runners have proportionately often been over 50 and under 30 years of age; in social classes IIIM, IV, and V; and first-time marathon runners in 1984. They also tend to have completed fewer events in 1984.

The remaining questions are ones of overrepresentation of those who compete more often at any event, of the effect this may have on analyses that make no allowance for this. Table 4 shows the average value of a number of characteristics according to the number of events completed (both full and half-marathons) in the extended sampling frame. This shows that training and performance vary in a systematic way with the number of events completed.

Although effects are not very large on an overall average, the overrepresentation of more serious trainers and better performers upwardly biases estimates of training in the population of marathon runners as a whole and downwardly biases estimates of average time taken. This is best seen in Table 5, which shows estimates of the average of each of these variables for Wessex residents in each of the full marathons sampled, taking no account of the overrepresentation of frequent competitors. We see that though the biases are small, there is almost always a consistent bias between the individual marathon results and the population average. This is a combination of the overrepresentation of frequent competitors and the omission of those who competed in a full marathon only at a distance from Wessex. Almost all individual marathons show an average

Table 3 Characteristics of Distant and Local Marathon Runners (in percentage)

	Sex and age groups						
	Male	Female	15–29	30–39	40–49	50+	Total
Distant	22.0	43.6	18.8	22.3	24.5	33.3	22.2
Local	77.8	54.4	81.2	77.7	75.5	66.7	77.8
Number	1,436	68	452	592	368	83	1,504

	Social classes						
	I	II	IIIN	IIIM	IV and V	Forces	Total
Distant	25.0	23.5	20.4	16.7	14.3	34.1	22.2
Local	75.0	76.5	79.6	83.3	85.7	63.9	77.8
Number	120	387	336	317	105	173	1,504

	First marathon and number of events on extended frame						
	First marathon in	before	Number of events on extended frame				
	1984	1984	1	2	3	4	5
Distant	13.2	25.1	25.1	24.8	18.1	9.7	11.1
Local	86.8	74.9	74.9	75.2	81.9	90.3	88.9
Number	365	1,066	642	456	233	110	63

Note. Estimated numbers in various categories may not total 1,504, because of nonresponses.

training mileage and maximum training mileage above the population average. Similarly, average times are systematically lower.

The overall bias due to overrepresentation of those who compete more often is not great. In part, this is because the survey was undertaken at the time when there had been a large growth in participation. A large proportion of marathon runners performed in only one event, and this dominated the biasing effects of more frequent competitors. With a smaller influx of new competitors or for some subgroup analyses the biasing effects may be much larger.

Conclusions

The results suggest that it is unwise simply to sample those who compete in marathons within a small area. A substantial increase in coverage is

Table 4 Average Value of Selected Variables for Marathon Runners, by Number of Events Completed

Variable	Number of events completed							Population average
	1	2	3	4	5	6	7	
Maximum weekly training mileage	35	43	43	45	49	53	55	40
Average weekly training mileage	25.3	30.1	30.5	32.7	34.5	41.4	46.0	28.6
Months of training	8.6	10.0	10.6	11.2	10.9	11.6	11.1	9.6
Marathon time[a]	242.7	223.1	223.1	221.8	206.8	204.6	194	230.5
Half-marathon time (where applicable)	99.4	95.8	92.6	91.9	86.5	84.8	83.4	96.1

[a]The best marathon time achieved in 1984 at a marathon on the sampling frame for local runners only.

Table 5 Unweighted Average Values of Variables, by Specific Marathon

Variable	Specific marathon[a]						Population average
	1	2	3	4	5	6	
Maximum training mileage	43.1	48.7	42.1	47.9	49.0	46.3	44.5
Average weekly training mileage	30.9	33.0	28.6	35.6	36.9	35.4	31.0
Months of training	11.3	11.6	11.4	11.4	11.6	11.6	11.4
Fastest marathon time	214.1	221.1	230.8	211.0	201.3	204.3	223.5
Fastest half-marathon time (where applicable)	89.0	90.9	92.9	89.1	88.7	89.6	93.4

[a]One selected marathon had such a small sample size that the results are not presented.

attained by extending the sampling scheme to events outside the area and by including competitors at half-marathons; the people who would be omitted, if this were not done, vary systematically from those who ran marathons within the region. A reweighting to allow for those who compete more often is desirable. Although the biasing effects are not large, samples from individual marathons showed consistent biases, compared with unbiased population estimates.

Acknowledgment

The project is funded by the Health Promotion Research Trust.

A Comparative Analysis of Results of the 1984 Los Angeles Summer Olympic Games

Herbert Haag
Guenter Riesinger

The mass media have a great responsibility in shaping public understanding of sport. However, this responsibility is not often recognized. All too frequently, the mass media sensationalize sport. The perpetuation of the "medal table" for the Olympic Games and world championships is an example, transmitting to the public a wrong impression of athletic performance being related to nationality.

Research in sport science, like any research, needs justification. The following are questions of a metatheory that is dealing with three aspects: What is the body of knowledge? What are the research methods? What is the function of the research? The last question can be answered in relation to the research with which this report deals. Research must deal with social problems—in this case, with the creation of a wrong perception of top-level athletics given by the mass media. Research must also offer alternative answers in order to improve social perceptions, for example, through better mass media reports on top-level athletics.

The hypothesis for this research was that the medal table used in all mass media to report on athletic success by nationality in Olympic Games is incorrect and misleading. First, the gold, silver, and bronze medals are counted as of equal value for ranking countries (see Table 1).

Four alternatives that have a much higher degree of objectivity can be developed:

1. Distribution of 3 (gold), 2 (silver), and 1 (bronze) points.
2. Distribution of 8 to 1 points for the places in the finals.
3. Relating the gained points (3, 2, 1) to each country's total population.
4. Relating the gained points (3, 2, 1) to the number of competitors.

A summative score was also calculated. In an earlier study (Haag & Riesinger, 1985), correlation with the gross national product was calculated, but it could not be obtained for every country; therefore, it was omitted in this analysis.

Table 1   Comparison of Results in the 1984 Summer Olympic Games Using Alternate Methods of Scoring

Country	Traditional medal table Rank	Medal points[a] Rank	Medal points[a] Points	Final points Rank	Final points Points	Medal points per inhabitant Rank	Medal points per inhabitant Points	Medal points per number of competitors Rank	Medal points per number of competitors Points	Summarized ranking 1 to 4 Rank	Summarized ranking 1 to 4 Points
U.S.A.	1	1	401	1	1,592	14	1.774	1	767	2	4.25
Rumania	2	3	109	5	466	5	4.954	3	206	1	4.00
Germany	3	2	112	2	716	11	1.806	2	261	2	4.25
China	4	5	70	7	379	42	0.070	6	134	13	14.50
Italy	5	6	66	6	383	17	1.157	7	118	4	9.00
Canada	6	4	82	3	508	8	3.416	5	153	3	5.00
Japan	7	7	60	10	323	26	0.512	12	72	11	13.75
New Zealand	8	14	31	16	137	2	10.333	15	55	8	11.75
Yugoslavia	9	12	36	13	169	15	1.636	4	161	7	11.00
South Korea	10	11	37	12	183	20	0.973	8	111	9	12.75
Great Britain	11	8	57	4	470	18	1.017	13	62	6	10.75
France	12	9	44	8	372	21	0.814	9	107	8	11.75
The Netherlands	13	15	25	14	164	13	1.785	11	74	10	13.25
Australia	14	10	40	9	327	9	2.666	10	77	5	9.50
Finland	15	16	24	15	146	6	4.800	19	23	12	14.00
Sweden	16	13	34	11	220	7	4.250	16	54	8	11.75
Mexico	17	18	13	22	59	36	0.180	21	13	22	24.75

18	Morocco	23	6	34	16	29	0.300	24	6	26	28.50
19	Brazil	17	15	19	90	38	0.121	14	59	19	22.00
20	Spain	21	9	19	90	30	0.243	18	35	19	22.00
21	Belgium	23	6	30	29	25	0.600	23	9	23	25.25
22	Austria	24	5	23	51	24	0.625	26	4	21	24.25
23	Portugal	26	4	32	19	27	0.400	25	5	26	28.50
24	Kenya	33	3	26	38	35	0.187	26	4	30	30.00
25	Pakistan	33	3	40	8	46	0.037	17	39	33	34.00
26	Switzerland	19	12	17	131	10	2.000	20	14	14	16.50
27	Denmark	21	9	20	78	12	1.799	21	12	15	18.50
28	Norway	26	4	21	68	19	1.000	26	4	20	23.00
29	Jamaica	33	3	27	36	16	1.500	22	10	24	27.00
30	Greece	33	3	24	46	29	0.300	27	3	25	28.25
31	Puerto Rico	33	3	33	18	22	0.750	27	3	27	28.75
32	Nigeria	42	2	31	22	47	0.027	24	6	36	36.00
33	Syria	42	2	39	10	31	0.222	28	2	34	35.00
34	Colombia	42	2	43	7	41	0.074	28	2	39	38.50
35	Peru	42	2	37	12	39	0.111	28	2	37	36.50
36	Ivory Coast	42	2	43	7	3	10.000	28	2	28	29.00
37	Thailand	42	2	43	7	45	0.042	28	2	41	39.50
38	Egypt	42	2	29	31	44	0.047	28	2	35	35.75
39	Ireland	42	2	39	10	23	0.666	28	2	33	34.00

(Cont.)

Table 1 (Cont.)

Country	Traditional medal table Rank	Medal points[a] Rank	Points	Final points Rank	Points	Medal points per inhabitant Rank	Points	Medal points per number of competitors Rank	Points	Summarized ranking 1 to 4 Rank	Points
Venezuela	40	33	3	28	35	32	0.214	27	3	30	30.00
Turkey	41	33	3	26	38	43	0.068	27	3	32	32.25
Algeria	42	42	2	37	12	40	0.105	28	2	38	36.75
Taiwan	43	47	1	47	6	34	0.200	29	1	40	39.25
Iceland	44	47	1	37	12	4	5.000	29	1	29	29.25
Cameroon	45	47	1	47	6	34	0.200	29	1	40	39.25
Zambia	46	47	1	47	6	37	0.166	29	1	42	40.00
Dominican Republic	47	47	1	47	6	1	12.499	29	1	31	31.00

[a]Gold = 3, silver = 2, bronze = 1. [b]First place = 8 points to eighth place = 1 point.

The data (sport results) were collected from *Zeitschrift Sport*, published in Zurich. The sociocultural data were gained from the *Statistical Yearbook* of the United Nations Organization (UNO) (1981). Computer programs were developed in order to calculate the four alternative tables.

This report describes the transmission of results in athletics; alternative forms of reporting success in Olympic Games, with rank-orders according to points; alternative forms of reporting success in Olympic Games with rank-orders according to sociocultural factors; and summarized ranking. The report ends with some concluding comments.

Transmission of Athletic Results

Before transmitting results to the public, one must first assess athletic performance.

Modes of Performance Assessment

Methods of sports performance assessment are dependent on the sport category, for example, team sports and individual sports. In regard to the given research topic, criteria that relate to modes of performance assessment are of interest. Three such modes can be delineated:

1. Centimeter/gram/second sport disciplines (measurement as the form of assessment)
2. Art sport disciplines (estimate as the form of assessment)
3. Games (One form of assessment is counting goals by number. Furthermore, measurement and estimate are also forms of assessment of games.)

Thus, modes for assessment of athletic performance vary. On the basis of such an assessment, the judgment is made, which is then transmitted to the public.

Value Judgments of Athletic Performances

Before the results can be transmitted, a value judgment must be made. In this regard, the comparisons are used. The following comparisons can be made: (a) with oneself (self-evaluation), (b) within a group, (c) between groups of similar nature, (d) with relative norms (e.g., AAHPERD percentile norms), and (e) with absolute norms (e.g., world record). The educational value of these comparisons decreases from (a) to (e). Reporting athletic performance using within-group and absolute-norm comparisons are mostly applied in order to produce information.

Alternate Methods of Reporting Success in the Olympic Games

The first alternative model is based on the distribution of points. There is a wide range of possible methods of point distribution. The following two seem appropriate. One alternative is to award points for medals as follows: gold, 3; silver, 2; bronze, 1. The distribution of points (compare column 2 in Table 1) results in clear changes in the rank order, because the majority effect of gold medals with regard to ranking is taken away. Two examples: Switzerland moved from 26th to 19th, and Kenya fell from 24th to 33rd. Rank order on the basis of 3, 2, 1 points is also used to calculate the alternatives based on points related to number of inhabitants and points related to number of competitors.

Awarding points based on final places in competition is another alternative. By distributing 8 points, eight for first place, seven for second place, one for eighth place, and so forth, the breadth of top performance is better illustrated. Furthermore, it is legitimate to consider 8 places, because many states have as a selection criterion for sending athletes to the Olympic Games, the chance to reach finals. Two examples: Great Britain moved from 11th to 4th; Morocco fell from 18th to 34th.

Another alternative is to determine success based on sociocultural factors. Sociocultural factors within teaching-learning processes in physical activity include situations related to (a) the individual, (b) the group, (c) the institution, and (d) the time (e.g., 1980s). For athletics, the following are important sociocultural factors: economy, size of the population, religion, climate, education, and so forth. In this investigation, the number of inhabitants and the number of competitors have been taken as underlying sociocultural factors.

Points may be awarded in relation to the number of inhabitants. The basis here was the calculation with 3, 2, 1 points. If one is judging the athletic performance in a realistic way, the number of people should be considered. Two examples: With this calculation, Iceland moved from 44th to 4th, and the U.S., with a huge population, fell from 1st to 14th.

Points may be awarded in relation to the number of competitors. Competition in sport disciplines are distinguished by the number of competitors involved. All sport disciplines can be divided into individual, dual, and team sports. Thus, it makes a difference if a medal is won by a single competitor in long jump, by a crew of two in sailing (tornado), or by a basketball team with 12 players. Therefore, the sociocultural variable of number of competitors was considered in calculating 3, 2, and 1 points for a medal. It is felt that this procedure contributes to a much fairer and more objective perception of a medal won. Two examples: Pakistan moved from 25th to 17th; New Zealand, from 8th to 15th.

A summarized ranking system provides another alternative. Every form of ranking has deficiencies and shortcomings. The summation of four rankings, divided by four, provides an index that should be the most appropriate expression of the real performance of a country at the Olympic

Games. There can be observed interesting changes in the rank order (e.g., Australia moved from 14th to 5th; Mexico, from 17th to 22nd). There is not 100% objectivity; however, it is important to try to present quantitative data as objectively as possible in order to give an adequate interpretation.

Conclusions

Four final comments can be made:

1. Proposals made in the form of alternatives are a sincere attempt to provide more justice in the reporting of top-level athletics, because the reports so far given are neither fair nor legitimate.
2. The results of this investigation are furthermore seen as a contribution to judging teams relatively, rather than always judging absolutely. This seems to be an important attitude, needed to promote fairness and tolerance.
3. This research project will be continued by developing rank-orders on the basis of other sociocultural factors, such as, putting a country in one of several classes according to its number of Olympic competitors in 1984 or its number of sport club members in a respective sport discipline.
4. For now, a possible overall rank-order might be a fair average indication of performance level as it relates to the summer Olympic Games of 1984.

It is hoped that this kind of research will help promote fair and reasonable judgments related to sport, especially on a high performance level. This, in turn, will benefit athletics and the Olympic movement.

References

Haag, H., & Riesinger, G. (1985). Der medaillenspiegel ist ausdruck einer ungerechtfertigten bevormundung durch die großmächte. *Olympische Jugend*, **3**, 12-14.

Haag, H., & Riesinger, G. (1988). A comparative analysis of results of the 1984 Los Angeles Summer Olympics. (To be published in the Congress Proceedings of the ICHPER Congress, London).

Seppänen, P. (1972). Die rolle des leistungssports in den gesellschaften der welt. *Zeitschrift Sportwissenschaft*, **2**, 133-155.

United Nations Organization. (1981). *Statistical Yearbook*. New York: Author.

A Comparative Study of Interschool Competition in England, Greece, and the United States

Ken Hardman
March Krotee
Andreas Chrissanthopoules

At the fourth ISCPES seminar in 1984 in Malente, Federal Republic of Germany, there was general acknowledgment of the need for comparative research concerning competitive sport in schools. Internationally, concern has been expressed by physical educators about the ethos of competition within and between schools, and about the internal and external pressures to which this ethos is being subjected. The situation is nowhere better reflected than in the English and American school systems, where sport has traditionally played an integral role. A plethora of articles, editorials, and letters in a number of publications exemplifies the concern and the debate that is taking place (Krotee, 1980; *British Journal of Physical Education*, 1983). It was from the seeds of the ideas sown at Malente that this investigation emerged. To minimize problems of comparative research, it was decided (a) to focus the investigation on the relationship between participation in interschool competition and school values; (b) to gather data on secondary and subsidiary themes, in order to meet the special needs of other countries; (c) to limit the investigation to random samples of equal numbers of 14-year-old girls and boys enrolled in similar levels and types of schools; and (d) to review the development of interschool competition and the historical background against which it evolved, in order to provide a clearer understanding of the context and, hence, facilitate a more meaningful basis for comparison.

Purposes of the Investigation

The primary aim of this investigation was to discover whether students who participate in interschool competition have greater identity with school values than nonparticipants. Hendry's (1978) and Eitzen's (1976) research has suggested that the way in which students identify with the school and its values is an important factor in determining the influence of the school and its physical education on the pupils. On this basis, it was hypothesized that pupils who participate in school teams do identify with the school value system more than nonparticipants. Four areas related to the hypothesis were addressed: (a) pride in the school's success, (b) prestige for the school emanating from success, (c) the place of interschool competition in the life of the school, and (d) students' and teachers' perceptions of sports team members.

The secondary aim was to determine teachers' and students' perceptions of the purposes of interschool sport. This aim was prompted by the traditionally held view that interschool competition has fulfilled the claimed purposes of character building and moral education, as well as enhancement of physical and psychosocial skills.

The investigation's subsidiary aims were (a) to determine the number and proportion of students involved in interschool competition, (b) to ascertain the number and range of competitive activities, (c) to determine the proportion of students gaining representative honors, (d) to establish the extent of teachers' and students' commitment to preparation for competition, (e) to discover whether competition enhances social status, (f) to estimate parental approval and support, (g) to determine teachers' selection criteria for competitive sport, and (h) to establish the mode and effect of financing for interschool sport.

Discussions at Malente and subsequent exchanges of ideas revealed a number of special needs in some countries for information on various related aspects of interschool competition. The above aims reflect those needs as well as further issues raised in the survey of literature.

Methods

Two methodological criteria were considered important in designing the research strategy. First, a variety of categories including different areas and aspects of attitudes were addressed in order to examine their possible interrelationships. Second, a variety of variables were used. For pupils, membership or nonmembership on school sport teams and gender were examined in relation to aspects of attitudinal relationships. Gender of teachers was also considered. School and academic ability (England only) of pupils were other variables considered, but the data were not correlated for the purposes of this paper.

After pilot surveys (Baker, 1985), two questionnaires were devised—one for teachers and one for students—the main aims of which were to assess teacher and student attitudes about interschool competition. It was assumed that there is a correspondence between attitude and behavior, and safeguards were taken (e.g., asking the same question in a number of ways) to minimize the possibility of the respondent "doing one thing and saying another."

Questionnaires

Student and teacher questionnaires were developed. The first section of the student questionnaire attempted to establish to which variable group each student belonged and sought largely quantitative data on a number of subsidiary themes (refer to earlier mentioned aims). The second section comprised 18 statements concerning sport in school and interschool competition. The statements were constructed so that the respondent's "agreement" did not always correspond to a "positive" attitude.

The first part of the teacher questionnaire sought to establish an overall picture of staff involvement in interschool sports competition, the scope of competition itself, and the means of financing it. The second part aimed at determining teachers' perceptions of outcomes of their physical education programs, of the educational values of interschool competition, and of the characteristics of "good performers." The third part of the teacher questionnaire comprised 19 statements related to interschool competition. As with pupil responses, "agreement" did not necessarily reflect a "positive" attitude. The only variable used was gender.

Subjects

A sample of students was selected from a suburban township in a metropolitan area in each of the three countries studied. In England, 100 students were randomly selected from Bolton, Greater Manchester, to ensure a representative sample of team members and nonteam members. The otherwise random selection was divided equally between the genders. In Greece, 132 students from Nea Philadelphia, Attica, all of whom were team members, were chosen. The selection was divided equally between the genders. In the United States, 140 students from Wayzata, Minnesota, were randomly selected to give a representative sample of team members and nonteam members. The selection comprised 64 males and 76 females. (N.B. For ease of reporting, the countries, rather than the townships, are referred to in this paper.)

Results

Data were analyzed to compare (a) identity with school values for interschool sport competitors and nonparticipant students, (b) student and teacher perceptions of interschool competition, and (c) characteristics of interschool competitive programs. Refer to Tables 1–3 for summaries of the responses.

Identification With School Values

All countries' variable groups, except English nonteam members, responded positively to questions regarding pride in school's success,

Table 1 Summary of Student Questionnaire Responses for Team Membership and Gender

Question	England					Greece[a]				U.S.				
	T	NT	M	F	All	T	M	F	All	T	NT	M	F	All
7	2.5	2.3	2.3	2.42	2.4	1.87	2.08	1.67	1.87	2.81	3.39	3.05	3.03	3.0
8	4.1	3.5	3.62	3.78	3.7	3.48	3.62	3.33	3.48	4.43	4.33	4.19	4.57	4.3
9	3.4	3.1	3.36	3.04	3.2	1.86	1.80	1.92	1.86	3.64	3.26	3.59	3.41	3.4
10	2.7	2.4	2.88	2.06	2.47	2.62	2.89	2.35	2.62	3.35	2.94	3.34	3.07	3.1
11	4.0	3.2	3.36	3.60	3.48	3.96	3.74	4.18	3.96	3.63	3.65	3.55	3.71	3.6
12	4.2	3.0	3.80	3.88	3.84	4.40	4.47	4.33	4.40	4.29	4.02	4.05	4.30	4.1
13	3.0	2.6	2.68	2.92	2.8	2.18	2.48	1.88	2.18	3.27	2.89	3.08	3.16	3.1
14	3.2	3.3	3.04	3.52	3.28	3.75	3.89	3.61	3.75	3.95	3.65	3.48	4.13	3.8
15	3.9	3.6	4.44	3.66	3.9	3.30	3.38	3.23	3.30	3.88	3.63	3.69	3.87	3.7
16	3.5	3.2	3.3	3.26	3.28	3.92	3.83	4.00	3.92	4.08	3.44	3.77	3.89	3.8
17	4.2	3.7	4.04	3.74	3.89	4.26	4.14	4.38	4.26	4.23	3.89	3.88	4.29	4.1
18	4.0	3.8	3.78	3.92	3.85	3.95	3.88	4.02	3.95	4.03	3.98	3.83	4.17	4.0
19	3.2	2.9	3.34	3.38	3.36	1.74	1.79	1.68	1.74	2.78	2.67	3.08	2.45	2.7
20	3.6	2.4	3.0	2.88	2.94	3.70	3.77	3.62	3.70	3.47	3.15	3.34	3.34	3.3
21	4.2	3.3	4.04	3.92	3.98	3.77	3.86	3.67	3.77	3.92	3.87	3.83	3.96	3.9
22	3.6	2.5	3.14	2.48	2.81	2.45	2.27	2.62	2.45	3.02	3.59	3.00	3.45	3.2
23	4.4	3.7	4.0	3.86	3.93	4.48	4.52	4.44	4.48	4.35	3.94	4.03	4.33	4.1
24	4.5	3.5	4.0	3.58	3.79	4.45	4.44	4.44	4.45	4.33	3.50	3.78	4.20	4.0

Note. T = team; NT = nonteam; M = male; F = female.
[a]Nonteam scores were not available for Greece.

with nonteam members scoring lowest. It is perhaps significant that the scores of the variable groups are quite close together, except for the margin of difference between nonteam members' scores and those above them. This may well suggest that nonteam status and its converse are major features underpinning attitudes about competition, and this presents some evidence to support the hypothesis.

Positive responses to questions about prestige for the school emanating from success indicate recognition that the school's image is enhanced through sports competition. In England and the U.S., 22% and 44%, respectively, agreed that gaining prestige for the school is the main reason for competition (question 7); 90% of Greek, 63% of English, and 37% of American pupils disagreed with the statement. Disagreement was taken to reveal a positive attitude about interschool competition; agreement,

Table 2   Summary of Student Questionnaire Agreement-Disagreement Responses

Question	England			Greece			U.S.		
	A	D	DK	A	D	DK	A	D	DK
7	22	63	15	10	120	2	62	52	26
8	75	18	7	94	38	0	134	2	4
9	52	35	13	19	111	2	88	33	19
10	22	63	15	52	79	1	67	42	31
11	29	59	12	18	109	5	26	98	16
12	79	17	4	124	8	0	123	4	13
13	47	51	2	29	103	0	67	47	26
14	45	54	1	28	95	9	18	107	15
15	70	18	12	85	40	7	92	13	35
16	30	53	17	24	104	5	21	98	21
17	69	13	18	120	8	4	112	7	21
18	80	10	10	116	14	2	120	4	16
19	53	30	17	9	117	6	36	67	37
20	44	30	26	101	26	5	63	25	52
21	87	9	4	106	22	4	110	9	21
22	44	35	21	37	91	4	68	30	42
23	81	5	14	130	2	0	121	8	11
24	25	64	11	7	125	0	21	99	20

Note.   A = agree; D = disagree; DK = don't know.

though showing a recognition of one aspect of sporting activity, failed to register an appreciation of the wider implications of participating in school teams. Hence, English and, in particular, Greek pupils might be said to have a wider appreciation of the values of interschool competition. It is interesting to note, however, that American team members tended toward disagreement and, hence, can be identified with the wider values.

Whereas English and American students similarly agreed that a school is judged by performances of its sports teams, the Greek subjects strongly disagreed; this may reflect a cultural difference. All countries' variable groups considered success conducive to more community awareness of the school. Overall, in this category of responses, there was positive support from all variable groups (nonteam marginally higher than team members) in the American sample and from all except nonteam members of the English sample.

Table 3 Summary of Teacher Questionnaire Responses

Question	England M	F	All	Greece M	F	All	U.S. M	F	All	England A	D	DK	Greece A	D	DK	U.S. A	D	DK
12	4.0	3.6	3.8	2.5	2.0	2.4	3.6	4.2	3.9	16	4	0	1	4	0	7	3	0
13	3.7	3.3	3.5	3.5	4.0	3.6	4.0	4.2	4.1	14	3	3	4	1	0	8	0	2
14	3.7	3.6	3.65	3.75	4.0	3.8	4.6	4.2	4.4	16	4	0	4	0	1	10	0	0
15	3.4	4.0	3.7	4.25	4.0	4.2	3.4	3.6	3.5	16	4	0	5	0	0	8	2	0
16	4.0	3.8	3.9	4.5	4.0	4.4	2.8	2.0	2.4	16	2	2	4	0	1	2	7	1
17	1.8	1.8	1.8	2.25	2.0	2.2	1.6	1.6	1.6	3	17	0	1	4	0	0	9	1
18	4.2	4.0	4.1	2.75	1.0	2.4	4.4	3.8	4.1	20	0	0	1	3	1	7	3	1
19	4.0	3.3	3.65	3.75	4.0	3.8	3.0	2.8	2.9	14	4	2	4	1	0	4	5	1
20	2.1	1.6	1.85	3.5	2.0	3.2	1.8	1.4	1.6	0	19	1	3	2	0	0	9	1
21	2.0	1.5	1.75	2.5	1.0	2.2	1.8	1.2	1.5	1	18	1	2	3	0	1	9	0
22	2.7	3.3	3.0	4.25	2.0	3.8	2.4	1.8	2.1	8	11	1	4	1	0	2	8	0
23	2.0	1.6	1.8	1.5	1.0	1.4	1.4	1.4	1.4	3	16	1	0	5	0	0	10	0
24	3.7	2.6	3.15	3.75	2.0	3.4	2.0	1.4	1.7	11	7	2	3	2	0	1	9	0
25	4.2	4.6	4.4	5.0	5.0	5.0	3.4	3.2	3.3	20	0	0	5	0	0	5	4	1
26	4.4	4.3	4.35	4.5	4.0	4.4	4.4	4.6	4.5	20	0	0	5	0	0	9	0	1
27	2.6	2.0	2.3	3.25	2.0	3.0	3.6	4.0	3.8	15	5	0	2	3	0	6	2	2
28	3.2	3.2	3.2	3.25	2.0	3.0	3.4	2.8	3.1	11	8	1	2	3	0	6	4	0
29	4.2	4.8	4.5	4.0	5.0	4.2	4.4	4.4	4.4	19	0	1	4	1	0	9	0	1
30	3.8	2.7	3.25	4.5	4.0	4.4	4.0	3.2	3.6	14	5	1	5	0	0	7	3	0

Note. M = male; F = female; A = agree; D = disagree; DK = don't know.

English teachers unanimously recognized, along with 70% of American (Greek only 20%) teachers, that success enhances the reputation of the school. However, all three countries rejected the statement that failure in interschool competition reflects an unsuccessful physical education program. In addition, 90% of English and American teachers denied that interschool competition results are the equivalent of examination or academic course work success.

Teachers from both England (75%) and the U.S. (60%) thought that too much importance was attached to success in interschool competition. Furthermore, all teachers in the Greek and American samples, and 80% of the English, were in favor of instruction for all-around competence, rather than for excellence in one sport only. English and Greek teachers supported the notion that professional satisfaction is derived from interschool competition, but American teachers were divided on this issue.

English female teachers were less concerned than the males with this aspect; moreover, they did not feel status was enhanced by success, a sentiment expressed by 90% of all American teachers and the one Greek female respondent. English and Greek males expressed the opposite view.

With regard to the place of interschool competition in the life of the school, English team members had the most positive mean score in this category. American team members scored highest in response to questions on importance of competition in school life and degree of interest in competition. All countries' variable groups gave strong support to interest in interschool competition and its important role in school life. Of the English and Greek variable groups, only English team members and males agreed that interschool competition was the most important extracurricular activity. This does not necessarily imply indifference or dislike by the other groups. Rather, it may reveal a preference for other activities in place of, or in addition to, sports competition. In the U.S., all variable groups supported the importance of other activities; significantly, nonteam members were the most supportive.

In this category, with the teachers' responses there was no significant difference between males and females. Apart from American teachers, who did not regard interschool competition as important to the physical education program and who had some general reservations on proportions of students benefiting from extracurricular attention, there was a strong consensus between the countries on the value of additional coaching for talented pupils, the influence of teachers on performers, and the importance of the inherent values of participation being greater than only winning. Interestingly, the latter accords well with students' attitudes toward winning, especially in Greece and the U.S.

Pupils' and teachers' perceptions of sports team members were analyzed. Team members scored higher than nonteam members in all questions in this category. It would seem that the former possess a more realistic perception of their position within the school community. Unlike their Greek and American counterparts, English students (nonteam members excepted) believed teacher esteem was higher if one was a member of a team. English and Greek pupils did not consider that team membership enhanced peer respect, whereas American pupils' responses (nonteam members excepted) indicated it did.

Teachers from all three countries agreed that there is a relationship between sports participation and identity with school values. Additionally, English and American teachers held that school sports team members have more favorable attitudes to school than nonparticipants. Greek teachers, however, disclaimed this; indeed, they reinforced their stance when ranking qualities related to perceptions of purposes of interschool competition. English teachers, on the other hand, rated skill, fitness, and competitiveness more highly than qualities such as reliability, leadership, and a positive attitude to authority.

There was difference between teachers' views on the value of encouraging poorer performers to join teams. Greece was most strongly in agreement, and the U.S. most strongly in disagreement, with such encouragement; England took an almost middle-of-the-road stance, but marginally supported the U.S. position. Generally, the countries denied (U.S. and England strongly so) that team members receive extra attention in physical education classes. It is worth noting that over 80% of all pupils agreed that team members do have additional opportunities to improve skills—perhaps these occur in extracurricular time or informal practice sessions.

Analysis of all relevant responses in the primary aim categories using a one-tail t test indicated that for both England and the U.S., there was support for the hypothesis at .05 and .01 levels of significance. For England $t = 84$ 1.645 (significant at the .05 level) and for the U.S. $t = 17.88$ 2.33 (significant at the .01 level).

Teacher and Student Perceptions of the Purposes of Interschool Competition

Teacher responses clearly indicated differences between all three countries. A statistical analysis using the Kendall coefficient of concordance *(W)* reinforced by the Spearman rank order correlation coefficient of means *(r)* provided evidence of the lack of overall relationship between the countries' responses. Indeed, England and Greece expressed opposite views on both "outcomes" and "characteristics." A Spearman rank order correlation coefficient analysis did, however, reveal a highly positive relationship between English and American teachers on "educational values" $(r = .9)$.

There was little real difference between student responses from all variable groups, though English and American females were less concerned than males with winning and fitness. Team members were less inclined than other variable groups to view physical fitness as the main aim of competition: In the English sample, they were perhaps less than idealistic in their attitude to winning.

Characteristics of Interschool Competition

The number and proportion of students involved in interschool competition were determined. The U.S. had the highest proportion of pupils participating in interschool competition—61% of the sample; teachers, on average, estimated participation at 40%. The English data indicated a closer relationship between actual percentage of participants (31%) and mean teacher estimates (26%). Clearly, the Greek student sample could not be used for comparative purposes, but teachers estimated the proportion of participants at 30%.

The number and range of competitive activities were also ascertained. Teachers indicated a wide scope of competition, with the U.S. having the widest and Greece the smallest. Pupils' responses paralleled teachers' estimates in England and the U.S., but the Greek pupils' responses bore no relationship to those of the teachers. Such a discrepancy warrants further investigation. All countries had activities common to both sexes as well as single sex only—the Greek sample being an exception to the latter, in that there were no interschool activities that were exclusive to females.

The proportion of pupils gaining representative honors was determined. The data suggest similarities between Greece and the U.S. of representative honors beyond selection for school teams. The English sample had the lowest proportion.

The overall picture of students' and teachers' preparation for competition was one of considerable commitment. The U.S. had a significantly higher proportion of students spending more than 5 hours per week on preparation for competition; teachers, on average, spent 13.5 hours of extracurricular time per week on coaching school competitors. The English competitors spent less time on preparation than American and Greek students, and the teachers devoted half the time of their American counterparts to extracurricular coaching. Greek teachers spent minimal time in extracurricular coaching; this may suggest that time is devoted to competition preparation during class time. Indeed, Greek teachers' responses on the importance of competition would support this suggestion. The data for American students and teachers may point to the status of competition in the American "ethic" and to possible additional renumeration for extracurricular work.

All variable groups supported the idea that competition enhances social contacts. In the U.S., some 96% of all respondents agreed with this; figures for England and Greece were 75% and 71%, respectively.

There was little difference in the responses of all pupil variable groups to parental approval and support, and these were positive. In England, 69%, Greece, 91% and the U.S., 86% felt that selection for a team would bring parental approval. Teachers were generally of the opinion that parental support had a positive influence on involvement of students in interschool sport. Again, the U.S. presented data that is probably a reflection of the status of competition in some sectors of American society.

All teachers responded that skill was the main selection criterion for competitive sport participation. Enthusiam, reliability, and team spirit were other criteria mentioned. In England ($n = 4$) and the U.S. ($n = 2$), 20% of teachers indicated that "poorer performers" are encouraged to join school teams; in Greece ($n = 4$), though, 80% of teachers indicated such encouragement.

The modes and effects of financing interschool competition were compared. In England, six means of financing interschool sport were listed: school and departmental funds were the most prominent (70%); capitation (35%); "tuck-shops" and vending machines (together 20%); pupil contributions (30%); parent-teacher associations (20%). In Greece, the sole source of finance listed was the state. In the U.S., school funds taxation and student/parent contributions were listed. Contrary to trends in sport as a whole, there was no mention of commercial sponsorship.

In England, all male teachers agreed that lack of finance often limits the scope of interschool competition, whereas only 49% of female teachers felt this to be the case. In Greece, all teachers agreed that lack of finance limited the scope of interschool competition. In the U.S., 80% of male teachers and 60% of female teachers agreed on the relationship between lack of finance and limitation of the scope of interschool competition.

Conclusions

Clearly, participation in school sports activity is related to a variety of factors. Some British studies (Emmett, 1971; Sillitoe, 1969) have shown that socioeconomic status is a determinant of participation in extracurricular activities. If, as Murdock and Phelps (1973) have postulated, the underlying values and assumptions of the school are class bound, then it can be assumed that pupils who participate in interschool competition are more likely to identify with the school value system than nonparticipants.

Conversely, it is possible to hypothesize that a number of families and cultures possess value systems that may be counterproductive to children's progress through school. Parental encouragement must then positively influence involvement in school physical activities. Most teachers in this investigation believed this to be the case. It is interesting to note that involvement of females in interschool competition in the U.S. and, especially, in England is substantially lower than that of males. This feature supports the findings of Hendry and Singer (1981), Emmett (1971), and Talbot (1979), which indicated lower participation rates by females in extracurricular activities and may well reflect cultural factors and attitudes (Sharpe, 1977).

A controversy that surrounds interschool competition embraces antagonists who charge teachers with devoting considerable amounts of time to relatively few numbers of selected athletes, usually the most able and skillful performers. It is further argued that a disproportionate amount of money is expended on a selected few and that the best equipment and facilities as well as prime time are often reserved for these privileged few. This study did highlight some related contentious issues: the considerable commitment of staff time in coaching and preparation for competition of a few participants in all three countries; the almost inevitable emphasis on selecting the most skilled performers (Greek pupils endorsed this, despite their teachers' strong indication of support for encouragement of poorer performers); and all teachers were of the opinion that the extent of interschool competition was largely determined by available finances, though there was no evidence presented (or even sought) on proportional distribution of spending.

Many top-class athletes have been nurtured through networks of interschool competition and have benefited from teachers' commitment. The importance of such competition is, to some, undeniable: It is properly an outlet for students' abilities and skills; it can stimulate a lasting enthusiasm for sport; others can take delight in sporting achievements; the general ethos of a school can be enhanced in the public eye by success in sport; results may be seen by others as a barometer of effective teaching or coaching; and producing successful performers may be regarded as a measure of the quality of the teachers.

Some of these features were borne out in this investigation. In contrast with Greek teachers, who on the whole disagreed that prestige of the school is enhanced by competitive sports success and yet placed it first in the list of objectives of their program, English and American teachers did agree that the prestige of the school is so enhanced, despite placing it last in the objectives of their programs. It would appear that success is a by-product of the physical education program, not a primary aim (at least as far as English and American teachers are concerned); nevertheless it does have its place.

Many student participants were less inclined to regard winning as a principal aim of competition and were more enthusiastic about concepts of self-esteem, support for the school, affiliation, and establishing new social contacts. The highly positive responses lend support to the claims for competitive activity with regard to development of social relationships, contrasting with the views of Glew (1983) on social contact and positive interaction. Perhaps the students overestimate the social outcomes of interschool competition, but at least they attach value to it.

Notably, in this exploratory investigation, team members overall revealed the most positive attitudes toward interschool competition. This was carried over into the notion of pride in the school and support for its standing in the community. Hence, there is an indication of some relationship between participation in interschool competition and identification with school values; this supports the findings of earlier studies.

Although the analysis of responses does indicate support for the main hypothesis, the evidence is not entirely conclusive, and, certainly, correlation must not be confused with causation. There are a number of cross-cultural differences, as well as similarities, that could only be properly understood in the light of substantial knowledge of the underlying ideological and sociocultural factors, among others. Such comprehension would facilitate a qualitative interpretation of the data assembled and bring out the comparison. In any event, features such as the weakness of the questionnaire method in identifying individual and small group variations, sample size, and its micro focus, as well as discrepancies between the individual countries' samples, render it unwise to draw more than tentative inferences from the results.

Nonetheless, the data collected and collated provide a valuable starting point for further investigation. The results and limitations of the study suggest several areas for possible future research:

1. A range of themes related to school value systems as a whole
2. The place and implications of competition in physical education programs
3. Socioeconomic factors: financing, and distribution of funds by sport, sex, or cultural prescription
4. Correlation or causality of participation and character development
5. A range of studies dealing with competition and cooperation within physical education and sport programs

References

Baker, C.A. (1985). *Pupil involvement in inter-secondary school sports competition and identity with the school value system.* Unpublished master's dissertation, University of Manchester, Manchester, England.

Board of Education (1920). *Annual Report.* London: Her Majesty's Stationary Office.

Eitzen, D.S. (1976). Sport and social status in American public secondary education. *Review of Sport and Leisure,* **1,** 139-155.

Emmett, I. (1971). *Youth and leisure in an urban sprawl.* Manchester, England: Manchester University Press.

Glew, P.A. (1983). Are your fixtures really necessary? *British Journal of Physical Education,* **14**(4), 100.

Hendry, L.B. (1978). *School, sport, and leisure: Three dimensions of adolescence.* Lepus Books.

Hendry, L.B., & Singer, F.E. (1981). Sport and the adolescent girl. *Scottish Journal of Physical Education,* **9**(2), 18-29.

Krotee, M.L. (1980). The effects of various physical activity situational settings on the anxiety level of children. *Journal of Sport Behaviour,* **3,** 158-164.

Murdock, G., & Phelps, G. (1973). *Mass media and the secondary school.* Macmillan.

Physical Education Association (1984) *British Journal of Physical Education,* **14,** 4-6.

Price, A. (1979). *Young people's perceptions of the influence of school and other socialising agents on participation in physical activities.* Unpublished master's dissertation, Manchester University, Manchester, England.

Sharpe, S. (1977). *Just like a girl: How girls learn to be women.* Penguin.

Sillitoe, K.K. (1969). *Planning for leisure.* London: Her Majesty's Stationary Office.

Talbot, M. (1979). *Women and leisure.* S.S.R.C./Sports Council.

A Comparative Study of the Research Systems of Sports Science in Different Countries

Xiong Douyin

Every country advanced in sports pays great attention to the development of the sports sciences. The research system of sports science of a country includes the organizational form and the administrative regulations by means of which scientific research on sports are made. It is often restricted by the social system and the economic condition of a country. By comparing the research systems of sports science in various countries of the world, this study has attempted to find a system of research best suited to China.

Types of Research Systems in Sports Science

The systems of research in sports science in various countries of the world at the moment can roughly be classified into three types, which can be called *concentrated, decentralized,* and *combined* systems. In the countries adopting the concentrated system, scientific research is carried out mainly by the special organizations of the state under the guidance of the government, with colleges of physical education, athlete training centers, and other scientific units playing a supporting role. The Soviet Union and the Eastern European countries represent this type of system, as does China.

In countries adopting the decentralized system, no nationwide research organization of sports science is established, nor is any such unified organization set up by the government. Scientific research is carried out separately by sports associations, departments of physical education in universities and colleges, medical institutions, and other research units in all parts of the country. The United States, Japan, and most of the western countries have adopted this type of system.

In countries adopting the combined system, the governments cooperate with mass organizations. In the past 10 years or so, France has taken this approach, and the Federal Republic of Germany and Switzerland are adopting similar systems.

The Concentrated System

Scientific research on sports in the Soviet Union and Eastern European countries has usually been done under the unified leadership of the physical culture and sports committee of the government of each country. In some of the countries, the sports committee cooperates with the academy of sciences or other government organizations. In Romania, for instance, scientific research on sports has been done jointly by the sports committee, education department, and public health department of the government.

These sport science committees consist of experts from all over the country. They convene one or two conferences each year. Under some science committees, there are many subcommittees of different branches of learning and a subcommittee of each significant special topic. The science committee's job is to draw up and determine long-term programs of scientific research, link the channels between scientific research and practice, appraise the training effects of the national sports teams, supvervise the experiments of special topics carried out in laboratories, and so on.

The Central Research Institute of Sports Science of the Soviet Union is not only the largest sport scientific institute in the country, but also the largest in the world. According to a report in 1985, the staff of the Institute consisted of 700 people (it reached 1,200 at its height), including 500 researchers and technicians. They not only do their own research but also guide and coordinate the research done by other institutes and colleges of physical culture. In addition, there are two research institutes of sports science in Leningrad and Tbilisi, which have more than 130 people in all.

The Research Institute of Sports Science of the Soviet Union aims at research in two areas: (a) the problems of mass sports, such as studying the methods of organizing mass sports, working out syllabuses of physical education for preschool and school children, setting up criteria for the "Ready for Labor and Defense" programs, designing fitness exercises for factory workers, and drawing up athletic training programs for ordinary citizens of different ages and different physical conditions; and (b) the methods of high performance athlete training for the purpose of raising the technical standards of sports throughout the country. The Institute attaches great importance to talent identification of athletes and the selection of individual events, the method of high-level athlete training, clinical practice of sportsmedicine, the methods of mathematical simulation and analysis, and the study of sports information.

The Decentralized System

Up to now, the United States and most of the Western nations have not set up any comprehensive research institute of sports science with various branches of learning. Currently, each branch of learning develops its research of sports science independently; within each branch, there are many units doing their research separately. Nevertheless, the West has had a lengthy history of development of sports science research.

Sports science research in the United States, like the sports in that country, is not controlled by the government. No research institute of sports science under the government has been set up so far. Scientific research is done separately in all parts of the country, especially in universities. It is reported that in the United States at present, there are at least 450 universities having colleges, or departments, of physical education. Many of these engage in scientific research on sports by themselves, because there is not any unified program in the country. The development of each branch of learning is often affected by economic aid from outside. The laboratory funds given by universities are quite limited, and research often depends upon the financial aid provided by industries or enterprises; thus, research efforts are often uncoordinated.

A new indication of the development of scientific research into competitive sports in the United States is the establishment of Olympic Training Centers, where training is combined with research. The first Olympic Training Center was established in 1977 in Squaw Valley. Later on, a new training center was built in Colorado Springs in preparation for the 1984 Olympic Games in Los Angeles. Since 1984 the Olympic Committee of the United States has made some changes in the scientific research organizations under the aegis of training centers and has formed a committee with three sections, namely, sportsmedicine, sports science, and education.

The Combined System

In recent years some Western European countries have incorporated the experience of the Soviet Union and the Eastern European countries and have adopted a kind of system in which the government and the people's organizations join together to do scientific research on sports. This type of system is used in France, and the Federal Republic of Germany and Switzerland are also adopting this approach.

In 1975 the French government issued a decree that merged the National Institute of Sports and the Teachers' College of Physical Education into the National Institute of Sport and Physical Education, and a new system of teaching and training combined with scientific research has come about. The research department of the National Institute, the high-level sport department, the personnel training department, and the medical department are parallel units maintaining close links with one another. The subjects they have studied in recent years are (a) the problem of the selection of athletes, (b) athletes in top form, and (c) the problem of children's physical activities.

Sports science research in France is by no means limited to the National Institute of Sport and Physical Education. The French Society of Sports Medicine has a long tradition. It makes academic exchanges through its periodical, *Medicine du Sport*, and some symposia it convenes.

The three different types of research systems of sports science in the world have been briefly discussed above, and some research activities in selected countries have been briefly introduced as well. Table 1 provides a comparison of the three types of sports science research systems.

Table 1 Comparison of Three Research Systems of Sports Science

	Concentrated	Decentralized	Combination
Organizer/leadership	Government sports department	Mass sports organizations or academic societies	Government organization of researchers from colleges of physical education and research institutes
Personnel	Researchers or teachers appointed by the government	Volunteers advertised for or invited by public bidding	Some researchers appointed by the government; most researchers invited by the government or mass sports societies
Funding	Government budget	Most provided by mass organizations, individual researchers, or enterprises entrusted with the research; some government aid	Government and mass organizations share expenses

Subject planning	Government assigned according to the country's needs; some decided, with government approval, by researchers	Mass organization invitations; researchers' free choice	Usually decided according to the demand of the mass organizations combined with the government; some assigned by the government; some, researchers free choices
Application of results	Applied and spread under the unified arrangement of the government	Spread by means of academic exchanges and publications	Applied and spread either by the government arrangement or by academic exchanges and publications
Comparisons	1. Manpower and material resources concentrated 2. Comprehensive research easy to make 3. Practice easy to service 4. Choice of subjects restricted	1. Manpower and material resources scattered, funds limited 2. Comprehensive research difficult to make 3. Practice difficult to service 4. Free choice of subjects	1. Manpower and material resources partially concentrated, funds ensured 2. Comprehensive research conditions and combinations of research with teaching favorable 3. Practice well combined 4. Rather free choice of subjects

The Research System of Sports Science in China

The research system of sports science in China is of the concentrated type on the whole. The science and education section of the State Physical Culture and Sports Commission leads and coordinates the research of sports science throughout China. There are now 30 research institutes of sports science all over China. Apart from the National Research Institute of Sports Science under the State Physical Culture and Sports Commission, the Research Institute of Electronic Sports Installations in Kunming (with 127 people, including 116 researchers and technicians) and the Research Institute of Sports Injury in Chengdu (with 160 people, including 99 researchers and technicians) are directly affiliated with the Commission.

Generally speaking, there is a research institute of sports science, or a similar organization, in every province or major city in China, but each is small in scale and embraces rather few branches of learning. In addition, 13 sports institutes, the university departments of physical education, and a number of teachers' colleges are doing scientific research as well. There is also a research institute of sportsmedicine in the Third Hospital of the Beijing Medical College, which is affiliated with the Department of Public Health of the Chinese government. At present, the number of full-time research personnel of sports science in China is more than 600.

The National Research Institute of Sports Science is the largest comprehensive research institute in China. It has a staff of 276 people, including 189 researchers and technicians. Within the Institute are eight research departments, namely, athletic training, ball game training, sports biomechanics, sportsmedicine, exercise physiology, mass sports (in which the topics of physical culture in schools, and spare-time training of children and youth are also studied), sports information, and sports instruments. Two other departments, sports psychology and sports theory, are about to be set up.

Besides the institutes mentioned above, a number of sports science societies exist. The China Sports Science Society (CSSS) is an organization affiliated with the Chinese Association for Science and Technology. Within the CSSS there are 10 subordinate societies focusing on sports theory (including sports philosophy and social sciences), athletic training research, sportsmedicine (including exercise physiology and biochemistry), sports psychology, sports biomechanics, sports information, sports instruments research, physical fitness research, sports statistics, and competition arena construction research. According to statistics at the end of 1984, the societies had a total membership of 5,600 people. There are branches of the societies, and some specialized subject committees subordinate to the societies, in 24 provinces and major cities in China. In order to disseminate research findings and make academic exchanges, the societies organize various kinds of public lectures, symposia, and classes for advanced studies. They also publish the periodicals *Sports Science, Chinese Journal of Sports Medicine,* and *Life Depends on Movement.* (Magazines and journals are also published by provinces, major cities, and colleges.) The societies make international academic exchanges with foreign academic organizations. They are members of the International Council of Sports Science and Physical Education. The activities of the societies have promoted the development of research in sports science and, especially, have drawn the attention of researchers in the domains of other sciences.

The research system of China at the moment is in keeping with the national conditions. Academic activities have been lively in recent years, and new branches of learning are absorbed one after another into research on sports science. For example, in the 1985 all-China symposium on sports philosophy and social sciences, there was a section on comparative physical education and sports. Now some provinces and major cities are preparing to set up their own comparative sports research groups, so as to form an all-China research organization on comparative sports. They have already found support from the China Sports Science Society.

Conclusions

In short, sports science is a new branch of science, and its research system has not fallen into a pattern yet. The three types of systems are influencing one another (the third type to a certain extent is a combination of the other two types). For a research system of sports science anywhere the following three principles must be taken into account.

1. The organizational structure of the research on sports must be set up according to the characteristics of sports science and the regularity of the research. Quite a lot of problems in sports science today must be studied comprehensively through varied branches of science, so that some good results can be achieved. No organization with only a single branch of science can do such research. A comprehensive research institute with various branches of science is obviously in an advantageous position.
2. Sports science is an applied science. Its research system must be able to help serve the administration of sports, sports teaching, sports training, physical exercise, the production of sports instruments and equipment, the construction of competition arenas, and so on. It must, of course, be able to help mainly in sports training and competition.
3. The research system of sports science must be favorable for establishing and strengthening the research systems of other pertinent branches of science. Sports science involves natural science, social science, technology, and administration. In case many and varied branches of science are not already brought together in one research organization, a nationwide unified program should be drawn up and concerted action must be taken among different research organizations, so that the development of various branches of science can be well balanced and coordinated. The work of applied research and basic research should be divided up as well.

Secondary Schools and Oxbridge Blues: From the 1950s to the 1980s

Timothy J.L. Chandler

In 1965 John Eggleston published a study entitled "Secondary Schools and Oxbridge Blues," which was an analysis of the relationship between preuniversity schooling and athletic achievement at Oxford and Cambridge ("Oxbridge"). Eggleston attempted "to discover if the well-established differential in chance of admission to Oxbridge between the public [independent] school and local education authority grammar school population [was] matched by similar differences in chance of award of a 'blue' [or 'letter']" (p. 233). Eggleston's analysis covered the years 1953/4 to 1962/3 and concentrated on the major sports of association football [soccer], rugby football, and cricket.

As Berryman and Loy (1976) observed in their comparative replication of Eggleston's study for Harvard and Yale, there have been markedly few sociological investigations into "the relationship between preuniversity schooling and achievement in several important non-academic sectors of higher education" (p. 61). Eggleston (1965) noted that such a situation is curious "in view of the widely held beliefs in the social and other non-academic advantages to be gained from university life" (p. 232).

One important measure of nonacademic achievement is athletic performance. As the results of Eggleston's study have shown, different educational backgrounds have clearly afforded differential chances of gaining a blue. Furthermore, these chances are further differentiated in terms of the differing status of the three sports reviewed.

The purpose of this study was to continue Eggleston's analysis of Oxbridge blues for the decades 1963/4 to 1972/3, and 1973/4 to 1982/3. Eggleston's study can be viewed as a benchmark against which to judge attempts to democratize Oxbridge as a result of the recommendations made in the Robbins Report on *Higher Education* (1964). The present analysis is, in some measure, a test of the effectiveness of Robbins to make the selection process for entry to higher education more equitable, thereby democratizing Oxbridge.

Data from the present study also provide a benchmark for future analysis of the effectiveness of recent changes in admission procedures at

Oxford, following the Dover Report (1983), and at Cambridge, following the decision by that university's colleges—following the example of Magdalene College—to join the national admissions consortium, the University Central Council for Admissions (UCCA). It has been predicted that these two changes will have an enormous impact on all aspects of university life, including sport, because they are attempts to erode finally the differential in chance of admissions to England's two most prestigious universities.

Blues are of particular interest in Britain because of their elitist associations within the universities and also, and perhaps more importantly, because of the leverage they provide in terms of the future occupational and social status of their holders. Again, as Eggleston (1965) notes, "university lore is rich in tales which equate the value of an Oxbridge blue with that of a 'first' " (p. 232), a 'first' being an honors degree equivalent to Summa Cum Laude. As such, the data presented here may help provide further information about the role of sport in educational settings as an avenue of social mobility.

Procedure

Investigation of the schools of origin of blues presents no major problem for the researcher, because such information is available in the national press and other appropriate annual sporting almanacs. However, to facilitate direct comparison with Eggleston's analysis, it was necessary to classify the blues' schools of origin using the categorization that he had used from Kelsall (1957). This classification contained five categories. These were one category of overseas students (O) and four of students at home schools, which were (a) independent Headmasters' Conference (HMC) schools; (b) Direct Grant schools, many of which were also HMC schools; (c) secondary schools maintained by local education authorities; and (d) other private schools not in membership with the HMC.

Limitations

Such categorization, although facilitating relative comparisons, slightly distorted the figures in terms of absolute comparison. This was because membership of HMC is by headmaster and not by school; thus, (although only rarely) when a school changes headmaster, it may no longer be a member of HMC. More serious was the problem of the categorization of Direct Grant schools for the years after 1978/9. During that year, because of the actions of the Department of Education and Science, a number of such schools became independent schools in membership of HMC. Twenty-nine became maintained local education authority schools. For the purposes of this study, schools have been categorized using Eggleston's criteria and their pre-1978/9 status, because direct comparison with his analysis was the primary purpose of this study. Thus, care should be taken in drawing conclusions based on absolute differences for the decade 1973/4-1982/3.

Results

The results both of Eggleston's study and the present survey are set in Tables 1 and 2. The numbers are numbers of blues awarded and not numbers of individuals, because some individuals were awarded more than one blue. An extreme case in the 1970s is A.J. Hignell of Denstone College, who was awarded eight blues for Cambridge—four in rugby football and four in cricket. Such a possibility only intensifies the relevance of this study as a model of nonexpanding status availability in a period when conditions of expanding demand existed, due to the growth in the number of students in higher education.

The tables indicate that the interesting variations in the membership of teams in each sport and between the universities that Eggleston highlighted have continued to some degree. In all three sports at both Oxford and Cambridge, the number of blues awarded to boys from maintained secondary schools has increased (see Table 2). By contrast, in all three sports at Oxford and in all football at Cambridge, the number of blues awarded to boys from independent HMC schools has declined. Only one Oxford cricket blue was awarded to a 'maintained' schools pupil in Eggleston's study. Yet, in the decade 1973/4–1982/3, 25 were awarded to boys from these schools. A similar increase from 5 cricket blues in the period 1953/4–1962/3 to 18 in the period 1973/4–1982/3 was experienced by boys from maintained schools at Cambridge. However, running counter to this trend was the number of cricket blues awarded to independent school students at Cambridge, which increased from 57 to 74 (+13.8%) during the three-decade period (see Table 3). Figures for the total number of blues in all three sports show quite clearly that the absolute chances of a boy from an independent school gaining a blue have been diminished over the period covered, whereas the absolute chances for a boy from a maintained school have increased (see Table 2).

Because accessible data were not available, it was not possible to compare these survey figures with the contribution of the five categories of schools to the total male undergraduate population of Oxford and Cambridge for all of the years between 1963/4 and 1982/3. However, as Eggleston noted, it is possible to achieve a basis of calculation by assuming that the figures for the total first-year undergraduate population for the years 1968/69 and 1978/79 are representative of the total undergraduate populations of the following years—that is, of the total entry for the years 1968, 1969, and 1970; and 1978, 1979, and 1980. Evidence of the slow change of the relative distribution of the schools of origin of Oxford and Cambridge undergraduates noted by Eggleston (1965) has continued (Tanner, 1983) and again suggests that the error involved in this assumption is likely to be more an absolute, than a relative, one. Therefore, in keeping with Eggleston (1965) the number of 1969 first-year students has

Table 1   Summary of Schools of Origin of Oxford and Cambridge Blues in Association Football, Rugby Football, and Cricket for the 1953/4–1982/3 Seasons

Sport	Oxford school of origin											Cambridge school of origin										
	1	%	2	%	3	%	4	%	O	%	Total	1	%	2	%	3	%	4	%	O	%	Total
1953/4–1962/3																						
Association football	39	35.5	8	7.3	63	57.2	–	–	–	–	110	21	18.9	22	19.8	65	58.6	3	2.7	–	–	111
Rugby football	65	42.7	13	8.6	31	20.4	11	7.2	32	21.1	152	88	58.7	8	5.3	26	17.3	24	16.0	4	2.7	150
All football	104	39.7	21	8.0	94	35.9	11	4.2	32	12.2	262	109	41.8	30	11.5	91	34.9	27	10.3	4	1.5	261
Cricket	61	56.5	21	19.4	1	0.9	–	–	25	23.2	108	57	53.3	13	12.1	9	8.4	5	4.7	23	21.5	107
All blues	165	44.6	42	11.4	95	25.7	11	2.9	57	15.4	370	166	45.1	43	11.7	100	27.2	32	8.7	27	7.3	368

1963/4–1972/3

	1 (n)	1 (%)	2 (n)	2 (%)	3 (n)	3 (%)	4 (n)	4 (%)	O (n)	O (%)	Total
Association football	14	12.7	14	12.7	81	73.6	1	1.0	–	–	110
Rugby football	61	40.7	19	12.7	32	21.3	6	4.0	32	21.3	150
All football	75	28.8	33	12.7	113	43.5	7	2.7	32	12.3	260
Cricket	51	46.4	12	10.9	16	14.5	1	0.9	30	27.3	110
All blues	126	34.0	45	12.2	129	34.9	8	2.2	62	16.7	370

	1 (n)	1 (%)	2 (n)	2 (%)	3 (n)	3 (%)	4 (n)	4 (%)	O (n)	O (%)	Total
Association football	20	18.2	7	6.3	78	71.0	5	4.5	–	–	110
Rugby football	68	45.3	13	8.7	63	42.0	–	–	6	4.0	150
All football	88	33.8	20	7.7	141	54.3	5	1.9	6	2.3	260
Cricket	56	50.9	11	10.0	20	18.2	3	2.7	20	18.2	110
All blues	144	38.9	31	8.4	161	43.5	8	2.2	26	7.0	370

1973/4–1982/3

	1 (n)	1 (%)	2 (n)	2 (%)	3 (n)	3 (%)	4 (n)	4 (%)	O (n)	O (%)	Total
Association football	13	11.8	18	16.4	71	64.5	6	5.5	2	1.8	110
Rugby football	50	33.3	30	20.0	37	24.7	3	2.0	30	20.0	150
All football	63	24.2	48	18.5	108	41.5	9	3.5	32	12.3	260
Cricket	56	51.0	11	10.0	25	22.7	1	0.9	17	15.4	110
All blues	119	32.2	59	15.9	133	35.9	10	2.8	49	13.2	370

	1 (n)	1 (%)	2 (n)	2 (%)	3 (n)	3 (%)	4 (n)	4 (%)	O (n)	O (%)	Total
Association football	14	12.8	13	11.8	81	73.6	2	1.8	–	–	110
Rugby football	75	50.0	16	10.7	42	28.0	6	4.0	11	7.3	150
All football	89	34.2	29	11.2	123	47.3	8	3.1	11	4.2	260
Cricket	74	67.3	7	6.4	18	16.3	3	2.7	8	7.3	110
All blues	163	44.1	36	9.7	141	38.1	11	3.0	19	5.1	370

Note. 1 = independent Headmasters' Conference schools; 2 = direct grant schools; 3 = locally maintained secondary schools; 4 = other private schools; O = overseas students.

Table 2　Total Number of Blues Awarded for Association Football, Rugby Football, and Cricket

Year	School of origin					
	1	2	3	4	Overseas	Total
1953/4–1962/3	331	85	195	43	84	738
1963/4–1972/3	270	76	290	16	88	740
1973/4–1982/3	282	95	274	21	68	740

Note. 1 = independent Headmasters' Conference schools; 2 = direct grant schools; 3 = locally maintained secondary schools; 4 = other private schools.

Table 3　Percentage of Net Gains and Losses in Number of Blues Awarded for Oxford and Cambridge, Seasons 1953–1983

Year	Oxford					Cambridge				
	1	2	3	4	Over-seas	1	2	3	4	Over-seas
Association football										
1953/4–1962/3	35.5	7.3	57.2	—	—	18.9	19.8	58.6	2.7	—
1963/4–1972/3	12.7	12.7	73.6	1.0	—	18.2	6.3	71.0	4.5	—
1973/4–1982/3	11.8	16.4	64.5	5.5	1.8	12.8	11.8	73.6	1.8	—
Direction of change	Down	Up	Up	Up	Up	Down	Down	Up	Down	—
% Change	23.7	9.1	7.3	5.5	1.8	6.1	8.0	15.0	2.9	—
Rugby football										
1953/4–1962/3	42.7	8.6	20.4	7.2	21.1	58.7	5.3	17.3	16.0	2.7
1963/4–1972/3	40.7	12.7	21.3	4.0	21.3	45.3	8.7	42.0	—	4.0

(Cont.)

Table 3 (Cont.)

	Oxford					Cambridge				
Year	1	2	3	4	Over-seas	1	2	3	4	Over-seas
1973/4–1982/3	33.3	20.0	24.7	2.0	20.0	50.0	10.7	28.0	4.0	7.3
Direction of change	Down	Up	Up	Down	Down	Down	Up	Up	Down	Up
% Change	9.4	11.4	4.3	5.2	1.1	8.7	5.4	10.7	12.0	4.6
					Cricket					
1953/4–1962/3	56.5	19.4	0.9	—	23.2	53.5	12.1	8.4	4.7	21.5
1963/4–1972/3	46.4	10.9	14.5	0.9	27.3	50.9	10.0	18.2	2.7	18.2
1973/4–1982/3	51.0	10.0	22.7	0.9	15.4	67.3	6.4	16.3	2.7	7.3
Direction of change	Down	Down	Up	Up	Down	Up	Down	Up	Down	Down
% Change	5.5	9.4	21.8	0.9	7.8	13.8	5.7	7.9	2.0	14.2

Note. 1 = independent Headmaster's Conference schools; 2 = direct grant schools; 3 = locally maintained secondary schools; 4 = other private schools.

been increased threefold to form a basis for calculating the rates shown in Table 4. Direct comparison with Eggleston's figures is not possible, because data equivalent to those for the years 1963/4–1972/3 and 1973/4–1982/3 are not available. However, the figures (see Table 4) give an indication of the relative differential between students from the five groups of schools. These figures suggest that at Oxford the relative chances of an independent school pupil gaining a blue have declined between the decades 1963/4–1972/3 and 1973/4–1982/3, whereas the relative chances for the maintained school student have risen. By contrast, the situation at Cambridge for the same periods is exactly reversed.

Major interest has continued to center on the relative chances of the independent and maintained school student, to which the recommendations of the Robbins Report (1964) and the recent efforts of the Dover Committee attest. Eggleston (1965) reported that "the absolute chance of the independent school pupil [achieving a blue] was greater in 1961/2 than

Table 4   Estimated Comparisons of the Differential Admission Rates and Differing Percentages of Blues Awarded to Students at Oxford and Cambridge

1963/4–1972/3	Oxford school of origin					Cambridge school of origin				
	1	2	3	4	O	1	2	3	4	O
General student population	40.3	16.1	37.0	1.3	5.3	40.5	16.3	37.2	1.9	4.1
Association football	12.7	12.7	73.6	1.0	0.00	18.2	6.3	71.0	4.5	0.0
Rugby football	40.7	12.7	21.3	4.0	21.3	45.3	8.7	42.0	0.0	4.0
All football	28.8	12.7	43.5	2.7	12.3	33.8	7.7	54.3	1.9	2.3
Cricket	46.4	10.9	14.5	0.9	27.3	50.9	10.0	18.2	2.7	18.2
All	34.0	12.2	34.5	2.2	16.7	38.9	8.4	43.5	2.2	7.0
1973/4–1982/3										
General student population	39.6	18.8	36.8	2.1	2.7	39.7	18.9	36.9	2.0	2.5
Association football	11.8	16.4	64.5	5.5	1.8	12.8	11.8	73.6	1.8	0.0
Rugby football	33.3	20.0	24.7	2.0	20.0	50.0	10.7	28.0	4.0	7.3
All football	24.2	18.5	41.5	3.5	12.3	34.2	11.2	47.3	3.1	4.2
Cricket	51.0	10.0	22.7	0.9	15.4	67.3	6.4	16.3	2.7	7.3
All	32.2	15.9	35.9	2.8	13.2	44.1	9.7	38.1	3.0	5.1

Note. 1 = independent Headmasters' Conference schools; 2 = direct grant schools; 3 = locally maintained secondary schools; 4 = other private schools; O = overseas students.

in 1956/7. . . . [T]he maintained grammar schoolboy's main source of blue opportunity is concentrated . . . in the lower status sport of association football. This has indeed compensated for their lower chance in rugby and has given them a higher overall chance of football blues than the independent schools'' (p. 239). The present survey findings suggest that at both universities, but more particularly at Cambridge, the absolute chances of a student from a maintained school gaining a blue for association football have increased. At Oxford the chances of gaining a soccer blue were higher in the decade 1963/4–1972/3 than in the preceding or subsequent decade, as were the chances of gaining a football blue at either university.

The chances of a student from an independent school gaining a rugby blue have decreased in the periods covered by Eggleston (1965) and the present study, although the independent school student has better chances at Cambridge than at Oxford for the honor of an appearance at Twickenham in early December. Oxford has a tradition of attracting overseas players to this event; students from this category account for at least one-fifth of the dark blues awarded for rugby during the three decades reviewed (see Table 4). Similarly, Oxford has continued to select a significant percentage of its cricketers from overseas (15%), whereas Cambridge has reduced its overseas contingent at Lord's by almost two-thirds, from 21.5 to 7.3%. Nevertheless, blues from overseas are still over-represented at both universities.

It is in cricket, the sport common to all of the home schools, that the maintained schools have made the least progress in overcoming the differential in the chances of gaining a blue. There is also a severe difference between Oxford and Cambridge in this category. Over the 3 decades surveyed, the percentage of Oxford cricket blues from maintained schools has risen 21.8 to 22.7%, yet maintained school undergraduates made up approximately 40% of the total undergraduate population in 1980. By 1982/3, as Tanner (1983) has shown, the ratio of independent to maintained school boys at Oxford was 51:49; yet, only 18% of Oxford cricket blues were won by maintained school pupils in that year.

The situation regarding cricket at Cambridge is even more severe. Not only has the percentage of cricket blues from independent schools risen over the course of the 3 decades, it has risen faster than the corresponding rate of growth for maintained schools' pupils (13.8 vs. 7.9%, respectively). The differential in cricket has widened both in absolute and relative terms over the course of 3 decades, and even in the decade 1963/4–1972/3, when the differential was eroded somewhat. Perhaps as a result of the adoption of the Robbins recommendations, independent school blues were still an absolute majority (50.9%, see Table 4).

Only in rugby football at Cambridge have independent school students maintained their dominance of footballing blues into the 1980s, whereas in cricket for the most recent decade independent school students maintained an absolute majority at both universities. Therefore, although there has been relative change in the differential with regard to both codes of football, in cricket—with the inferior chances of a blue for a boy from a maintained school, which Eggleston (1965) highlighted as being "the major factor in the overall inferior chance of boys from maintained grammar school within the universities" (p. 239)—the differential has continued.

Discussion

Social observers have long recognized the class overtones of Oxbridge sport. In keeping with Eggleston's (1965) findings, this study indicates that the type of school attended is still closely associated with differential chances of gaining a blue. Again following Eggleston (1965), this study shows these chances to be further differentiated by sport status, which are in themselves an indirect index of social class. However, because the social background of blues was not ascertained, and because there is at best only a moderate fit between school of origin and social class, the veracity and utility of such an index as a measure of status mobility must remain the subject of further study.

Eggleston (1965) was at pains to point out that there is no evidence of any kind of overt bias in the selection procedures of university teams. He noted that "the selection procedure is usually carried out in a highly public manner in the various trial games and seems to embody a genuine attempt to ensure objective assessment of the candidate's prowess" (p. 239). Such a proposition, he suggested, could be tested "by examining the number of blues achieving 'caps' " (p. 239), awards given to players representing England in international competition in rugby, soccer, or cricket. However, it might also be of interest to review the college affiliation of blues to see whether the major unit of influence in these universities has any effect on blue selection.

Oxford and Cambridge produced five cricketers in the decade 1973/4–1982/3 who played international cricket and many more who elected to play cricket professionally for a period of time. Cambridge produced the majority of these professional cricketers, most of whom came from independent schools. This fact somewhat explains the very high percentage of cricket blues gained by independent school students at Cambridge during the most recent decade.

However, despite the influence of such an exceptional group of individuals, the figures for Cambridge cricket blues require further explanation. Whereas Eggleston attempted to explain such differences as being covert and "differences of social experience rather than sporting ability" (an explanation that was undoubtedly appropriate for the 1950s and early 1960s), I believe that an explanation for the figures for the 1970s and early 1980s must be based on differential sporting experience. First, independent schools have long encouraged athletic endeavor as an integral part of their educational philosophy, and this continues to be one of their attractions for parents.

Second, boys from independent schools, who can spend as much as 25 hours per week practicing and playing, are far more likely to come under the influence of old blues and international players, who are overtly recruited by such establishments as coaches and role models for future generations. From the schools' point of view, such individuals, being "big names," are likely to attract future generations of aspiring athletes.

Third, in cricket, in which long hours of practice and expensive facilities are prerequisites, blues—referring to the recipient of the award—are familiar with the regimen necessary for success. Additionally, independent schools often employ the services of a retired professional cricketer to help foster the skills and attitudes necessary for success in "the noble game."

Fourth, expenditure on games also distinguishes the schools with regard to cricket, the condition of the practice nets in many independent schools being superior to "the square," or playing field, in most maintained local authority schools. Finally, as Eggleston noted, "the immediate economic obligations of university team membership, both in actual expenses and forfeited . . . work earnings, also tend to constitute a greater problem to the pupil from the maintained . . . school" (p. 241).

All these factors militate against the maintained school student, whereas they obviously favor the student from the independent school. The very talented cricketer from an independent school has a mentor with experience of the Oxbridge cricket system to advise him when he goes up to university. He also has a former professional cricketer to tutor him in the subtleties of the game while at school and to help him break into professional cricket after he comes down, or graduates. Furthermore, since Oxford and Cambridge are the only university teams to play regular first-class fixtures, or matches, against professional teams, blues have an advantage over others who might wish to become professional cricketers in that they understand the occupational subculture of the professional cricketer and have increased access to the occupational status of the professional cricketer. I believe that these are some of the reasons for the continuing advantage that independent school students have in gaining cricket blues.

Conclusions

This study of the relationship between preuniversity schooling and athletic achievement at Oxford and Cambridge indicates that the ex-pupils of maintained local education authority schools are still at a disadvantage when compared to ex-pupils of independent schools in cricket and rugby, and at an advantage in terms of the lower status sport of association football. These results parallel those of Eggleston (1965) in kind, though not in degree, and suggest that the differential in the chance of gaining a blue between the independent and maintained school pupil— and the possible status mobility that may accompany it—has been somewhat eroded.

It is in cricket at both universities, but particularly at Cambridge, that the differential has not been eroded. Reasons of similar sporting experience and "structural conduciveness" between the independent schools and Oxbridge were posited to explain this phenomenon.

Those who believed that the recommendation of the Robbins Report would, if implemented, make Oxbridge more a meritocratic, than a social, elite can take some satisfaction from the maintained school student's improved chance of gaining a blue in the decade 1963/4-1972/3. There appears to have been some regression in his chances in the decade 1973/4-1982/3, and perhaps the effects of the Dover recommendations at Oxford and the changed admissions policy at Cambridge will reverse this trend during the next decade.

The present study can provide a benchmark against which to judge the effects of these very important changes on sport at England's two most prestigious institutions of higher learning. For an Oxbridge blue, although perhaps less valuable than in the past still, as Eggleston has suggested, "seems to be of considerable importance in view of its likely association with social opportunities in university life and social and occupational prospects in later life" (p. 241).

References

Berryman, J.W., & Loy, J.W. (1976). Secondary schools and Ivy League letters: A comparative replication of Eggleston's "Oxbridge Blues." *The British Journal of Sociology*, **27**(1), 61-77.

Department of Education and Science. (1964–1984). *Statistics of education 1 – 6*. London: Her Majesty's Stationary Office.

Eggleston, J. (1965). Secondary schools and Oxbridge blues. *The British Journal of Sociology*, **16**(3), 232-242.

Kelsall, R.K. (1957). *Report on an enquiry into application for admissions to universities*. London: Association of Universities of the British Commonwealth.

Robbins Committee. (1964). *Higher Education*. Parliamentary Papers Cmnd—2154—II. London: Her Majesty's Stationary Office.

Tanner, N.W., & Tanner, J.S.G. (1983, April 29). University entrance: Is there a selection bias? *Times Higher Education Supplement*, p. 1-3.

A Comparison of Changes in Women's Intercollegiate Sports Between 1974 and 1984 in Selected Colleges and Universities in the United States and Canada

Donna R. Marburger

The past decade has brought many changes in women's sports throughout the world. Increased participation at all age levels, expansion of women's interscholastic and intercollegiate programs in many countries, more Olympic sports for women, and, particularly in the United States, more female Olympic contenders are all important indications of the changes in women's athletics.

The strongest catalyst for change in programs in the United States was the passage of Title IX of the Educational Amendments Act of 1972. This law mandates that no person in the United States shall, on the basis of sex, be excluded from participation in, be denied benefits of, or be subjected to discrimination in, any educational program or activity receiving federal funds. As schools and colleges came into compliance with Title IX, there was a great expansion of athletic opportunities for women. Many myths about the female athlete were dispelled. Psychological, physiological, and sociological research regarding the female athlete gave impetus to the expanding programs.

Although Canada has not had legislation such as Title IX, this country, too, has seen an increase in interest and concern about women in sport. The Royal Commission on the Status of Women (1970) made recommendations in this area. Likewise, the National Conference on Women and Sport (1974) and the Female Athletic Conference (1980) also identified problems and proposed areas for action.

Because the United States and Canada have been in a period of change in women's athletics, and because the United States has had legislation affecting women's athletics, but Canada has not, it seemed worthwhile to compare the changes that took place in selected colleges and universities in the two countries between 1974 and 1984.

Historical Review

United States

In the early years of the United States, few women participated in competitive sport. This was in part due to the Puritan work ethic so strongly ingrained in the early settlers. Appropriate dress for physical activity was a problem, as was the idea that athletic participation just was not feminine.

Eventually, sports for women became more accepted, and many institutions of higher education for women—such as Mount Holyoke, Smith, Vassar, and Wellesley Colleges—provided exercise classes, gymnastics, and sports for their students. Likewise, sports for women became more obvious in community programs.

By the late 1800s many women's academies and colleges were involved in intercollegiate athletic contests. Since there were few women's teams, competition was not well organized. College teams played against high school teams or teams made up of women in the area or community. Except in the case of women's colleges, many teams were coached by men. This, coupled with unchaperoned travel arrangements, questionable uniforms, and a feeling of exploitation of women athletes, concerned women physical educators. Criticism from women physical educators also hit the lack of good sportsmanship and the inappropriate use of women in sport advertising. Men's intercollegiate programs were accused of being too professional, and many women did not wish to follow this pattern.

As a result of these concerns, in 1920 the Association of Directors of Physical Education for College Women denounced intercollegiate athletics for women in favor of Sports Days and Play Days. These athletic endeavors emphasized the social benefits of friendly competition, good sportsmanship, and fun. Instead of highly organized competition with regulation games and tournaments, short round robin tournaments and novelty events were held in the course of a day. Although Sports Day teams were made up of participants from the same school, most had little formal practice prior to competition. For Play Days, teams were picked at random from participating schools. Each team would include a player from each school represented. Competitive sports were considered unladylike by many, and those who competed outside the college arenas of Sports Days and Play Days risked having their femininity questioned.

The 1950s and 1960s brought a new wave of concern regarding women and sport. Many women physical educators developed a more positive attitude toward athletic competition, even though the needs of the highly skilled female athlete were largely unattended.

Finally, women physical educators and others interested in athletics modified their position. According to Oglesby (1978), this paralleled an expressed interest in women athletes by the U.S. Olympic Development Committee. The Division of Girls' and Women's Sports, with the support of the National Collegiate Athletic Association (NCAA), formed a commission to work on the problem of providing athletic opportunities, including national championships, for women. As a result of this effort, the Association of Intercollegiate Athletics for Women (AIAW) was formed.

Increased backing for women's sports was provided in the sixties by the civil rights movement. This was the basis for the passage of Title IX in 1972, which became law in 1975. In the past 2 decades, there has been considerable growth in women's sports in both amateur and professional ranks. Collegiate programs have had many significant changes, not the least of which was the demise of the AIAW. This occurred after a power struggle with the NCAA, which took control of women's intercollegiate athletics.

Canada

Although Canadian women were active in sport in the twenties and thirties and, according to Hoffman (1976), dominated the 1928 Olympics, they, too, have had difficulty overcoming sex discrimination barriers and myths regarding the female athlete. According to the National Conference on Women and Sport (1974), sport in Canada, as in the U.S., has historically been accepted as a male domain. Sport has not been considered conducive to femininity, and it has been thought that emphasis on winning was antithetical to the development of acceptable feminine characteristics. There has been a lack of financial support for women's athletics, and many higher level sport programs simply did not encourage the female athlete.

Although Canada did not have legislation such as Title IX, strong proposals for action came from the National Conference on Women and Sport (1974). These included recommendations that the government appoint several permanent sport consultants for women's affairs and that the Canadian Association of University Teachers (CAUT) intensify its activities concerning the status of women to ensure that the special problems of women in university physical education be considered. In addition, it was urged that the Canadian Federation of Provincial Schools Athletic Associations demonstrate commitment to the promotion of girls' and women's sport by working for an equitable distribution of funds to male and female programs. Other recommendations were made regarding preparation, certification, and improvement of women coaches and support of research regarding the female athlete. Acceptance of athletics for all girls and women was to be encouraged by hiring competent female coaches and sport administrators and by giving more positive press coverage to women's sports.

Prior to 1978, the administration of university athletics at the national level was undertaken by separate men's and women's organizations. However, in 1978 the Canadian Interscholastic Athletic Union (CIAU) was formed. This organization joined men's and women's intercollegiate athletics under one umbrella. Since that time the Women's Representative Committee of the CIAU has undertaken several studies to determine the status of men and women in sport and to identify increases and decreases in sport participation at the college level for each sex.

The results of these studies are most interesting. According to Vickers and Gosling (1984), data from the 1978–82 period indicates that there was a growth in the number of both male and female athletic participants in CIAU programs. The men outnumbered the women by a ratio of 2.4 to 1. During this period the total number of programs for men increased from 253 to 278, a gain of 25. Women's programs increased from 136 to 189, a gain of 53. In spite of a greater percentage gain in women's programs, the average of 6.1 programs for men per university was still significantly higher than the 3.8 programs for women per university.

It can be seen from this brief historical overview that Canada and the United States have indeed faced many similar problems related to growth in women's athletics. What changes have come about in women's inter-collegiate sports programs in these two nations in the past 10 years? The present study was conducted in an attempt to answer this question.

Methods

Prior to visits to schools, the researcher developed a questionnaire to ascertain changes in women's athletic programs in the past 10 years. The questionnaire covered such areas as number of male and female participants, available sports, club sports, scholarships, funding, gate receipts, recruitment of female athletes, facilities, availability of an athletic trainer, increases in coaching staff, grievances, and lawsuits. The questionnaire was sent to 89 Canadian and 270 U.S. colleges and universities listed in the 1984–85 Women's Edition of the National Directory of College Athletics. Thirty-two (36%) Canadian colleges and 130 (48%) U.S. colleges responded. On-site visits were conducted at 10 Canadian schools and 37 U.S. schools. Information was also secured from CIAU and Sport Canada as well as the NCAA. Based on the return of the questionnaires and the follow-up visits, the following information was gained. It is based on all of the Canadian returns and 111 of the 130 U.S. returns. Nineteen U.S. schools were excluded because in 1974 or in 1984 they were single-sex institutions. A summary of the data gleaned from the questionnaires can be seen in Table 1.

Discussion

It should be noted that a greater percentage of Canadian schools had a general enrollment increase (both males and females) between 1974 and 1984 than did American schools. In light of this, it is interesting to observe that in all areas of change in women's athletics studied, with the exception of gate receipts, figures for the U.S. showed greater percentage increases than Canada. These figures would lead one to speculate that the greater number of U.S. increases are due at least in part to Title IX legislation.

Although not included in Table 1, the data revealed that three Canadian schools (9%) had an increase in the number of sports for females and a

Table 1 Percentage of Schools Showing Increases in Selected Aspects of Women's and Men's Athletic Programs in the United States and Canada, 1974–1984

Program aspects	Canada (n = 32)		United States (n = 111)	
	%	n	%	n
Female varsity athletes	56	18	85	94
Male varsity athletes	44	14	45	50
General enrollment	90	29	62	69
Varsity sports for women	66	21	83	92
Varsity sports for men	34	11	37	41
Women's sports with scholarships	22	7	42	47
Men's sports with scholarships	9	3	19	21
Women receiving athletic scholarships	31	10	45	50
Club sports for women	44	14	47	52
Club sports for men	40	13	48	53
Funding increase for women's sports	63	20	88	98
Full-time coaches for women's sports	38	12	63	70
Part-time coaches for women's sports	19	6	55	61
Female athletes recruited	40	13	67	74
Athletic trainer for women's sports	63	20	78	87
Gate receipts for women's sports	44	14	34	38
New/remodeled facilities for women's sports	40	13	58	64
Grievances and lawsuits	3	1	13	14

decrease in the number for males. The U.S. figures were slightly higher. Twenty-one schools (19%) showed an increase for females and a decrease for males. Most schools in both countries increased programs for both males and females, or at least maintained 1974 levels for men's programs while increasing women's programs.

In both countries, increases in club sports for men and women seemed to be positively correlated to increases in varsity athletics. There was a slightly greater increase in individual sports for both sexes than team sports. Because many schools used successful club sport status for a 2- or 3-year period as one criteria for a sport to qualify as a varsity sport, it seems reasonable that club sport programs would increase. It is encouraging to learn that varsity sports have not replaced club sports in either Canada or the U.S.

A number of Canadians who were interviewed felt that the passage of Title IX in the U.S. had a positive influence on the growth of women's sports progams in Canada. Some women coaches believed that the growth of women's intercollegiate athletics in Canada was in part due to self-policing actions. In a country with such a sparse population and a relatively small number of colleges and universities, it is not as easy to cover inequities between men's and women's programs. On the other hand, schools in the U.S., with its larger population and greater number of programs, found it feasible to attempt to correct inequities on the basis of the Title IX legislation. This has been highlighted by grievances, lawsuits, and affirmative action investigations in a number of U.S. schools.

Another facet of Canadian programs that is different from many American programs is the general attitude toward all intercollegiate sports, male and female. Canadians do not seem to put as much emphasis on varsity athletics as Americans. They are not involved in heavy scholarship programs to the extent the U.S. is, and they encourage varsity athletes to go out for other extracurricular activities. Academic achievement takes precedence over athletics for most students. It is doubtful that the same can be said for many American athletes.

Until 1981, according to Bennett (1983), Canadian universities with one exception, did not give athletic scholarships to either males or females. In that year, the CIAU voted to lift this restriction; even so, the provinces of Ontario and Quebec chose not to give athletic scholarships. Even now this policy is being questioned in these provinces, and it will be interesting to see how long the policy will remain. One of the problems, of course, is that many fine Canadian athletes, male and female, are enticed to U.S. schools on full-ride athletic scholarships.

In conclusion, it can be said that women's intercollegiate athletic programs in both the United States and Canada have experienced considerable growth in the past decade. Although many schools have achieved equality in women's and men's programs, a number of schools in both countries still lag behind in providing athletic programs for female students that are equal to those provided for males.

References

Bennett, B., Howell, M., & Simri, U. (1983). *Comparative physical education and sport*. Philadelphia: Lea & Febiger.

Fitness and amateur sport Canada. (1974). *The report of the National Conference on Women in Sport*. Ottawa: Author.

Hoffman, A. (1976). *About-face: Towards a positive image of women in sport*. Toronto: Ontario Status of Women Council, Ontario Secretariat for Social Development, and Ontario Ministry of Culture and Recreation.

Information Canada. (1970). The report of the Royal Commission on the Status of Women. Ottawa: Author.

Oglesby, C. (1978). *Women and sport: From myth to reality*. Philadelphia: Lea & Febiger.

Popma, A. (1980). *The Female Athlete: Proceedings of a National Conference about Women in Sports and Recreation*. Burnaby, BC: Continuing Studies, Simon Fraser University.

Vickers, J., & Gosling, B. (1984). *The changing participation of men and women in the CIAU (1978-1982)*. Ottawa: The Women's Representative Committee of the CIAU.

A Comparison of the Reasons for Marathon Participation of British and Australian Non-Elite Runners

Gerald V. Barrell
David Holt
Jill M. MacKean

One of the most notable developments in sports participation during the last decade has been the enormous increase in the number of people who take part in marathon events. In 1978 the number of runners who completed at least one marathon event in Britain was 1,789. By 1985 participation had grown to an estimated 250,000 competitors, with over 16,000 finishers in the London Marathon alone. The marathon boom has not been limited to Britain; increases on a similar scale have occurred in many other countries throughout the world.

Yet, despite the worldwide growth of marathon running, few investigations have considered the reasons why individuals take part in marathon events. Furthermore, no attempt has been made to discover whether the motivations of runners vary from country to country. The present study examines this latter problem. In particular, the investigation compares the motives of British runners for competing in marathon events and for starting running with those reported by Summers, Machin, and Sargent (1983) for Australian participants.

Methods

Subjects

In the Australian study, a mail questionnaire was sent to a random sample of one in six entrants in the 1980 Big M Melbourne Marathon. Because only 4% of the 5,423 entrants were female, questionnaires were also sent to all women entrants who were not included in the initial one of six selection. A total of 1,093 entrants were sent questionnaires, and a response rate of 42% was obtained.

In the British investigation, a two-stage sampling strategy was employed. First, through stratified sampling procedures, 14 of the 26 marathon and half-marathon events held in, or close to, the Wessex region of England in 1984 were selected. Second, the results of the selected events were used to stratify competitors into four ability levels for both full and half-marathon events. A total of 1,435 subjects were then selected randomly from the different strata and sent a mail questionnaire. In order to minimize the problem of nonresponse, a team of interviewers followed up on respondents who did not return questionnaires. A response rate of over 93% was thus achieved.

Our sampling method allowed us to relate the survey data to the population of Wessex participants who ran in marathon and half-marathon events in the region in 1984 (Barrell, Holt, and MacKean, 1985). In order to make comparisons with the Australian study, the British results are based on the data of the 789 runners in our population whose first ever running event was a full marathon.

Questionnaire

The Australian questionnaire consisted of several different sections, one of which was concerned with the psychological aspects of marathon running. In this section, subjects were asked in an open-ended question to give three reasons why they were attempting a marathon. In the subsequent analysis, the reasons given were grouped into the following seven categories:

1. Goal achievement (personal challenge, sense of achievement)
2. Test of personal worth (test of physical/mental capabilities, personal satisfaction, to prove to myself I can do it)
3. Physical health (improve fitness)
4. Others' influence (peer pressure, family influence)
5. Curiosity (for the experience, gauge reaction of body/mind)
6. Enjoyment
7. Miscellaneous reasons (too infrequent to classify)

The British questionnaire used the first six categories identified in the Australian study. These six factors were listed, and respondents were required to indicate whether each item had a strong influence, some influence, or no influence on their initial decision to run a marathon. After piloting the question, we added two additional motivational factors, namely, raising money for charity and the influence of television and newspapers. Runners were also asked to specify any additional factors that had influenced their decision to run a marathon. The important methodological difference between the two studies was that British respondents were offered eight specific factors that may have influenced them, whereas the Australian runners were asked to list three reasons without a list from which to choose.

Results and Discussion

The results for the Australian and British studies are given in Table 1, although the methodological differences between the two studies were so great that no importance should be attached to direct comparison. For the British study, the percentage of respondents who identified a factor as a strong influence or as a moderate influence are given, but for comparative purposes we emphasize the results in the strong influence category only. The point to note at this stage is that the British study has two main factors (goal achievement and personal worth) that more than 70% of respondents in each case identify as strong influences, whereas in the Australian study, goal achievement is clearly more commonly reported than personal worth (both are nevertheless much more important than the remaining factors). The Australian study makes no further distinction between minor factors (except that charitable causes was not identified as a factor), whereas the British study identifies a second tier of importance (physical health, enjoyment, curiosity, and charitable causes). The remaining factors are much less important.

Both studies analyzed their data according to the sex of the competitor. There are essentially no differences in motivation between the sexes identified in either study, and the patterns in Table 1 apply to both men and women. The data were also analyzed by age; these results are given in Table 2. The overriding impression for both studies is that any differences between ages are comparatively minor and that the basic pattern of results in Table 1 applies to all ages. There is some suggestion in the Australian results that the under-20 age group differs from the rest in several respects, but the sample size is small ($n = 47$) and the result may be due to sampling error. The British data do not mirror the Australian results in this respect. There is also a suggestion in the British results of the increasing importance of the marathon as a test of personal worth as age increases.

In overall pattern, the two studies arrive at similar conclusions, except for the distinction in importance between goal achievement and personal worth among Australian runners, which is not reflected among the British. However, there are actual number discrepancies in the two sets of results, which may be explained by the difference in sampling methods. A direct comparison between the Australian and British studies is impossible because of the methodological differences and the way of reporting the findings.

The Australian data represent the three reasons for attempting a marathon as identified by each respondent, whereas the British data reflect the separate response of each respondent to each factor in turn. In the British study, there was no constraint on the number of factors reported as having a strong influence. In fact, the average number of factors reported as having a strong influence was 2.6 per respondent; 77% of the respondents reported 2, 3, or 4 strongly influencing factors. This is one reason for concentrating on strong influences in the British data.

Table 1 Reasons for Running a Marathon Reported by Australian and British Competitors

Reason	Australian	British			
		Strong influence		Moderate influence	
	% of total responses	% of respondents reporting	% of total responses	% of respondents reporting	% of total responses
Goal achievement	54	75	29	23	8
Test of personal worth	20	72	28	51	18
Physical health	6	26	10	27	10
Enjoyment	4	25	10	57	21
Curiosity	6	28	11	51	18
Others' influence	8	8	3	28	10
Charitable cause	—	18	7	18	6
Miscellaneous	3	5	2	22	8

Table 2 Reasons for Running a Marathon Reported by Age of Competitors

Age (years)	Goal achievement %	Test of personal worth %	Physical health %	Enjoyment %	Curiosity %	Others' influence %	Charitable cause %	Miscellaneous reasons %
British								
20–29	31	27	12	9	11	4	3	2
30–39	30	30	10	10	10	4	3	2
40–59	31	31	9	11	11	2	3	2
Australian								
Under 20	44	14	10	3	14	12	—	2
20–29	57	19	7	4	5	7	—	1
30–39	55	22	4	4	5	9	—	1
40–61	50	21	4	5	7	5	—	8

Note. There were too few British respondents under 20 to justify reporting their results. Because the Australian sample contained no runners over 61 years old, the data of the small number of British competitors aged 60 and over have been omitted from the analysis.

It is well known in the survey literature that offering a specific list of possible factors, as was done in the British study, increases positive responses, because the question itself reminds the respondent of some factors. This effect is most marked for minor factors that might not occur to respondents if an open-ended question were used, as in the Australian study. In the Australian study, the open-ended question required 41 initial response code categories; these were subsequently grouped into the six factor categories reported in Summers et al. (1983). Assuming that each respondent followed instructions and offered three reasons for running a marathon, it is possible that more than one of these may have been coded to the same factor category. For example, a respondent who gave "physical fitness" and "to maintain health" would have had both coded to the factor category "physical health." This duplication of response must have occurred, because 54% of all initial responses were allocated to the "goal achievement" category. The British study, on the other hand, forced a response of some kind on each factor but effectively precluded the same factor from being reported under several guises.

The distribution of initial responses reported in the Australian study does not permit a direct estimate of the percentage of runners who responded at least once in any particular factor category. Nor do we know the average number of different factor categories offered per respondent. However, Summers et al. (1983) do give some information on the largest categories occurring among the 41 initial response codes. The main duplication seems to be within the goal achievement and personal worth categories.

By using this information, it is possible to calculate upper and lower bounds on the percentage of runners who reported each factor category. The true value will be close to the upper bound where little duplication occurs or close to the lower bound where duplication is extensive. These bounds are given in Table 3, together with the implied number of separate factor categories reported per respondent.

For the lesser categories, we would expect the true Australian result to be close to the upper bound. The British results appear to be a little higher, but this is consistent with the inflation in positive response that would occur among these minor factors due to specifically asking about each factor in turn. The obvious discrepancy is in the last category (charitable causes), but this may reflect the extensive recent publicity in Britain for people who run for charitable causes.

We expect the true Australian result to be closer to the lower bound for the goal achievement and personal worth categories, because these are the factor categories (especially goal achievement) where duplication occurred. The result for goal achievement seems comparable with the British results. It seems as if it is the personal worth factor that reveals the clearest difference between the two studies.

Conclusions

We have attempted to compare the results of two studies that investigate the reasons why non-elite runners take part in marathons. Both studies

Table 3   Percentages of Respondents Who Mentioned Each Reason in British Study and Estimated Maximum and Minimum Responses in Australian Survey

Reason	Australian Minimum	Maximum	British Reported Findings
Goal achievement	72	100	75
Personal worth	30	60	72
Physical health	12	18	26
Enjoyment	7	21	25
Curiosity	6	18	28
Others' influence	4	12	8
Charitable cause	—	—	18
Miscellaneous	2	6	5
Number of factor categories per respondent	1.33	2.35	2.57

show little difference between the sexes or age groups. The main influences are running for a sense of goal achievement and as a test of personal worth, but the main difference between the two studies appears to be that British respondents place more importance on the marathon as a test of personal worth, regarding this motivating influence as strongly as they do goal achievement.

Acknowledgment

This project was funded by the Health Promotion Research Trust.

References

Barrell, G.V., Holt, D., & MacKean, J.M. (1985). Is there a marathon boom? In T. Hale (Ed.), *Proceedings of Sport and Science Conference* (pp. 128-135). Chichester, England: British Association of Sports Science.

Summers, J.J., Machine, V.J., & Sargent, G.I. (1983). Psychological factors related to marathon running. *Journal of Sports Psychology*, **5**, 314-331.

School Sport in Poland From the 1950s to the 1980s

Pawel Kudlorz

The organizers of this symposium suggested presenting in the historical comparisons section selected problems concerning the development of school sports in the 1950s and 1980s. With respect to Poland, we decided to accept as the starting point the year 1945, the year of the end of World War II. Poland supposedly emerged from World War II as a victor, but there were enormous losses. Over 6,028,000 Polish citizens, or 220 out of every 1,000, died. Staggering material losses have been estimated at about $50 billion (38% of the country's prewar assets).

Education lost 60% of its material resources. All secondary and university schools were closed; 95% of all school library material was destroyed; 1,022 athletic fields were ruined, as were 7,621 school buildings, 371 swimming pools, and 1,061 gymnasiums. Some 16,000 teachers were killed, among them many outstanding physical education teachers, coaches, volunteers, and athletes, as well as 29 Olympic athletes. Poland was the only country where it was forbidden for the youth of the country to participate in sports. The results in the first postwar championships in track and field were lower than those achieved before World War I.

Considering these facts, one can imagine the improvement that has taken place during the past 40 years in the area of school sports and physical education in Poland. This paper, after a brief presentation of the current Polish school system, will examine the following topics: (a) the system of physical education and sport at primary and secondary schools, (b) the training of youthful athletes within specialized sport schools, and (c) the School Sports Union.

Polish School System

The Polish educational system includes schools at the preschool, primary, secondary, postsecondary, and university levels (see Figure 1).

There are general education schools that fall into the uniform 8-grade primary and the 4-grade general or academic secondary categories; vocational schools with 2- to 3-year basic vocational programs (practical farming

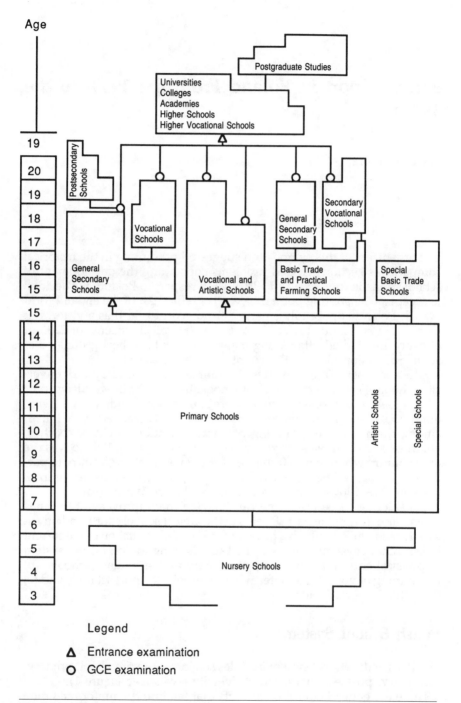

Figure 1. The school system in Poland.

and trade schools); 4- to 5-year technical secondary schools; 2- to 3-year postsecondary schools; and schools of higher education (colleges, academies, higher vocational schools, and universities) (see Figure 1).

All schools are operated by the state, the only exception being the Catholic University in Lublin. All the state schools are based on no tuition or fees, secular upbringing, and universal opportunities for the continuance of postelementary education.

Physical Education and Sport at the Primary and Secondary Schools

In the system of physical education and sport, one can distinguish two major forms of activities—required physical education classes and extracurricular activities. Extracurricular activities include extramural interschool sport clubs and the following forms of intramural activities: (a) sports preparation classes, (b) school sports circles (clubs), and (c) student organized "Hours of Sport."

Physical Education

Physical education classes are the basic means to achieve the aims and objectives of physical education. Classes are intended to provide the required physical education within the framework of hours specified in the teaching schedule of the schools where physical education is one of the subjects taught. As a rule, there were, and still are, 2 hours weekly of required physical education classes from the beginning of the primary schools up to and through the first and second years of study at the university level. The length of time of the structured (methodical) unit is 45 minutes.

Extracurricular Activities

There are various levels of intramural programs, which consist of nonrequired sports activities. This program underwent various transformations during the time period discussed. In the years from 1947 to 1955, the required physical education activity reached its peak level. Included were 2 hours of physical education and 2 hours of sports participation classes. In 1955 the sports participation program was canceled. It was again introduced in 1961, but only in the form of nonrequired activities and reduced to 2-4 hours of classes weekly per school. Since 1971 this sports participation activity has ceased to exist. The regular physical education activities continued during this period of time.

Sports preparation classes were held outside of the school schedule. Their aims were to increase the physical fitness of the students, to stimulate their interest in sports, and to familiarize the students with the basic organizational principles of sports activities and with the rules of the various sports.

In 1971, the Ministry of Education established another program of non-required activities at the schools—school sports circles (clubs). School sports circles (SSC) enable students to practice various sports after school. In the first years after WW II, a part of the SSC that operated before the war was reactivated in the grammar schools. Some of the circles were also created in the vocational schools. These circles were formally organized for the vocational schools in 1949 and for the grammar schools in 1950. Until the creation in 1953 of the sports union ZRYW (only within the vocational school system), and in 1957 of the School Sports Union (which took in the entire school system, including vocational schools), the SSC circles worked independently.

Today the SSC circles represent the basic way of bringing school sports to most students. SSC circles provide the initial opportunity for sports participation and, through sport, the development and improvement of youth's self-discipline, leadership qualities, and skills needed for a better social life.

The amount of time allotted to SSC activities is included in the teachers' annual salaries. The number of hours in the program is based on the number of students and the type of school. The growth and development of the SSC program for the years 1960 and 1971 is shown in Table 1.

The Hour of Sports is a planned hour of sports activities conducted each week for each grade in addition to the 2 hours of physical education. This is also in addition to the hours assigned to a given school for the non-required activities of the School Sports Circle. This Hour of Sports is con-

Table 1   Growth and Development of School Sports Circles, 1960–1971

Type of school	Number of pupils	Hours/week/school 1960	1971
Primary	≤ 200	2	6
	201–320	4	8
	321–600	8	12
	> 600	12	18
Secondary	≤ 200	4	8
	201–320	8	12
	321–600	12	16
	> 600	16	18

Note. In 1947 there were 529 SSC Circles, whereas in 1980 there were 13,247.

ducted exclusively by students titled *youth sports organizers*. These activities represent active play and games as well as contests in individual and team sports, which are adjusted to the age groups and fitness levels of the participants—within the scope of activities and/or sports that were learned and performed at an earlier time.

The Hour of Sport was introduced in 1974 by the Minister of Education for students from the fifth grade up to and including all types of secondary schools. The implementation of this idea initially met with such obstacles as the lack of facilities and inadequate number of qualified youth sports organizers. The Hour of Sports program was conducted in some 5,900 schools in 1980.

Interschool Sports Clubs provide opportunities for high-level intramural competitors. Until the coming into existence and the development of Sports Schools, the main place to initiate interest in sports, to search for talented individual athletes, and to give specialized basic training and instruction was in Interschool Sports Clubs. The School Sports Union was created in 1957, with one of its purposes being the organization and administration of the Interschool Sports Clubs for competition at the highest level. From its beginning in 1958, some 175 clubs belonged to the union. This increased to 300 in 1962, and at present some 360 clubs belong to the union and represent about 800 different sport teams.

Training of Youthful Athletes Within Specialized Sport Schools

In 1969 formal approval of the first special physical education expansion program in schools took place. In 1971 and 1972, several additional primary and secondary schools were added to the program. These were the first schools with broadened physical education classes. Previously, a school in Lodz, Poland, had adopted a similar program as early as 1965.

As far back as 1955, the Presidium of Ministers passed a bill (#327) approving the creation of youth sports schools, but this was not realized until the school year 1973/74, with the establishment of many of these schools. In 1974 the Ministry of Education presented the first document, "Outlines for the Organization of Sports Schools." These outlines included aims and objectives, principles of recruitment, teaching programs, organization of activities, and other principles and practices of such schools. In 1977, five schools were established for the training of world class athletes. These were called Championship Sports Schools.

Organization of the System

The lowest level and most common schools are those with expanded physical education programs of a total of 6 hours per week. Their objective is the practice of activities, general overall physical fitness, and determination of any predisposition to sports activities by the schoolchildren.

The second group are sport schools (Table 2). These schools prepare students in some 25 different areas of sport. The majority of these schools are concerned with more than one sport. The training schedules in their respective activities include from 8 to 18 hours of practice each week.

The Championship Sports Schools provide the highest level of instruction and are concerned with preparing athletes for international competition. Weekly training schedules depend upon the particular sport and the level of international competition. These athletes train from 25 to 40 hours per week in addition to their academic work. In view of this fact, it is expected students here take 5 years, instead of the normal 4, to complete their education.

Recruitment

Until this time, nothing has been developed in the way of principles of recruiting criteria. Schools are using general physical fitness, suggestions from respective school programs, and personal recommendations of individual coaches. Students are recruited from schools with extended physical education programs, from championship games and competition among athletes, upon the recommendations of the various Polish sports federations.

System of Competition

The main aim of competition is to attract the talented to participate. Competition immediately after WW II was dominated by two characteristics: massive participation in various activities, such as distance running and cross-country skiing, and separate organized competition for vocational, primary, and grammar schools.

The above separate organizations united in 1957. In the 1960s, the School Sports Union initiated a competitive program, which was transformed into a system of winter and summer games called the "Youth Sports Festival." Athletes participate in the following:

Table 2   Sport Schools, 1969–1985

School year	Schools with extended PE programs	Sport schools[a]	Championship sport schools
1969–70	3	—	—
1974–75	230	65	—
1979–80	1,100	146	7
1984–85	2,000	153	14

[a]The first 40 sport schools were introduced in 1973–74.

- Individual School Sports Festival—games and competition among the various classes held through the entire school year. To conclude these activities, a special sports holiday is declared.
- Mass games and competition among schools—organized for primary and secondary schools of all types.
- Voivodeship (similar to the Canadian *province*) competition among schools. These are winter and summer games that are held according to the national sports festival rules.
- National youth sports festivals, organized and held every two years until 1980. The best student athletes competed in nearly every Olympic event.

In the years 1981 and 1982 only the voivodeship festivals were held. From 1983 the Youth Sports Festivals were held in eight regional competitions.

It is by agreement of all the school authorities that the championships of sport schools at the national level are conducted for young athletes in swimming and gymnastics. Other sports include skiing (alpine and cross-country), ski jumping, figure skating, track and field, and ice hockey. In the many other activities of sport, the sport schools conduct a general system of competition for the children and youth of the country.

Teaching and Coaching Staff

The opportunity for employment of physical education graduates, as a rule, was—and still is today—greater than the number completing their degrees. Between the two World Wars, the departments of physical education at the two universities and the Physical Education Academy in Warsaw produced nearly 1,000 teachers. In 1945 only 180 of them were available to teach in the secondary schools, and several dozen at the primary level. In the next few years, their number increased slowly to several hundred. The first 34 postwar physical education teachers graduated in 1947. By 1952 the number of graduates from all the higher schools exceeded 1,000. In 1972 some 3,800, in 1972, 6,000 had competed their studies. During the 1980s, the six Academies of Physical Education and two branch schools have about 10,000 students attending annually, with about 2,000 graduating each year.

During the postwar period, some 37,000 have completed their studies at the higher level physical education institutions, with about 86% becoming teachers of physical education. Even with this number of graduates, there were only 19,000 physical education teachers working in 1980, and there is a need for another 10,000. Even with a law passed by the Polish Parliament in 1973 to enable preparation of future teachers at the master's level, Poland had to reactivate about 20 postsecondary 2-year normal school teachers to meet this shortage.

During the course of study, the Polish schools of higher education make it possible for the students to get additional qualifications as instructors and coaches in the basic sports included in their program of studies. In part by this method, some 16,000 coaches earned their certification during the postwar period. These additional qualifications—apart from the master's degree—are required of staff members of schools with extended physical education programs as well as the Sport Schools. In the Sport and Championships Sport Schools, of the 900 teachers of physical education, 650 are certified coaches, and 240 are certified instructors.

Facilities

The needs of the schools with respect to facilities for physical education and sport are always greater than the facilities available. Over 50% of all school buildings were destroyed during WW II, and much of what remained was devastated during the occupation. After the war there remained 674 gymnasiums. This was less that 32% of the prewar total. By the year 1950, there were 2,900 gyms; in 1960, 6,500. In 1970 there were more than 8,000 gyms; in 1980, about 9,500. By the end of 1983, 2,000 of the 12,000 primary schools were lacking gyms, while 500 of the 3,500 secondary schools were without similar facilities. In recent years there has been an increase in school-age population. This has created a need for another 9,000 new gyms. The Youth Sport Schools, by the way, either have their own facilities or are provided use of club gymnasiums.

School Sports Union

The School Sports Union is probably one of the very few such organizations in existence, responsible for all the organization, administration, and training of the youth in primary and secondary schools of all types. This Union was organized in 1957. Four years previously, this type of union had been organized for the vocational schools.

Immediately following the war, there were no organized sports for children and youth. The years 1958 to 1964 were characterized by stagnation, because the Sports Union was concerned only with interschool sports clubs that had the more talented athletes, whereas nothing was being done with the general school population.

During the years 1965 to 1970, the Union became more active, taking over the organization of all the school youth sports programs, rather than only those of the interschool sports clubs. During this time School Sports Circles, the basis of all the common sports programs, became full members of the Sports Union.

From 1971 to 1979, there was a dynamic growth and development of the School Sports Union. In 1974 the name of the School Sports Circle was changed to *School Sports Clubs*. They initiated a program of training youth sports organizers and instituted the promotion of massive school sports competitions. In this same year, the position of the union was strengthened by the declaration of the Minister of Education that the leading organization cooperating with the schools concerning the free time of the children and youth was the School Sports Union.

Up to 1974 the Minister of Education was responsible for funding this program. Since then, the General Committee for Physical Culture and Sport has been responsible for the financial support of the program. Therefore, the director of the School Sports Union no longer can control the program. Now the director serves only as the agent for information, consulting, and instruction.

The change of placing the School Sports Union under the General Committee of Physical Culture and Sport did not weaken the association with the overall school system. However, it introduced new accents—particularly since 1978, when the School Sports Union was transferred from the department of general physical education of the General Committee of Physical Education and Sport to the department of competitive sports. In this same year, the Ministry of Education and General Committee of Physical Education and Sport signed an agreement establishing a single permanent system of sports competition, recruitment, and schooling, and a calendar of events.

In ensuing years the School Sports Union became a highly specialized and general organization for education and sport. It united the teachers, parents, coaches, volunteers, and sympathizers of school sports. In close coordination and cooperation with the youth sports organizations, educational and sports institutions, and their authorities at all levels, the School Sports Union established aims and objectives of a general nature: a well-rounded education of each student's personality, promotion of the health of the individual, and organization of the free time of children and youth. In addition, the chief specific goal was to increase participation in sport.

The School Sports Union should not be looked at as one of many organizations, but as the basic unit for the entire sports program of the country. In this way, the School Sports Union is not only concerned with competitive sport, but with all aspects of the general well-being of physical education and sport in all school systems.

Conclusions

In spite of the many attainments in the development of school sports in the 40-year period of the People's Republic of Poland, there are still some scarcities and shortcomings. In the not too distant future, Poland should: educate the necessary number of highly qualified teachers of physical education, instructors, and coaches; and build adequate facilities in every school to meet modern requirements.

Poland must also strive to have 1 hour of required physical education class daily for each student, accent individual lifelong sports, and encourage greater participation in sports by girls. It must work out an optimal model of the school sports club and a plan of creating schools with expanded physical education programs, sport schools, and championship sport schools.

Finally, Polish science must become interested in the state of health and the role of sports in the balance of the free time of pupils, the theory of sports for children and youths, and the humanization of champion school sports.

A Comparative Analysis of Early East-West Sport Diplomacy

Victor E. Peppard

Sport diplomacy between East and West has now become a well-established feature of the conduct of foreign relations. In some instances it is even possible that sports diplomacy can become a dominant factor in international relations. As James Riordan (1980) has pointed out, in the Soviet Union, the leaders apparently believe that "sports emissaries can sometimes do more than diplomats to recommend a political philosophy and way of life to the outside world." The purpose of this paper is to compare the motives and goals of both sides in the beginnings of East-West sport diplomacy, in order to understand better how it became such a significant means of conducting foreign relations. As it turns out, the early practice of sport diplomacy created certain precedents, tendencies, and models that are largely still in effect in the present day.

Sport Diplomacy in the East

Soviet goals and motives are generally more unified and somewhat easier to discern than those of the West. This is not to say, however, that the Soviet situation has not been without its own internal controversies. Among the early Soviet administrators of physical culture, there was a split into different factions over the desirability of competitive sport. Among the so-called hygienists and proletarian culturalists, there were those who believed that competitive sport was harmful because it was a product of bourgeois culture. This group was never able to gain control of Soviet physical culture, however, and advocates of competitive sport generally held the upper hand. For example, Nikolai Semashko (1967), one of the first leaders of Soviet physical culture, stressed the close link between physical culture and preventive medicine, and maintained that sport and games were in fact an essential part of physical culture and that they helped to draw attention to it.

Soviet political motivation for the employment of sport diplomacy followed two parallel tracks that operated simultaneously. The first of these was to help secure the recognition of the bourgeois states. Together with other kinds of cultural and commercial contacts, sporting events were intended to help break down resistance to official recognition of the Soviet state and help to give it legitimacy in the eyes of the Western nations. The other track concerns the Soviets' desire to gain increased control over the international workers movement. The formation of the Red Sport International in 1921 as a parallel to the Comintern had the following goals, as stated by its president, A. K. Mekhanoshin, in an interview with *Izvestiia* on July 25, 1923: to draw foreign athletes away from bourgeois clubs, to organize worker sections inside sport unions with the ultimate goal of creating independent Red sportinterns, to strengthen contact with foreign athletes, and to organize international competitions and physical culture holidays. These political considerations will be discussed in greater detail shortly.

Even stronger than the desire to organize the international proletariat was the Soviet Union's need to reorganize and revitalize an economy that had been devastated by years of war, revolution, and civil war. A *Pravda* editorial urged the need of both the Soviet Union and capitalist countries to "reestablish economic ties that had been broken off by the war and revolution" (SSSR, 1923). At this time the Soviets were particularly interested in renewing trade relations with their Scandinavian neighbors, such as Finland, Sweden, and Norway. The editorial just mentioned even advocated establishing the cultivation of trade relations with the so-called small powers as a special part of foreign policy. This editorial concluded that these small powers had found that the U.S.S.R. was someone with whom "it is not dangerous to do business," and that, for its part, the U.S.S.R. had found in the small powers "merchants ready to view the union of workers and peasants as a merchant, as a side of equal power." Consequently, the first major act of sport diplomacy between East and West, the Russian Federated Republic's soccer tour of Scandinavia and Germany in August and September of 1923, cannot be considered outside of the Soviet Union's great desire to enhance trade with the "small powers" of Norway and Sweden.

There were still other powerful motivating factors for the Soviets' early conduct of sports diplomacy. One of these was the natural desire to reestablish cultural relations with the West outside of commercial considerations. Despite periods of isolation and officially sponsored hostility to Western culture, since the Revolution the Soviets have never lost their keen interest in both the popular and the high culture of the West. Andrei Starostin (1980) has remarked on the great respect the Soviet players enjoyed among the public when they returned from the Scandinavian tour attired in the latest Western European fashions.

Finally, among Soviet athletes and coaches, there was the desire to compare themselves with strong international competition. Success in competition with foreign sportsmen not only served to raise the confidence of Soviet athletes in themselves but also to raise the prestige of Soviet sport among its domestic followers (Starostin, 1980).

Sport Diplomacy in the West

The motives and goals of the Western countries for engaging in early sport diplomacy with the Soviet Union are naturally more diverse than those of the Soviet Union, because each country had its own special needs. Furthermore, within each country, different groups and factions had their own agendas. Some of the Western sport groups in the early 1920s greeted the visiting Soviet athletes with the singing of "The International" and generally festive atmospheres. Another attitude was evident in the Lucerne Sport International, which was founded expressly for the purpose of combating the influence of the Red Sport International (*Sportintern*) within the international sporting movement of workers.

Many of the Western needs and goals are reflected in the situation of Sweden in the early 1920s. One of the central issues confronting the Swedes was whether to renew trade relations with the Soviet Union. The Right still considered Russia, now the dominant part of the Soviet Union, to be its traditional enemy, whereas the Left did not believe that reestablishing trade would put Sweden in any danger (Tingsten, 1949). As often happens in such cases, the events of the day began to overtake purely political considerations. For example, it was reported in the Soviet press that some Swedes were in favor of establishing *de jure* recognition of the Soviet Union as well as trade with the Soviets in order to keep up with Denmark, which had already resumed commercial contacts (SSSR, 1923).

One of the strongest motives on the part of Western countries in the early 1920s in participating in friendly sporting contests with the Soviet Union was plain curiosity. In circles that were opposed to engaging the Soviets in sport, there were those who were fond of calling the Soviet athletes "red agitators." These people saw Soviet sport tours as nothing more than the exercise of Bolshevik propaganda. Other, more fair-minded people, however, were extremely curious to find out just who the Soviet diplomats of sport were. The Stockholm newspaper *Dagens Nyheter* reveals this particularly graphically in its description of the Russian players at the first game of the 1923 tour.

How did they look? Starved, emaciated, and exhausted, or like bandits who had committed all kinds of crimes? Oh, no, they looked like any nice, good-looking young men, blond or darkhaired, as is the case even in Sweden, neither giants nor dwarfs. The red shirts with white pants did not suggest blood or agitation, but made a nice-looking uniform. They could just as well have been from Copenhagen. (Nej, det blev, 1923)

East-West Sport Diplomacy

The political ramifications of early East-West sport diplomacy are especially complex and deserve further examination. It has been stated that sport has "no intrinsic political value" (Lowe, Kanin, and Strenk, 1978, p. v). For this reason, contests that take place in connection with sport diplomacy can have a multiplicity of meanings, political and otherwise, depending on who is investing what in them.

The experiences of the 1920s bear this out, particularly the Soviet soccer tour of Scandinavia in 1923. When the Russian players had returned from their triumphant tour (15 wins, 3 draws), it was clear that—for the Soviets, at least—the trip had had important political implications. This was evident in a controversy that took place over the flying of the Soviet flag. It was apparently the policy of the Swedish Foreign Ministry to allow the Soviet flag to be flown in other places, but not in Stockholm. Although one source has reported that the Russians would not play the last match in Stockholm until the Soviet flag was raised at Queens Stadium (Korshak, 1975), it has not been possible to verify this in contemporary press accounts. In any event, even if the Swedish sportswriters were not especially interested in where and when the Soviet flag was flown, the Soviets were.

The situation in the Stockholm press with regard to the Soviet visit is most revealing of the different political sympathies and perceptions concerning sport diplomacy that existed at that time. The leftist paper *Folkets Dagblad Politiken* was actually a sponsor of the Russian soccer players' visit. *Politiken* wanted to highlight a labor day holiday in Göteborg with the visit of the Soviet soccer emissaries. According to the newspaper *Dagens Nyheter*, there were accusations from the Right that the Swedish team selected to play the Russians in the final match had deliberately been made a weak one in order to assure that the Russians returned home as winners— supposedly an important part of Russian propaganda (Ryssmatcherna, 1923). For its part, *Dagens Nyheter*, the main organ of the liberal press, chose to see no political connotations or overtones whatsoever in the soccer matches. An article on the first match of the tour asks rhetorically, "Why should a political view be taken about a Soviet visit? No one assumes this about Hungary or Finland as they travel about" (Den svenska fotbollsrörelsen, 1923). Another article about the same match concluded by saying, "Very nice and without a breath of revolution!" (Nej, det blev, 1923).

The various and conflicting views on the Russian-Swedish matches demonstrate clearly that in connection with sport diplomacy, political significance is in the eyes of the beholder. People, politicians, and press make of such contests and tours exactly what they wish to make of them. Here, then, is the special attraction and power of sport diplomacy, for its greatest asset is its inherent flexibility, its ability to deliver several messages— sometimes even contradictory ones—simultaneously.

Sport diplomacy is, of course, not without its potential drawbacks. As Kanin (1978) has pointed out in reference to more recent history, in certain cases—such as the U.S.-U.S.S.R. sporting contests—these events have "not enhanced the process of 'detente' so much as the competition in sport has reminded people of the continuing rivalry between the two sides."

This downside of sport diplomacy was already evident in the early 1920s. For example, during the Soviet visit to Sweden in 1923, not only were there charges of "red agitators" hurled at the Soviet players, but when the Russian team turned out to be much stronger than anticipated, there were, as noted above, recriminations in the Stockholm press over the selection of the Swedish sides. In this instance, the Russians obliged the Swedes in helping them to find their strongest team by agreeing to an additional farewell game against a select Stockholm side. The Russian victory by a score of 2–1 gave them a final tally of seven wins and two draws for the tour. Nevertheless, *Dagens Nyheter* continued to complain that "the Swedish team chosen did not measure up to par" (Ryssarna vunne, 1923).

Finally, it should be noted that the German leg of the tour was far less successful than the Scandinavian part. The Russians could take little satisfaction in the three overwhelming victories they scored because they were at the expense of relatively weak workers' clubs. Furthermore, they were reported to have received a poor reception, and their accommodations were not up to standard (Russkie futbolisty, 1923).

The most important precedents set by early East-West sport diplomacy have to do with its role as a means of signaling or symbolizing a positive change in relations, new beginnings, or even full-fledged detente. For example, the first U.S.-U.S.S.R. track and field meets signaled something of a thaw in the Cold War relations that had prevailed between the two countries.

Certainly the most graphic instance of sport signaling change was the famed "Ping-Pong diplomacy" that heralded the new relationship between the U.S. and the People's Republic of China. Interestingly enough, in this case the Chinese, either consciously or unconsciously, were following the Soviet example of beginning sporting contacts with foreign countries in their own strongest sport, for table tennis is the most developed Chinese sport, just as soccer was the most popular Soviet sport in the early 1920s.

Finally, the East-West detente of the 1970s included not only the much ballyhooed Canadian-Soviet hockey games but also some less well-publicized friendly soccer matches between the Soviets and the teams of the now-defunct North American Soccer League.

It should be pointed out, however, that just as the commencement of sporting contacts can herald better East-West relations, their termination can be a sure sign that relations have changed for the worse. As Kanin (1978) has pointed out, the cancellation of the U.S.-U.S.S.R. track and field meets in 1966 was probably a means for the Soviet Union to protest the U.S. involvement in Vietnam.

Conclusions

Experiences of early East-West sport diplomacy are a vivid reminder that although sport diplomacy may sometimes assume powerful political dimensions, it is not the real substance of politics and cannot by itself be expected to reconcile fundamental differences between opposing political systems. Sport diplomacy can be effective only when, as at times during the 1920s and subsequently, both sides have compelling reasons unrelated to sport to come to some sort of an accommodation.

In the final analysis, the Soviets had better defined and more urgent goals in their conduct of early sport diplomacy than did the West. This does not mean that the Soviets had at that time a thoroughly articulated political program for sport diplomacy. Yet, they seemed better able to recognize and develop rationales for their sport diplomacy as the events of the day unfolded. Here, too, it would seem that early practice has set an enduring precedent, for, as contemporary analysis has shown, the Soviets continue to be far better organized and more resourceful in their political exploitation of sport diplomacy than the Western countries (Jefferies, 1985).

This points to a poignant paradox in East-West cultural relations. Although first the Russians and now the Soviets have continued over the centuries to look to the West for the enrichment of their own technology and culture, in the modern day the West often looks to the Soviet Union for the development of its own systems of sport and physical culture.

Acknowledgment

I am extremely grateful to the Russian Summer Research Laboratory of the University of Illinois and the Slavic and East European Library and Applied Life Sciences Library of the University of Illinois Library for making the research for this paper possible. The translations from Russian are my own, and the translations from Swedish have been done by Monica Foreman.

References

Den svenska fotbollsrörelsen her fätt sin Don Quijote [The Swedish soccer alliance has got its Don Quixote]. (1923, August 4). *Dagens Nyheter*.

Jefferies, S. (1985, July, August). Games within games: Soviet sport diplomacy. *Coaching Review*, p. 43.

Kanin, D. (1978). Superpower sport in cold war and "detente." In B. Lowe, D. Kanin, & A. Strenk (Eds.), *Sport and international relations* (pp. 249-262). Champaign, IL: Stipes Publishing.

Korshak, Yu. (1975). *Staryi, staryi futbol* [Old, old soccer]. Moscow: Fizkul'tura i sport.

Lowe, B., Kanin, D., & Strenk, A. (1978). *Sport and international relations*. Champaign, IL: Stipes Publishing.

Mekhanoshin, A. (1923, July 25). Interview with Mekhanoshin, president of Sportintern. *Izvestiia*.

Nej, det blev ingen sensation! [No, it was not a sensation!]. (1923, August 4). *Dagens Nyheter*.

Riordan, J. (1980). Sport and physical education in West and East: A comparative study of approaches to sport and physical education in Britain and the U.S.S.R. In C. Pooley & J. Pooley, (Eds.), *Proceedings of the 2nd International Conference on Comparative Physical Education and Sport* (pp. 1-37). Halifax, NS: Dalhousie University.

Russkie futbolisty za granitsei [Russian soccer players abroad]. (1923, September 26). *Izvestiia*.

Ryssarna vunne med 2-1. Det borde varit mer [The Russians won 2-1. It ought to have been more]. (1923, August 23). *Dagens Nyheter*.

Ryssmatcherna icke rent spel? Svär anklagelse [Russian matches not clean play? Difficult accusation]. (1923, August 24). *Dagens Nyheter*.

Semashko, N. (1967). Fizicheskaia kul'tura i zdravookhranenie v SSSR [Physical culture and public health care in the U.S.S.R.]. In N. Semashko, *Izbrannye proizvedeniia* [Selected works] (pp. 265-266). Moscow: Meditsina.

SSSR i "malye" derzhavy [The U.S.S.R. and the "small" powers]. (1923, July 5). *Pravda*.

Starostin, A. (1980). *Vstrechi na futbol'nom orbite* [Meetings in the soccer orbit] (2nd ed.). Moscow: Sovetskaia Rossiia.

Tingsten, H. (1949). *The debate on the foreign policy of Sweden, 1918-1939*. London: Oxford University Press.

A Comparison Between Sport in Britain in the 1950s and 1980s

Peter Wilfred Sutcliffe

The choice of dates for the comparison of sport in Great Britain is significant, for the 1950s was the last decade when the provision of sporting opportunities was regarded as the responsibility of private individuals playing in voluntary sports clubs under the control, or with the encouragement, of the Governing Bodies of Sport (GBs). Since then, government intervention, nationally and locally, has fundamentally changed sport in the United Kingdom to the form we see in the 1980s.

If we glance back only to 1980 and the buildup to the Moscow Olympics, a dispute arose between the Conservative government, led by Margaret Thatcher, and the GBs of the Olympic Sports, led by Sir Denis Follows, chairman of the British Olympic Association. The disagreement was whether or not a British team should take part in the Games. The majority of the GBs resisted government pressure. With the growing dependence of sport on government sources of finance, it is interesting to speculate on the outcome of any future disputes, should they arise.

By the conclusion of this paper, a case should have been made that sport in Britain is now within reach of every person, irrespective of class, age, or sex, whether able bodied or handicapped. This position of British sport is the result of financial support from statutory sources. Yet, financial dependence brings in its train political dependence, and it has long been a hallowed principle in British sport that there is no place for politics. Now that sport throughout the world is increasingly being regarded as part of the fabric of society, such a sentiment is, at best, naive and, at worst, foolish. As we have seen in Eastern Europe since 1945, and more recently in South Africa, sport can be used to propagate a political ideology or used as a weapon to destroy one. Too few people in Britain recognize that our Victorian forbears used sport for political purposes, overseas as a potent factor in building the Empire and domestically to promulgate upper- and middle-class social values. Politics is not new to sport in Britain.

Traditionally, sport in Britain has been thought to serve two functions: first, as a form of recreation, enjoyment, and entertainment; and second, as a means of achieving better health, both mental and physical. Although, as we now recognize, both are part of the same concept, they have led to separate strands of sporting development in Britain.

In a society devoted to the work ethic, the hedonistic motive for sport has been regarded in the past as a private matter. Thus, persons were expected to play in whatever leisure time was available and at their own expense. The choice of sport was dependent on opportunity and cost, rather than aptitude. In time, groups of players and clubs banded together to form associations, the GBs, which regularized the laws of competition.

In contrast, health has always been a concern of the state, more often than not stirred by the need to ensure a fit and active population well able to defend itself or its Empire. The most significant legislation prior to the 1950s took place at times when Britain felt itself threatened by force, first from the Russians, then the Boers, and twice in the twentieth century from the Germans. Perhaps there is hope for the future in the recollection that recent sports legislation was initiated not by the threat of armed aggression but by an event brought to the attention of Parliament: Britain's sole Olympic success in 1952 was by a horse!

State Intervention in Sport

Although different kings of England have from time to time banned football, made archery compulsory, and played tennis, the first sports legislation by Parliament, real or otherwise, came in 1846 with the Baths and Washhouses Act. This act enabled local authorities (LAs) to provide facilities for swimming. Successive Public Health Acts in 1875, 1890, 1925, and 1936, in addition to the Local Government Act of 1894, enabled LAs to equip, maintain, and service sporting amenities in towns and in the countryside. Unfortunately, the whole of this legislation was permissive rather than mandatory. Thus, at times when resources in LAs were stretched, spending on recreation was curtailed.

Nonetheless, by the 1950s all local authorities provided facilities for swimming at both competitive and recreative levels and maintained a good stock of outdoor playing pitches for field games, tennis, and bowls. Grounds for the last two were usually built in public parks and gardens, which had been a feature of municipal provision since Victorian times. Laying out playing fields was given a considerable boost by the King George VI charity, which ultimately changed to the very influential National Playing Fields Association.

The administration of plant was split within a number of departments in borough councils, something which was to cause difficulties at a later date. The Physical Training and Recreation Act of 1937 supplemented LA finance with grant aid from central government via the Board of Education and, most significantly, offered similar support to voluntary bodies at local and national level.

Provision for physical education in state schools followed a different pathway. Although Swedish drill had been encouraged in schools in the 1902 Education Act, it was not until the Fisher Acts of 1918 and 1921 that the building of school facilities for sport was encouraged by legislation. Meanwhile, teachers in the state system had seen the benefits of competitive sport in the private sector. As early as 1885, the South London Schools Football Association had been formed. It was the first of many school associations that were to mushroom over the next 50 years, often outside the jurisdiction of the GBs and under the control of teachers. The Amateur Swimming Association (ASA) had taken an enlightened view of its functions and established training courses for those wishing to teach swimming, as early as 1919. Because of its early involvement in teaching and teacher training, the ASA coaching scheme was the best developed of all GB schemes in the 1950s.

It was not until the 1944 Butler Education Act that the provision of physical education facilities in schools was made mandatory. It should be noted that these facilities were for children only and were not intended for the general community. Thus, in the 1950s, at a time of restricted recreational opportunities for the general public, many excellent gymnasia, swimming pools, and playing fields stood idle at times when not in school use. This situation still remains to be resolved in the 1980s, and it is proving to be an almost intractable problem.

The development of sport in the private sector of education and the subsequent growth of sport in voluntary clubs were scarcely touched by legislation until after the 1950s. At that time, as McIntosh and Charlton (1985) commented, the GBs provided a chaotic pattern of regulations and behavior, an example of which was the variety of definitions of amateurism, which had troubled de Coubertin at the close of the 19th century and which has not yet been completely resolved in the 1980s.

The first serious attempt to coordinate the work of the GBs was made in 1935 with the establishment of the Central Council of Recreation and Physical Training (CCRPT) (Evans, 1974). Public concern about the welfare of young people in the mid-1930s was exacerbated by the growing apprehension that national socialism in Germany might lead Britain into a war for which it was ill prepared. Comparisons were made between British youth and the well-drilled Hitler Youth, with its motto "I was born to die for Germany" (Dixon, McIntosh, Munrow, & Willetts, 1957). In 1934 an inquiry into sport was instigated by the Ministry of Health. The result was the CCRPT, but, consistent with the British attitude to sport and recreation, the Council had to rely on charitable donations for its finance. At its inception the CCRPT had 84 GBs in membership. In its first newsletter, the Council outlined its policies: "To help to improve the physical and mental health of the community through physical recreation, by developing existing facilities for recreative physical activities of all kinds, and also by making provision for the thousands not yet associated with any organization."

Britain's failure in the 1936 Berlin Olympics, allied with the growing threat from Nazi Germany, brought further government action that redirected the work of the CCRPT and enabled the voluntary sector of sport to make real progress. This was the passing of the Physical Training and Recreation Act in 1937 (PT&R Act). It urged the development and expansion of existing facilities and organizations in schools and places of work. LAs were required to establish committees to aid physical training and recreation. A National Grants Committee was established to grant aid for the provision of gymnasia, swimming baths, and campsites. LAs were encouraged to appoint staff to effect these policies, and grant aid was made available to assist national and local bodies in training personnel for this purpose. Finally, and perhaps most important of all, under Section 4, LAs were empowered to raise cash to pay for recreation by levying an "extra rate payable by owners and occupiers" (PT&R Act, 1937).

Just as real progress was being made, the war intervened, but in 1944 the CCRPT was reconstituted as the Central Council for Physical Recreation (CCPR). The CCPR influenced the GBs to establish coaching schemes in the postwar years. From 1947 the Ministry of Education offered grants of up to 80% toward the salaries and expenses of National Coaches and for the training and examination of coaches working at regional and local levels. The staff of the CCPR made their professional knowledge as teachers of physical education "tactfully available in working out the various schemes and with their administration generally, in cooperation with PE Organisers employed by local education authorities" (Evans, 1974, p. 72).

The title *National Governing Body* sounds grandiose, but in the 1950s the reality was far from grand. Apart from the major sports with large spectator followings, most GBs could afford little more than a modest secretariat, often working in an honorary capacity from the back room of someone's home (Sutcliffe, 1983). Nevertheless, irrespective of its size, every GB was recognized as the disciplinary and legislative authority for its sport.

With more resources, the larger GBs were better able to find the other 20% of the costs incurred in employing coaches. Thus, sports like soccer, swimming, and cricket expanded their coaching schemes with the help of full-time professional coaches. Considering that these coaches were former teachers, that coaching schemes were supported by the Ministry of Education, and promoted by the CCPR (whose staff was also recruited from the teaching profession), it is not surprising that their efforts were aimed at schoolchildren and teachers. The existing pattern of sport in school, therefore, was reinforced. At this time, coaching schemes barely touched adult players.

The smaller GBs, including many Olympic sports, were in a catch-22. Because they seldom attracted media coverage and had few resources to extend their activities, they had a low profile. Unable to attract more members, they could not increase their resources. Thus, the most popular sports in the 1950s remained the traditional field games: for men, soccer, rugby, and cricket; for women, hockey, netball, rounders, and tennis. Swimming was well supported as a recreational activity by both sexes and as a competitive sport in schools. Athletics was widely taught in schools but was less popular as a recreational sport.

Despite the valiant efforts of the "Wing PE Colleges" to introduce more variety into school programs, competitive sport in schools reflected the adult pattern. This situation was reinforced by growing television coverage, which also concentrated on the traditional, and often professional, sports. For example, the Lords Test Match or the Wembley Cup Final were the highlights of the sporting calendar.

In 1956 the physical education Department of Birmingham University published a short pamphlet called "Britain in the World of Sport." It analyzed the factors affecting British sport at that time, drawing attention to the handicap under which sporting bodies and amateur sportsmen and women labored in their preparations for international competition. The pamphlet placed sport in Britain in the wider context of world sport, pointing out that success in international competition had far-reaching political and educational implications. Participation at this level demanded a price that Britain would have to pay, both in money and in the sacrifice of traditional attitudes. The document foresaw the growing separation in standards of performance in countries enjoying state support and control, from those that left the organization of sport to nonpolitical bodies. In Britain, relative to the size of its population, standards were adequate, but compared to past success, standards were falling behind the rest of the world. The pamphlet concluded that British physical education in schools was unequaled, but there was little continuity once a boy or girl had left school. British sport suffered badly with regard to finance, when compared to many other countries where sport received massive support from the state, from lotteries or, as in the case of America, from commercially motivated university or high school organizations. The report concluded by suggesting that it was imperative for British sport to be funded by the central government, together with the inescapable conclusion that a sports council should be appointed that would "bear in mind not only international sports and its related problems but also the tremendous educational potential of sport and its social value to the average and less-than-average player."

The Birmingham report led directly to the appointment of the Wolfenden Committee in October 1957, for the following purposes:

> To examine the factors affecting the development of games, sports and outdoor activities in the United Kingdom and to make recommendations to the CCPR as to any practical measures which should be taken by statutory or voluntary bodies in order that these activities may play their full part in promoting the general welfare of the community. (Wolfenden, 1960, p. 1)

The Committee was convinced that Birmingham University had been correct in making the case for government support for sport. Yet it recognized that tradition persists in Britain, and it resisted recommending the establishment of anything that could be interpreted as a Ministry of Sport. The recommendation was that a Sports Development Council be formed so that "more people may be enabled to enjoy the recreative benefits of sport" (Wolfenden, 1960, p. 97). The Council was to consist of a body of advisers responsible to the Chancellor of the Exchequer. The report made over 50 other recommendations, one of which was that the CCPR had a vital role to play in helping the Council to effect its policies.

It was not until 1963 that the government implemented any of Wolfenden's suggestions. The Conservative government of the time agreed to allocate resources but resisted the idea of a Sports Council. In October 1964 a Labour government was elected; in the following February, it established an advisory, rather than an executive, Sports Council. In the course of time, an uneasy relationship developed between the advisory council, the CCPR, and government departments. Thus, in 1970 Dennis Howell, Labour government's minister for sport, recommended that the CCPR should fulfill several functions:

1. To service the Sports Council and newly established Regional Sports Councils
2. To administer the National Sports Centres
3. To assist GBs in the administration of their coaching schemes
4. To provide a "voice for sport" (Evans, 1974, p. 216)

The Conservative government was returned in June of that year and made positive efforts to rationalize the work of the Sports Council and the CCPR. In June 1971 it was announced that the Advisory Sports Council was to be re-formed as an Executive Body, with its independence guaranteed by Royal Charter. The new organization was to take over the assets of the CCPR, its staff, the National Sports Centres, and all equipment and office accommodation. On completion of this transfer, the CCPR would cease to exist. In theory, the Charter ensured that the new body would remain free from political interference.

At this point the British sporting tradition reasserted itself. The GBs demanded an independent voice and canvassed the President of the CCPR—the Duke of Edinburgh—to this effect. The press of the day reported, "The Duke opposes a sports takeover!" In short, the GBs resented government intrusion into sport. Royal patronage ensured the continued life of the CCPR, though with a different function and constitution from its predecessor, thus causing conflict within British sport, which has now come to a head in the 1980s. The difficulties have been caused by the overlapping aims of the Sports Council and the CCPR. For example, the CCPR "constitutes a standing forum where all GBs may be represented to formulate and promote measures to improve and develop sport and physical recreation." The Sports Council has as one of its aims "to develop and improve the knowledge and practice of sport and physical recreation in the interests of social welfare and the enjoyment of leisure among the public at large and to encourage the attainment of high standards in conjunction with the GBs."

Conflict between the two bodies was, therefore, inevitable without sympathetic and skilled leadership of both. In any event, the two bodies have been unable to work in harmony. The 1980s have witnessed a continual and escalating conflict between them, which has now become the subject of a parliamentary select committee inquiry. The committee's recommendation could lead to a drastic change in the CCPR's role in the future:

The CCPR called in question the need for a Sports Council in its present form. We were satisfied by their evidence that there is overlapping of functions and put the issues so raised to our other witnesses. The overwhelming response has been that the CCPR is the organization which should be called into question. . . . We can and do say we see no justification on the evidence for continuous public funding of the CCPR.

At this point it is necessary to consider a second area of development, one that has changed the face of sport in Britain more than any other factor. It is the reorganization of local government and the subsequent establishment of recreation departments in boroughs throughout Britain. The Cobham Report (HMSO, Department of the Environment, 1973) defined the responsibilities of LAs with regard to providing opportunities for recreation. It said, ''The provision for sport and recreational opportunities is indeed a social service that in its own way is almost as important to the well-being of the community as good housing, hospitals, and schools.'' The report pointed to the serious deficiencies in facilities for sport in Britain and suggested that LAs, with government assistance, were the best agencies to plan, build, and manage new facilities. It recommended that this should be a statutory duty.

The subsequent 1976 Local Government Act encapsulated all of the Cobham recommendations, except that provision was to be permissive, rather than mandatory. This did not, however, inhibit local authority development. It is estimated that LA spending in the 1980s on sport and recreation is in the order of £600M per annum.

In 1974 LA reorganization had led to smaller authorities being amalgamated to form larger units. Rather than handing over balances of funds, the disappearing authorities usually invested them in new facilities. This led to a boom in the provision of indoor recreation centers and coincided with the Sports Council's drive for new recreation facilities. It is estimated that in 1974/75, over 150 new swimming pools and 130 indoor sports centers were constructed. Between 1975 and 1981, an average of a further 50 indoor centers were built annually.

These developments and the formation of large, multidisciplinary departments overtook the experience of many officers working in local government recreational services. The Yates Report on recreation management suggested that one professional body with appropriate qualifications for membership should guide the future of the recreation management profession. The Institute of Leisure and Amenities Management (ILAM) has now been established in the 1980s, not without resistance from the previous institutes involved in baths and recreation management. However, there now exists a structure of recognized courses in module form to assist in the training of managers in this area.

In setting up an Executive Sports Council, the government provided the catalyst by which the energies, expertise, and resources in manpower and cash of LAs, GBs, and voluntary bodies could be harnessed for the benefit of the existing and potential sporting public. The aims of the Sports Council were wide, but can be briefly expressed:

1. to help more people play sport,
2. to help more people achieve higher standards of play,
3. to encourage the provision of more facilities,
4. to encourage research into sporting problems and topics,
5. to liaise with sports bodies in foreign countries.

In the 1970s the flood of requests for help from the LAs, GBs, and their constituent members left little time to do other than respond on an opportunist basis. An illustration of this fact is that between 1972 and 1981, when over 800 new indoor sports centers were built, vast numbers of voluntary sports clubs improved their pitches and changing accommodations. Following the government white paper, *Sport and Recreation* (HMSO, 1975), Centres of Sporting Excellence were established in cooperation with the GBs, new coaching schemes were launched, and existing schemes expanded. This expanding program was taking place alongside the Sports Council's own initiative to bring sport to the general public under the banner of "Sport for All."

The Sports Council's budget grew from £3M in 1972 to £16M in 1980, but its growth was insufficient to meet the demands made on it. In order to make the case for more resources, a strategy was produced in 1982 called "Sport in the Community: The Next Ten Years." This program included the construction of a further 800 indoor sports centers—some of which could stage major spectator events—50 new and 200 refurbished swimming pools, 3,000 new or upgraded sports pitches, and better access for countryside sports. One aspect of facilities already referred to, and featured in the 10-Year Strategy, was to bring into public use existing, underused school facilities.

It was perhaps in the area of participation that the Sports Council broke new ground by targeting its efforts at specific groups of people: those who live in areas of special need, the unemployed, the handicapped, and those who tend not to take part in sport—young women and school leavers. The estimate was that this program would cost £215M in the first 5 years, much of which would come from sponsoring agencies, LAs, and voluntary sports clubs.

Despite the financial stringencies in public spending, the annual budget of the Sports Council has increased in 1985/6 to £37M, well ahead of inflation. Voluntary sports clubs continue to improve their facilities with grant aid at a level of 50% of total costs, while many local authorities—particularly those qualifying for special government assistance in areas of urban deprivation—are responding to the call for improved provision. For example, the Liverpool City Council has built in the last 3 years 5 new indoor centers, and plans 2 more in 1986, plus 2 new leisure pools, a 25-meter competition pool, and a synthetic athletics track. The gratifying feature of this ambitious program is that Liverpool is building according to the recommendations of the Sports Council in its unique design for community sports halls, the Standardised Approach to Sports Halls (SASH, 1982).

Conclusions

Participation in sport in the 1950s took place within the traditional, competitive GB structure. Because of the social origins of sport, this usually meant being a member of a private single sport club, with all the class distinctions that this implies. Informal sport—a game of tennis in the park, a swim in the municipal baths, or perhaps a ramble in the countryside— was more likely to be the recreation of the many. Soccer was extensively played in local leagues on municipal pitches often without adequate changing accommodations. Few teams outside the league structure could afford their own facilities.

Sport in the north of England tended to be more democratic than in the south. Spectator involvement offered the chance for promising players at cricket, for example, to earn talent money. In Scotland, municipal provision for golf made it a working man's game; in England, golf was the preserve of the private member. There were sharp divisions in sport between classes, amateurs and professionals, men and women, for whom far fewer opportunities existed. In short, sport reflected the divisions and prejudices that existed in society.

Government intervention in the 1980s, through the medium of grant aid, has assisted private clubs to improve their facilities. However, in qualifying for a grant, many have had to become more democratic and less exclusive than in the 1950s. The major effect of legislation, however, has been seen in the provision of municipal facilities, particularly indoor sports centers. These can be booked on a casual basis, allowing members of the public to play a wide variety of sports without being committed to regular membership or competition in a club. Municipal provision has also spawned clubs in sports that otherwise would not have had access to facilities, for example, the martial arts, volleyball, basketball, handball, and many others.

With additional resources for coaching and development from the Sports Council, the GBs have been able to reach a wider public, particularly the minority sports. Since the 1950s squash has increased its membership tenfold. Similar figures could be quoted for badminton, judo, and basketball. In contrast, since 1950 the number of spectators supporting both professional soccer and cricket has halved.

Other examples of the influence of the Sports Council could be noted: the ambitious program of coach education, launched in cooperation with the British Association of National Coaches, to supplement the technical content of GB coaching awards; the development of a network of National Sports Centres for the major sports and outdoor pursuits; and research into a wide variety of sporting problems, not the least of which at the present time is the detection of drugs being used to enhance athletic performance.

The work of the Sports Council is bringing the benefits of sport to an ever-growing section of the population in Britain in the 1980s. As a government-sponsored agency, the Sports Council must, as it says in the Royal Charter, take cognizance of government policy. For many, this loss of independence matters little; for others, it is something not easily accepted.

References

Birmingham University, Department of Physical Education. (1956). *Britain in the world of sport.*

Dixon, J.G., McIntosh, P.C., Munrow, A.D., & Willetts, R.F. (1960). *Landmarks in the history of physical education.* London: Routledge and Kegan Paul.

Evans, J. (1974). *Service to sport.* London: Pelham.

Her Majesty's Stationary Office. (1937). *Physical training and recreation act 1937.* London: Author.

Her Majesty's Stationary Office. (1971). *Royal charter sports council.* London: Author.

Her Majesty's Stationary Office. (1972). *Local government act 1972.* London: Author.

Her Majesty's Stationary Office, Department of the Environment. (1973). *Sport and leisure.* London: Author.

Her Majesty's Stationary Office, Department of the Environment (1975). *Sport and recreation.* London: Author.

McIntosh, P.C., & Charlton, V. (1985). *The impact of Sport for All policy 1966–1984.* London: Sport Council.

Sports Council (1982). *Sport in the community: The next ten years.* London: Author.

Wolfenden, J. (1960). *Sport and the community* (CCPR). London: Author.

PART III

Physical Education

The Development, Evaluation, and Validation of Undergraduate and Graduate Curricula in Physical Education, Sport, and Leisure in the 1960s and the 1980s in Great Britain

Eric D. Saunders

In this short paper, it is impossible to completely delineate the influence of the complex social, political, and economic factors on the changing system of physical education, sport, and leisure. Essentially, an examination is made of institutional change and course development, rather than details of the curriculum. Nevertheless, attention is drawn to some changes essentially brought about by the validation of courses that have made a major impact upon physical education, sport, and leisure.

Structure of Higher Education in the 1960s and the 1980s

Until 1960 there were two distinct sectors in higher education: universities and teacher training colleges. The universities were autonomous, independent institutions, whereas the colleges were closely controlled by local authorities and the central government. In 1961—as a result of the need to create a more effective industrial base, an unprecedented rise in the demand for higher education caused by the postwar bulge in the birth rate, and the increasing number of pupils remaining at schools after the statutory school leaving age—the Conservative government set up a committee under the chairmanship of Lord Robbins to undertake a comprehensive inquiry into the field of higher education. The report, published in 1963, provoked the newly elected Labour government to expand the provision for higher education by increasing the number of universities to 46 by 1969, to create 30 polytechnics under local authority control, and to support the increase in the number of teacher training places in renamed colleges of education, which would also provide 4-year bachelor of education degrees. In essence, a binary system was established, with the universities retaining individual autonomy in what is now called the "private" sector, and polytechnics and colleges of education becoming "public" sector institutions under the control of local authorities.

In the early 1960s, Birmingham University, which had accepted physical education as a subject in general education in 1946, was still the only university to offer the academic study of the subject at undergraduate level. An advanced diploma course began in 1955 and, run jointly by the University of Leeds and Carnegie College of Physical Education, led the way for those who wished to pursue further full-time postgraduate study. Anyone who wished to pursue a career in teaching followed a 3-year professional course in a college of education, or a 4-year bachelor of education degree validated by the university but taught by college of education staff. Most colleges offered physical education in the new bachelor of education degree (BEd). About 10% took this route into teaching, the majority leaving with a 3-year certificate in education.

During the 1960s, higher education was dominated by uncertainties over the supply of teachers, and figures were constantly being revised. In 1970, with the return of the Conservative government, the secretary of state for education—Margaret Thatcher, the present prime minister—set up a committee of inquiry under the chairmanship of Lord James to examine the content and organization of courses to be provided; the possibility of prospective teachers being educated with students pursuing other careers; and the role of colleges of education, polytechnics, further-education institutions, and the universities in the training process. The James Report, "Teacher Education and Training" (Department of Education and Science, 1972), recommended a 2-year diploma in higher education and a 3-year bachelor of arts degree in education to be validated by the Council for National Academic Awards (CNAA).

These proposals were not accepted by Government, which set out its policies in December 1972 in the white paper *Education: A Framework for Expansion*, in which new 3-year ordinary or 4-year honors bachelor of education degrees were established as principal routes into teaching. Validation was made the responsibility of both the universities and the CNAA, thus establishing a binary system of validation. The white paper also dealt with the problem of reorganization resulting from a reduction in demand for teachers. It proposed that colleges should merge with other institutions and seek to diversify into new fields of study.

Between 1972 and 1982, 200 colleges were reorganized, 25 closed, 37 amalgamated with polytechnics, 12 joined the university sector, 59 colleges of higher education were established by merger, and only 28 remained as colleges of education (Pratt, Locke, & Burgess, 1985). Diversification and the rationalization of resources had a profound impact on course planning. It enforced a new system of first degrees that provided an entry into teaching through new-style BEd and the postgraduate certificate in education. Rationalization, on the other hand, had both a negative and positive impact. The amalgamation of colleges into larger institutions enabled course planners to draw on a wider range of resources, whereas a restriction of the number of students entering any one course threatened the viability of the curriculum in terms of coverage, group sizes, and options.

The move to diversification coincided with Government policy outlined in the white paper *Sport and Recreation* in 1975, which gave official recognition to the social value of sport and recreation in terms of physical well-being and community morale. It conferred on the state the duty of establishing institutions by which to secure this aim. This white paper also reiterated the need to ensure close personal and professional contact between education and recreation services, and that schools and sporting communities were not set apart.

It was also believed by many colleges that delayed vocational choice within a vocationally relevant framework, as outlined in the earlier James Report, was highly desirable both for students and potential employers, because choice of career could be more closely related to job opportunities and career aspirations. Rationalization of resources, the amalgamation of former colleges into polytechnics and universities, and the merging of others into colleges of higher education provided better staffing and facilities to realize aspirations toward course diversification. As befits a pluralistic society, a variety of different course patterns and structures emerged as a result of institutional policies and planning.

The late 1970s and the 1980s, therefore, saw fewer people entering teaching and an incremental rise in academic and vocationally relevant courses in sports science, sports studies, recreation and leisure, and human movement studies. By 1980 there were over 30 courses validated principally by the CNAA.

The 1980s also saw a dramatic cut in funding to universities and the public sector, with centralized control over numbers entering higher education. The Department of Education and Science in England and Wales, the Scottish Education Department, and the Department of Education in Northern Ireland operate a quota system to allocate places to universities, polytechnics, and colleges of higher education in England, Wales, and Northern Ireland, and colleges of education in Scotland. Diversified courses in sport, recreation, and leisure are not so closely confined by quotas, but the license to run courses is firmly in the hands of central government agencies. A measure of government control in England, Wales, and Northern Ireland can be gauged by the establishment of the Council for Accreditation of Teacher Education (CATE) by the Secretary of State. The Council evaluates all courses of initial training against specified criteria and can withdraw courses that do not meet prespecified conditions.

Fortunately, the license to run postgraduate courses, most of which are pursued part time, has not been subjected to such close scrutiny, although their viability is dependent upon the availability of finance and facilities within institutions where priorities are being more closely determined by market forces.

The Development of Undergraduate and Graduate Courses in Physical Education, Sport, and Leisure

In 1960, with the exception of the University of Birmingham, courses of physical education were subdegree and aimed specifically at a qualification to teach. The publication of the Robbins Report in 1963, which proposed the introduction of a new BEd degree, was a landmark in the development of degree-level study for those who wished to enter the teaching profession. By 1970, the majority of the departments in specialist colleges in England, Scotland, Wales, and Northern Ireland (11 male and 17 female) were offering both diploma and degree courses in physical education.

In addition, from the early 1960s to 1970, the number of colleges offering physical education as an element in general courses of teacher preparation expanded from around 47 in 1963 to 109 in 1970 (Physical Education Year Book, 1963–64, 1967–70). These courses were validated by universities, and the majority were located in colleges of education or specialist colleges of physical education. At the postgraduate level, where universities had strong physical education departments—for example, in Leeds, Liverpool, Newcastle, and Manchester—physical education was introduced into courses leading to diplomas in advanced studies in education and, later, to master of education degrees. With the exception of the advanced diploma in physical education taught jointly at Carnegie College and the University of Leeds and the MA in physical education begun in 1969 at Leeds, postgraduate study was closely aligned to the needs of primary and secondary education.

Developments in the 1970s and, in particular, the impact of CNAA, which countered the elitist and selective policies of the universities, resulted in a range of diversified courses that were not readily acceptable to most universities. Moreover, changes in validating and evaluation procedures ensured a range of models of courses based on sound rationales and a movement away from the monolithic academic/practical dichotomies that had dogged the development of courses in the 1960s. The 1980s, therefore, saw the introduction of a range of vocationally relevant courses tailored to the needs of a range of professions, including teaching, that were demonstrably more relevant and meaningful to students and to future careers outside teaching.

Patterns of Courses

In seeking to elaborate differences between the 1960s and the 1980s, it is necessary to differentiate teacher education courses from vocational or academic courses that lead to qualifications in leisure- and recreation-related spheres, undergraduate from postgraduate, education and initial training from in-service training.

In the 1960s the recreation service was still in its infancy, and the majority of courses led to careers or the enhancement of careers in teaching. The BEd recommended by Robbins was validated by 16 English universities on the "three plus one" model, a 3-year certificate course followed by a year of academic study. Postgraduate certificates were available for graduates in other subject areas. Graduates and selected nongraduates could seek higher level qualifications through full- and part-time study, through diplomas in the advanced study of education followed by a master of education, or by research for a master of philosophy or a doctor of philosophy degree. Others with certificate qualifications could return to college on a discretionary grant and undertake the fourth BEd year, followed by initial training students.

In the 1980s the picture has become more complicated. With the exception of Scotland, where there is an impending change in the organization of tertiary education, courses of study leading to careers in teaching and the field of leisure and recreation have become concentrated in a small number of institutions, mostly in the public sector. The number of "specialist colleges" engaged in teacher education has been reduced to 14 in the public sector and 4 universities. This policy has led to the demise of physical education in the work of the 107 colleges that offered physical education as a mainstream subject in the late 1960s.

Most undergraduate teacher education courses are now 4 years in length and lead to an honors BEd degree. Two universities offer a "two plus two" model—2 years academic study followed by 2 years academic and professional studies leading to BA or BS honors with a qualification to teach. Although it is still believed that the BEd is the most effective way of preparing for teaching, many institutes now offer a post-graduate certificate in education (PGCE) on completion of a degree in an area cognate to physical education. Postgraduate qualifications are still available through diploma in advanced studies in education (DASE) or MEds with varying degrees of specialization. A range of in-service BEd degrees for serving teachers can also be found on both sides of the binary line.

In the field of sport, recreation, and leisure, the normal undergraduate pattern is a 3-year full-time course leading to an ordinary or honors BA or BS. One university, Ulster, offers a 4-year course, with the third year spent in a paid employment placement. Most undergraduate courses are conceived as vocationally relevant, and the curricula are closely related to career outlets in the recreation service or as academic subjects that lead via a PGCE to teaching. Research leading to masters or doctorates can now be completed at universities, polytechnics, or colleges, provided adequate supervision can be found. The massive curriculum development that went into the planning of undergraduate courses is now being directed toward postgraduate qualifications; new courses in leisure practice, leisure studies, and physical education have recently been validated.

Course Curricula

Those interested in a detailed analysis of the contents of the curricula will find useful comparative material published elsewhere in books, theses, reports, and papers (Storey, 1980; Whitehead, 1969; Whitehead & Hendry, 1976; Hargreaves, 1982; HMI/BAALPE, 1980, HMI/NATFE, 1982; HMI, 1983, CNAA/SCOPE, 1985; Saunders, 1982).

Space does not permit an analysis of many curricular issues that have occurred over the last 20 to 25 years. However, it should be appreciated that course design in the 1980s is a sophisticated and developed system in which clear distinctions are made between initial and in-service courses; between teacher education and the academic education for sport, recreation, and leisure professionals; and between undergraduates and postgraduate qualifications. Despite the increase in demand for other sport- and recreation-related courses at undergraduate levels, postgraduate qualifications aimed at the enhancement of academic and/or professional development are still in their infancy.

Validation and Evaluation of Courses

In the 1960s, the validation of courses was under the control of universities, and there is an absence of documentary evidence that describes the process that led to course approval. The writer's own experience in two specialist colleges in the 1960s leads him to believe that there was not a typical set of course validation procedures and that the process was superficial and undemanding. Quality control was achieved by the university insisting that teaching staff had appropriate high-level qualifications in the subjects they taught, a consequence of which was a massive staff development exercise for those who aspired to teach at degree level and beyond.

In the late 1980s, it is still difficult to find a typical set of university procedures. On the other hand, the CNAA, which has a near-monopoly of course validation in physical education, sport, and leisure, has a clear-cut set of procedures. Despite the criticism that the CNAA has become overly bureaucratic, other important benefits have accrued to the profession. Any system of validation offers institutions both freedoms and constraints. CNAA regulations assert there is no single model for a course leading to a CNAA degree (CNAA, 1983), and submissions are judged on their own merits.

This contrasts with the catalogue of factors in universities that inhibit the development of innovatory degree schemes of any description. Although there may be common features of curriculum design that have been labeled academic, vocational, and professional, every CNAA undergraduate course in sports, physical education, or leisure studies has its own unique features.

The essence of this approach, therefore, is that there is no one single model. This openness is not a strong feature of the university sector, where these courses have not obtained much support from the academic hierarchy, who consider areas such as physical education, sport, and leisure to be academically suspect and, consequently, of low status. Yet, the logic of the concept of higher education is openness, the critical appraisal of any subject, and the assumptions and values underpinning it. The fact that there is no stipulated model for a course ensures this openness and encourages innovation in curriculum design.

In moving to this form of public scrutiny, not only has the system ensured the survival of the subject, it has encouraged major innovation in the design of courses in physical education, sport, and leisure and has given the subject an acceptable status in higher education—in the public sector, at least.

References

Council for National Academic Awards/Standing Conference of Physical Education. (1985, November). *Teaching quality and physical education.* Report of a conference held at Hohne-Pier-point, Nottingham, England.

Department of Environment. (1975). *Sport and recreation.* London: Her Majesty's Stationary Office.

Department of Education and Science. (1972). *Education: A framework for expansion.* London: Her Majesty's Stationary Office.

Hargreaves, A. (1982). *An analysis of selected B.Ed. degree courses in physical education validated by C.N.A.A.* Unpublished master's dissertation, University of Manchester, Manchester, England.

Her Majesty's Inspectorate. (1983). *The education and training of specialist teachers of physical education.* Report of a conference held at Bournemouth, England.

Her Majesty's Inspectorate/British Association of Advisors and Lecturers in Physical Education. (1980). *The education and training of specialist teachers of physical education.* Report of a conference held at Nottingham, England.

Her Majesty's Inspectorate/National Association of Teachers in Further and Higher Education. (1982). *The education and training of specialist teachers of physical education.* Report of a conference held at Leeds, England.

James Report. (1972). *Teacher education and training—Report of an enquiry.* **370**: 71. London: Her Majesty's Stationary Office.

Physical Education Association (1963–64). *Physical education year book.* London: Ling House.

Physical Education Association (1969–70). *Physical education year book.* London: Ling House.

Pratt, J., Locke, M., & Burgess, T. (1985). Central management of organic change: The college of higher education 1972-82. *Higher Education Review,* **17**(3), 35-48.

Robbins Report. (1963). *Higher education—Report of an enquiry.* London: Her Majesty's Stationary Office.

Saunders, E.D. (1982). Preparation for the profession. Mary Hankinson Memorial Trust Lecture. Proceedings of the 1982 study course *The Changing Curriculum of Physical Education.* Physical Education Association of Great Britain and Northern Ireland. London.

Storey, A. (1980). *The education and training of physical education teachers in England.* Unpublished master's dissertation, University of Birmingham, Birmingham, England.

Whitehead, N.J., & Hendry, L.B. (1976). *Teaching physical education in England: Description and analysis.* London: Lepus.

A Comparative Analysis of Undergraduate Professional Preparation in Physical Education in the United States and Canada (1960–1985)

Earle F. Zeigler

In this study, a preliminary comparative analysis was made of undergraduate professional preparation in physical education in the United States and Canada from 1960 to 1985. I hypothesize that there have been significant changes, some similar and others different, in the undergraduate professional preparation programs of both countries. I further hypothesize that changes came about in the U.S. first. Lipset (1973) pointed out that there has been reluctance on the part of Canadians ''to be over-optimistic, assertive, or experimentally inclined.'' Finally, it should be recognized that it is difficult, if not impossible, to obtain true historical perspective on at least the latter half of this 25-year period.

I have been concerned with both the theoretical and the practical aspects of this historical development of professional preparation (having spent equal time on an alternating basis in Canada and the United States at both the undergraduate and graduate levels during this period). In addition, I have carried out historical research on the topic of professional preparation and disciplinary scholarship commencing with doctoral dissertation work in the 1940s. These experiences may have equipped me uniquely to make this comparative analysis; nevertheless, highly competent men and women—people who have lived through these 25 years in both countries—have been called upon to buttress and expand upon the facts and opinions that are provided.

Interestingly, most people in my generation thought that progress in life, and accordingly in professional preparation in physical education, would be mostly an unhindered upward growth after World War I. However, such has not been the case, and many changes (some good and some bad) have undoubtedly been brought about by the prevailing *social forces* or *influences* that developed in each country (e.g., the influence of values, nationalism, economics) (Zeigler, 1975).

Also, a number of professional concerns (e.g., approach to professional preparation, curriculum content, instructional methodology) have been affected by these social forces. Therefore, I decided in 1984 to investigate developments in the United States since 1960 using descriptive methodology and a questionnaire technique (Good & Scates, 1954). The instrument was sent to a small group comprising 10 members of The American Academy of Physical Education, selected primarily on the basis of geographic location and known to have a deep interest in undergraduate professional preparation. The results of this preliminary survey about developments in professional preparation in physical education in the U.S. were reported at the convention of the American Alliance for Health, Physical Education, Recreation and Dance in 1985 (Zeigler, 1986).

The results of a similar investigation for Canada are now being reported. Leaders from across Canada who have been involved in professional preparation during the 1960s, 1970s, and 1980s were asked to describe what they believe took place in Canada during the same 25-year period (see Paton, 1975; Canadian Association for Health, Physical Education and Recreation, 1966). The Canadians were given the results of the earlier U.S. survey with which to begin the statements of descriptive characteristics and some preliminary comparisons.

Methodology

The investigation employed broad descriptive methodology together with the following techniques to gather and analyze data: a questionnaire distributed to approximately 10 authorities in each country; a comparative approach (recommended by Bereday, 1964, 1969) that included four steps explained as description, interpretation, juxtaposition, and comparison; and selected documentary analysis.

Five problems, phrased as questions, were included in the questionnaire: (a) What have been the strongest social influences during each decade? (b) What changes have been made in the professional curriculum? (c) What developments have taken place in instructional methodology? (d) What other interesting or significant developments have occurred (typically within higher education)?; and (e) What is the greatest problem in professional preparation? Respondents were asked to make any additional comments that they wished.

Description and Interpretation

The results of the first two steps of the Bereday technique (description and interpretation) within broad descriptive methodology were assembled according to the various categories of answers. The questionnaires distributed to respondents in the United States and Canada were identical, both asking the five questions relative to each of the three decades. So much detailed material was obtained that the results have been compiled in the form of tables. A table for each decade presents the results from the United States and Canada, respectively, for the first four questions.

Separate tables were required to list "the greatest problem in professional preparation." Based on these findings, tentative hypotheses were then postulated in the third step (juxtaposition) of the Bereday technique.

Juxtaposition

The third and fourth steps of Bereday's comparative technique of broad descriptive research are *juxtaposition* and *comparison*. In 1969, Bereday introduced two possible approaches for each of these steps—*tabular* or *textual* juxtaposition and *balanced* or *illustrative* comparison. In juxtaposition, the preliminary matching of data textually after a degree of systematization presented an opportunity for the orderly establishment of comparable topics. At this point one or more hypotheses are made "in terms of what the assembled data are likely to permit one to prove" (Bereday, 1969, p. 5).

In regarding this investigation as preliminary because of its extent and complexity, I decided to carry out an illustrative rather than a balanced comparison. Rather than matching each of the many items from one country to the other, a few *similar* and *dissimilar* practices or occurrences in each category in each country were selected randomly to illustrate comparative aspects of the two developments. Such an approach obviously has limited effectiveness because no subsequent principles can be reliably established.

With this limitation in mind, the data were assembled and juxtaposed textually, 11 broad hypotheses were established, and the data from both countries were compared illustratively in an effort to confirm, disconfirm, or refine the hypotheses established. An analysis of the related literature was helpful at this point.

Based on the textual juxtaposition and analysis of the data obtained for each country, the 11 tentative hypotheses were made from the categories examined:

Category #1 (Social influences)

1.1. The federal government has had much more influence on physical education and sport in Canada than in the United States.

1.2. Politics influence public higher education more in the United States than in Canada.

Category #2 (Curriculum)

2.1. Canada has developed a greater subdisciplinary orientation in its curriculum than has the United States.

2.2. Nonteaching, alternative-career options in degree programs have developed more rapidly in the United States.

2.3. Enrollment levels in physical education/kinesiology programs have held up better in Canada.

Category #3 (Instructional methodology)

    3.1. Development in instructional methodology has been comparable and concurrent in both countries.

    3.2. Pressure for improvement in the teaching act arrived somewhat earlier in the United States.

Category #4 (Other campus developments)

    4.1. The pattern of rotation for administrators in Canada has tended to preserve their scholarly competence, contrary to the situation in the United States.

    4.2. A smaller percentage of women in Canada have been acculturated to become university physical education and kinesiology professors and scholars.

Category #5 (Greatest problem/need)

    5.1. The need to control or lessen the impact of highly competitive athletics within the college and university structure is much greater in the United States.

    5.2. Different emphases are needed for the development of improved professional training for teacher/coaches in the two countries.

Comparison

My decision to carry out an illustrative rather than a balanced comparison of the data assembled in Bereday's Step #4 was made in an effort to tentatively confirm, disconfirm, or refine the broad hypotheses established as the final phase of Step #3 (juxtaposition).

The following similar and dissimilar practices, occurrences, or stated problems were selected randomly to illustrate the broad hypotheses designated above. See Table 9.

Conclusions

This comparative analysis of undergraduate professional preparation in physical education in the United States and Canada from 1960–1985 must be recognized as preliminary. I hypothesized generally at the outset that significant changes have occurred in undergraduate programs in the past 25 years and that similarities and differences between the two countries exist both because of and despite their contiguity. Also, earlier studies have shown Canadians to be generally more conservative than Americans toward change.

After carrying out the juxtaposition phase (Step #3) of Bereday's comparative technique, I established 11 tentative hypotheses involving the five different categories. Each is based on textual matching of comparable data. When illustrative comparisons were made in Step #4, the tentative hypotheses established were justified preliminarily by the data presented.

Although more in-depth comparative analysis of these developments is called for, this investigative technique has provided a good basis for further study.

Acknowledgment

I wish to express my deep appreciation to the following members of the American Academy of Physical Education for their assistance: Anita Aldrich (Indiana), Ted Baumgartner (Georgia), Jan Broekhoff (Oregon), Charles Corbin (Arizona State), Marvin Eyler (Maryland), M. Dorothy Massey (Rhode Island), and George Sage (Northern Colorado).

In Canada, the following colleagues were equally helpful in giving time and knowledge to this undertaking: P.J. Galasso (Windsor, earlier at Waterloo and Queen's), Patricia Lawson (Saskatchewan), Donald Macintosh (Queen's), Fred L. Martens (Victoria), John Meagher (New Brunswick), William Orban (Ottawa, earlier at Saskatchewan), and Garth A. Paton (New Brunswick, earlier at Western Ontario).

Table 1   The United States—The 1960s

The 1960s was a period of considerable social unrest in the U.S.; higher education was being criticized for a lack of academic rigor in its programs (Conant, 1963).

Strongest social influences

Aftermath of Sputnik.

Call to fitness for "soft" Americans.

JFK's plans for America; LBJ's "Great Society."

Civil rights movement.

Vietnam War involvement.

Hippie movement (a minority "opted out").

Students prioritize values; eschew materialism.

Carnegie Study states that teachers don't relate subjects to ongoing living.

Professional curriculum

Many undergraduate requirements opposed.

Beginnings of subdisciplines (scientific base).

Generalist concept challenged.

Academic rigor of programs questioned.

Beginning of individualized, specialized programs.

(Cont.)

Table 1 (Cont.)

Instructional methodology

  Efforts to improve laboratory experiences.

  Token student involvement typically did not result in intelligent modifications; faculty still reticent about allowing basic student contributions.

  Improved instructional materials (audiovisual, etc.).

  Decreased funding begins trend toward overly large lecture classes.

  Mosston's recommendations regarding teaching styles (from "command to discovery").

Other campus developments

  Student demand for input in decision making.

  Greater use of mainframe computers.

  Beginnings of subdisciplinary societies.

  A variety of inputs into proposed disciplinary models.

  Increasing demand for academic integrity begins rift between researcher-scholars and those primarily involved with teacher training.

  Physical education faculty members judged by same standards as other disciplines.

  Excesses in gate-receipt sports continue.

  Assessment of joint arrangements with intercollegiate athletics units on campuses.

  Spiraling costs of intercollegiate programs.

  Many faculty unprepared for new standards of accountability (including research output).

  Faculty on campuses beginning to organize unions.

Table 2 The United States—The 1970s

The 1970s saw an aftermath of the 1960s; a PhD glut; a generally slackening job market; "stagflation"; and financial cutbacks in education.

Strongest social influences

  Lingering effects of Vietnam War.

  Watergate; increasing distrust of politicians.

  Taxpayer revolt against increasing burden.

  Slowing of economy ("stagflation").

  Influence of oil cartel.

  Carter's leadership style deplored by some; Iranian hostage incident.

(Cont.)

Table 2 (Cont.)

Concern about falling birth rate.

Women's movement (role expectations of men and women beginning to blend).

Professionals beginning to break with tradition in dress, behavior, educational values.

Continuing threat of legal suits against teachers.

Enforced busing for racial mix.

Affirmative action hiring.

Legislation regarding education of handicapped.

Promotion of "competency-based curricula."

Variety of analyses about most notable improvements in U.S. undergraduate teaching (*change*).

Professional curriculum

Curriculum becomes more "scientifically" oriented; effect of physical fitness thrust.

Growth of opportunities for specialization (elective sequences or emerging tracks such as athletic training, fitness specialist, sport management, special physical education recommended as alternate careers).

Concern for a core program in physical education theory and practice (basic requirements).

Subdisciplinary areas continue to expand within departments (biosciences and social sciences and humanities).

Instructional methodology

More fieldwork opportunities.

Independent course experiences.

Demand for teacher evaluation grows with possible improvement in instruction as a result.

Impact at several educational levels of Mosston's work on teaching styles.

Courses taught by specialists to greater extent.

Computer-assisted instruction (e.g., PLATO).

Sport pedagogy thrust in Federal Republic of Germany with some later influence in U.S.

Other campus developments

Men's and women's departments merged by administrative fiat.

Title IX legislation (women in sport).

Improvement shown in faculty professionalism; younger faculty a "new breed," but without a definite interest in the broad picture of developmental physical activity in the schools.

(Cont.)

Table 2 (Cont.)

Other campus developments (Cont.)

    More graduate students because of fewer jobs.

    Splintering of departmental faculty, all "doing their own thing."

    Changing departmental titles reflect disciplinary emphasis and continued growth of allied professions.

    Concern for licensing and certification (*action?*).

    Job market in higher education grim; faculty face few opportunities to move except in highly specialized areas.

    Opportunities for faculty grievances increase.

    Pressure to "publish or perish."

    Grant monies less available.

    Retooling of faculty a definite concern.

    Excesses in gate-receipt sports seem to increase.

    Emergence of the "female jock"—a catch-22 situation!

Table 3 The United States—The 1980s

The 1980s thus far have shown financial recovery of a sort; the job market is still tight in higher education, but shortages are predicted at other levels; federal government decisions have made their impact on education and research funding.

Strongest social influences

    Conflicting world ideologies; how to combat spreading communism without invoking its methodology and techniques.

    Worldwide satellite communication.

    Impact of Reagan administration; many, including the young, praise his leadership style ("proud to be American," etc.).

    Rise of fundamentalist religious phenomenon (TV evangelists).

    Urban populations soar in desirable areas of the country; cities suffer as crime rates increase.

    Increasing numbers of elderly.

    Enormous increase in health care costs.

    Federal government establishes Health Objectives, 1990 (for all five stages of life).

    Impact of high technology (e.g., computer software—the "knowledge industry").

    Certain major industries suffering greatly; recovery of automobile industry.

    Enrollment declines begin to affect many colleges and universities.

    Federal funding for education decreases.

(Cont.)

Table 3 (Cont.)

Cost of education soaring at all levels.

Presidential Task Force on Education proclaims mediocrity in secondary schools.

Continuing concern that "teacher can't teach."

Demand for accountability at very high level.

Steady call for "back to basics" in education.

Concept of mastery teaching is catching on.

Greater cooperation between the public schools and higher education.

Competition among institutions for top students.

Federal government eases off on Title IX enforcement.

Less than one third of the school population ages (10–17) receive daily physical education.

Professional curriculum

Concern for greater teacher effectiveness.

Continued expansion of nonteaching programs; importance of job orientation; decline of liberal education.

Continued concern for improved standards (regular certification or voluntary accreditation?).

Need for improved scholarship stressed.

Need to eliminate superfluous courses.

How to generate increased revenue?

Faculty positions lost due to inadequate funds.

Intrainstitutional research funds drying up.

Instructional methodology

Larger lecture groups/combining of sections.

Need to streamline learning experiences.

Introduction of microcomputers into curriculum.

Continued concern for teacher/coach effectiveness.

Continued retooling of faculty to improve level of instruction.

Some stress on education for "human fulfillment," with teacher as facilitator.

Other campus developments

Salary schedules still at low ebb at all levels.

Pressure to get grants whether or not there is time to complete the research.

Creative "early semiretirement" schemes needed.

Many faculty find outside means to supplement substandard salaries. Environment too stressful.

(Cont.)

Table 3 (Cont.)

Other campus developments (Cont.)

    Faculty subdisciplinary specialization increases in large universities; in smaller institutions (because of heavy workloads?) faculty are still broadly based (less research and publications; heavier teaching/coaching loads).

    NASPE Task Force working on revision of NCATE accreditation standards for undergraduate physical education teacher preparation.

Table 4 The Greatest Problems in the United States Professional Preparation

Need to develop *consensus about a disciplinary definition* from which should evolve a more unified, less fractionated curriculum (i.e., a greater balance among the bio-scientific aspects, the social science and humanities aspects, and the "professional aspects" of our field).

Need to develop *a sound body of retrievable knowledge* in all phases of the profession.

Need to implement the educational possibilities of a *competency approach* within the professional preparation curriculum.

Need to develop *a variety of sound options for specialization* within a unified curriculum (extending to a fifth year of offerings?). This involves expanding alternate career options in keeping with our goal of serving people of all ages and abilities.

Need to develop a format for *regular planning for the future* by staff and students.

Need to graduate *competent, well-educated, fully professional physical educator/coaches* who have sound personal philosophies embodying an understanding of professional ethics.

Need to seek *recognition of our professional endeavors* in public, semipublic, and private agency work through state *certification* and national *voluntary accreditation*.

Need to help *control or lessen the impact of highly competitive athletics within the college and university structure* to foster a finer type of professional preparation program.

Need to *recognize the worth of intramural recreational sports* in our programs and to make every effort to encourage administrators of these programs to maintain professional identification with the National Association for Sport and Physical Education.

Need to continue implementing in educational institutions *patterns of administrative control fully consonant with individual freedom* within our society.

Need to work for maintenance of *collegiality among faculty members* despite lack of adequate funding, faculty unionization, pressure for publication and obtaining grants, and extensive splintering within the profession.

(Cont.)

Table 4 (Cont.)

Need to develop an attitude that will permit us to *"let go of obsolesence."* Somehow how we must apply new knowledge creatively in the face of an often discouraging political environment.

Need to dispel any malaise in our professional preparation programs in regard to *the future of the profession.* If we prepare our students to be certified and accredited professionals in their respective options within the broad curriculum, we will undoubtedly bring about *a service profession of the highest type* within a reasonable period (Zeigler, 1986).

Table 5 Canada—The 1960s

The 1960s was a period of some unrest in Canada, but rarely as much as in the U.S. (except possibly in Quebec). There was considerable expansion within education at several levels.

Strongest social influences

Era of "economic sufficiency."

Evidence of nationalism (e.g., concern for independence from the U.S.).

Social unrest due to world situation.

Beginning of "women's liberation."

Education more highly valued.

Continued faith in government to solve societal ills; resulting governmental expansion and involvement in education.

Developing rift in Canada—a "quiet revolution" leading toward "Western separatism."

Growing concern with the use of leisure—resulting improvements in municipal recreation.

Lack of fitness indicated; poor showing in international competition decried; Bill C.131 enacted (Fitness and Amateur Sport Act).

Growth of professional sport.

Professional curriculum

Aftermath of 1966 Physical Education and Athletics Conference in Toronto.

Oriented to producing high school teacher/coaches.

Gradual expansion of curriculum offerings.

Emergence of social science aspects of physical education and sport.

More electives, fewer requirements in curriculum.

(Cont.)

Table 5 (Cont.)

Professional curriculum (Cont.)

Significant growth of the number of professional programs.

Division of task in Ontario: Physical education units adopt a disciplinary approach, while teacher education is allotted to professional education schools or departments; the arrangement in Western provinces is a combined one similar to that offered in the U.S.

Outdoor recreation and orienteering added to curriculum.

Instructional methodology

Quality of teaching mediocre; little effort to evaluate performance as faculty members "do their own thing."

Increased use of seminars and laboratories.

Introduction of reading texts.

Audiovisual aids stressed.

Other campus developments

Expansive development of universities, community colleges, and secondary education.

Student unrest on campuses, but PE students' demands for greater involvement are limited.

Governing boards submitted to variety of pressures.

Only "strongest" top administrators survive.

Physical education develops somewhat higher profile in Canadian universities.

Concern for "academic respectability" drives wedge between researcher/scholars and those concerned mainly with teacher/coach preparation.

Gradual entry into graduate education in physical education/kinesiology in the late 1960s.

Prospective faculty members work toward specialized programs for their doctoral degrees.

Very few well-qualified faculty to cope with newer disciplinary approach.

Federal funding to competitive sport and, to a lesser extent, physical education (e.g., undergraduate scholarships).

Job market open; very difficult to predict future developments.

Team sports grow in popularity; gymnastics declines.

Continued struggle to make the Canadian Association for Health, Physical Education and Recreation a fully viable professional society.

Expension of facilities (e.g., swimming pools, racquet courts).

Table 6   Canada—The 1970s

The 1970s saw the aftermath of the 1960s; beginnings of the PhD glut in higher education (not physical education initially, however); declining job market at the secondary level; and the beginning of financial cutbacks in education at all levels.

Strongest social influences

Faith in the "just and rational" society (early impact of Trudeau).

Economic downturn ("stagflation").

Further development of the "Cold War"; proliferation of the hydrogen bomb.

Oil shortage (OPEC).

Increased impact of the women's movement.

Separatist movement in Quebec (FLQ).

Falling birth rate; predictions of enrollment slump at university and community college levels.

Developing isolation of western Canada.

Physical activity promoted by federal government (e.g., Participaction, a crown corporation), promoted to ultimately reduce health costs.

Federal government promotes elite sport nationally and internationally as an aid to the promotion of national unity and world status.

Continued struggle between provincial and federal governments threatens federal support to higher education.

Professionals break from traditional values and behavior patterns (e.g., dress, grooming).

The professional curriculum

Opportunities for greater specialization (including fitness options) because of governmental influence.

Concern for a core program in physical education/kinesiology theory and practice.

Increasing interst in administrative theory as a subdiscipline (and accompanying recognition of the importance of the "mother disciplines").

A significant increase in the sophistication of the field's knowledge base.

Federal government's attention to elite sport brings a demand for training programs and a national certification plan for coaches.

Universities pressured to develop high performance athletes (with methods including testing centers and various types of laboratories).

Deemphasis on teacher training per se as discipline-based curriculum receives steadily increasing emphasis (with courses often designed seemingly to meet teachers' needs).

(Cont.)

Table 6 (Cont.)

The professional curriculum (Cont.)

Deemphasis of the activity-based aspect of total curricular offerings.

Steady increase in female enrollment in programs.

Departments, schools, and faculties called by a variety of names (e.g., kinesiology, human kinetics).

Instructional methodology

Larger classes result in fewer seminars and fewer essays to correct (i.e., less individual attention).

Audiovisual emphasis has a big impact on activity teaching.

Play increasingly recognized as learning.

Greater opportunity for laboratory experiences (including individual help from teaching/research assistants).

More field work opportunities (e.g., internships).

Significant decrease in the use of ever-more-expensive textbooks as professors develop their own texts and study guides.

Demand for teacher evaluation grows, with seemingly greater emphasis on the teaching process.

Courses taught typically by professors with greater specialization (at the upper undergraduate level at least) using a greater theoretical orientation.

Attempts were often made to use new technologies in teaching, but profession seemed slow to pick them up.

Other campus developments

Faculty gradually developing more areas for research and scholarly investigation.

Earlier altruism and professional dedication declines significant.

Some faculty disillusionment due to aging, outmoded equipment.

Most growth stops in the mid-1970s due to the increasingly stringent financial situation.

Decrease in the emphasis on health and safety education within many curricula.

Sport Administration Centre in Ottawa continues to grow in size, scope, and influence.

Participaction, as a crown corporation, increases in influence through sound marketing approach.

Increase in the number of students enrolled in graduate study; this is to a considerable extent due to the job market.

Significant change did not occur rapidly enough when the climate was right for such innovation.

Grantsmanship develops increasingly because of the need for external funding.

Table 7   Canada—The 1980s

The 1980s thus far have brought financial recovery of a sort; nevertheless, education continues to be underfunded (especially at the university and community college levels); the job market still tight; the decline of the Canadian dollar has affected education.

Strongest social influences

Constitution Act becomes law in 1982; includes Canadian Charter of Rights & Freedoms; will influence all areas of living.

Heating up of the Cold War (terrorists, Central America, Middle East conflict, Afghanistan, Libya, etc.).

Satellite communication is a boon, but incipient problems for the world loom large.

Impact of high technology (the "knowledge industry").

Conservative political control at the national level and in certain provinces.

Increasing financial crises at federal and provincial levels despite recovery from recession of the early 1980s.

Unemployment a problem, especially for the young; fewer government jobs available.

The "haves" and the "have-nots" grow further apart.

Enormous increase in health care costs.

Increased awareness of the need for preventive medicine.

University and community college enrollments do not drop off as predicted; some actually increase.

The "computer age" is upon us.

Professional curriculum

Lack of curriculum aims and objectives.

A back-to-basics emphasis (core courses).

Debate over which courses should be required and which elective.

Continued expansion of nonteaching options and concentrations with curricula (e.g., sport management, athletic training, fitness testing and aerobics, coaching).

Continuing decline of teacher education.

Concern for improved program standards and scholarship.

Some recognition that each university can't "be all things to all people" with its program offerings.

Inability to predict what curricular changes will best equip our graduates for job placement.

Students are typically more serious and goal-oriented.

(Cont.)

Table 7 (Cont.)

Professional curriculum (Cont.)

    More students with poor physical skills in the professional program.

    New emphasis on special physical education.

    Call for lengthening of curricular program in some universities.

Instructional methodology

    Computer instruction slowly being incorporated into pattern of instruction.

    Larger lecture groups/combining of sections.

    Instruction based more on research findings and improved theory.

    Improved research/teaching facilities and equipment.

    Continued concern for teacher/coach effectiveness; many faculty taking teaching responsibilities more seriously; improved level of creativity and innovation.

    Some retooling of certain faculty to improve instruction and to make them more valuable.

    Increased use of videotaping.

    More Canadian educational materials.

Other campus developments

    Physical education/kinesiology has achieved greater respectability on most campuses.

    Some faculty pessimism and cynicism present.

    Salary schedules have not kept pace with other professions and occupations; pension schemes inadequate.

    Sharp increase in faculty unionization (to more than 50%).

    Early retirement schemes appearing, but limited by lack of creativity and illegality of mandatory retirement in certain provinces.

    Requirements for promotion and tenure more stringent; moreover, faculty positions are threatened by continued economic pressures.

    Circumstances have created managers rather than "old-style" department heads.

    Lack of dedication to the established profession.

    More students going on for degrees in other fields.

Table 8   The Greatest Problems in Professional Preparation in Canada

Need *regular turnover* in faculty to change the "collective staleness" that has developed.

Need *more money* to carry out an improved level of professional preparation.

(Cont.)

Table 8 (Cont.)

Need *a sharper focus* in professional preparation programs to counter "aimless wandering."

Need to zero in on the *best ways of preparing teachers and coaches* (i.e., improve the teaching/learning process).

Need to provide meaningful, relevant, challenging, professional *preparation for those seeking alternative careers* employing purposeful physical activity in sport, exercise, dance, and play.

Need to *graduate competent, well-educated, fully professional physical educator/coaches* who have sound personal philosophies and professional ethics.

Need to develop *a more selective admission process* to undergraduate programs in physical education and sport.

Need to achieve a *consensus about what constitutes the core* of the curricular subciplines.

Need to *convince qualified women that there are places for them at the university level—* and then find them!

Table 9 Comparisons Between the United States and Canada

United States	Canada
Category #1 (Social influences)	
1. Federal government has more directly been involved financially with higher education.	1. Education has been established as belonging to the provinces; the federal government's influence is more indirect because funding must be granted through the provinces.
2. State legislatures often become directly involved with state university operations and programs.	2. A hands-off relationship has been established traditionally at the provincial level.
Category #2 (Curriculum)	
1. Most teacher education occurs in the four-year bachelor's degree program in a school of education.	1. Much teacher education begins after the "disciplinary" degree has been granted.
2. The teacher surplus developed earlier, creating pressure for alternative career options. It is more difficult for U.S. students to gain admission to degree programs in other fields.	2. The pressure for alternative career options came later than in the U.S.; changes are difficult to implement within the present program because of a stronger arts and science and disciplinary orientation.

(Cont.)

Table 9 (Cont.)

United States	Canada

Category #2 (Curriculum) (Cont.)

3. The slumping job market caused a sharp drop in enrollment in many colleges and universities; the financial outlook caused retrenchment that affected physical education.

3. Despite a slumping job market and the predictions of statisticians, enrollments have held up; this may have been due to the liberal arts nature of the programs (i.e., many students could switch to other fields more easily).

Category #3 (Instructional methodology)

1. Responses in both countries indicate that developments and improvements in instructional methodology have been comparable and concurrent. This finding seems reasonable in that politics and other factors do not appear to have been a consideration for this area (with the possible exception of inadequate funding for physical education at the local level).

2. Social unrest of the 1960s apparently impacted higher education sooner in the U.S., with resultant demands for more attention to the teaching act on the part of professors.

2. Social unrest in Canada was evident primarily in Quebec, with fewer demands for teacher accountability elsewhere.

Category #4 (Other campus developments)

1. Deans, directors, heads, and chairpersons are rarely appointed for defined periods; study or administrative leave is a rarity.

1. A specified number of years is associated with each category of appointment, and study leave is usually available.

2. Graduate study was established in the early 1900s; women typically had separate departments and earned professorial rank at all levels.

2. Graduate study did not begin until the 1960s. Women were not acculturated to carry on to the doctoral level in physical education; as a result there are very few female professors.

Category #5 (Greatest problem/need)

1. Gate receipts in athletics and the extracurricular nature of highly competitive sport brought many negative influences to teacher training in physical education; in many cases it has become necessary to separate athletics from the educational unit.

1. Universities & colleges still control their own destinies in interuniversity athletics; it has been fully possible to maintain unified departments and schools, including a division of intercollegiate athletics.

(Cont.)

Table 9 (Cont.)

United States	Canada

Category #5 (Greatest problem/need) (Cont.)

United States	Canada
2. Admission to programs for teacher/coach education is more selective and requires a stronger arts and social science background; more professional theory and practice are often needed as well.	2. Students have a longer period of training that includes considerable arts and science work; deficiency exists in internship experiences for nonteaching options.

Note. These illustrative comparisons relate directly to the 11 hypotheses already described.

References

American Alliance for Health, Physical Education, Recreation and Dance. (1962). *Professional preparation in health education, physical education, recreation education*. Report of national conference. Washington, DC: Author.

American Alliance for Health, Physical Education, Recreation and Dance. (1974). *Professional preparation in dance, physical education, recreation education, safety education, and school health education*. Report of national conference. Washington, DC: Author.

Bereday, G.Z.F. (1964). *Comparative method in education* (pp. 11-27). New York: Holt, Rinehart and Winston.

Bereday, G.Z.F. (1969). Reflections on comparative methodology in education, 1964-1966. In M.A. Eckstein & H.J. Noah (Eds.), *Scientific investigations in comparative education* (pp. 3-24). New York: Macmillan.

Bookwalter, K.W., & Bookwalter, C.W. (1980). *A review of thirty years of selected research on undergraduate professional preparation physical education programs in the United States*. Unionville, IN: Author.

Canadian Association for Health, Physical Education and Recreation. (1966). *Physical education and athletics in Canadian universities and colleges* (pp. 14-21). Ottawa: Author.

Conant, J.B. (1963). *The education of American teachers* (pp. 122-123). New York: McGraw-Hill.

Good, C.F., & Scates, D.E. (1954). *Methods of research* (pp. 255-268). New York: Appleton-Century-Crofts.

Lipset, S.M. (1973). National character. In D. Koulack & D. Perlman (Eds.), *Readings in social psychology: Focus on Canada*. Toronto: Wiley.

Paton, G.A. (1975). The historical background and present status of Canadian physical education. In E.F. Zeigler (Ed.), *A history of physical education and sport in the United States and Canada* (pp. 441-443). Champaign, IL: Stipes.

Proceedings of the 6th Commonwealth Conference. (1978). *Sport, physical education, recreation proceedings* (Vols. 1 and 2). Edmonton, Alberta: University of Alberta.

Van Vliet, M.L. (Ed.) (1965). *Physical education in Canada.* Scarborough, Ontario: Prentice-Hall.

Zeigler, E.F. (1951). *A history of undergraduate professional preparation in physical education in the United States, 1866-1948.* Eugene, OR: Oregon Microfiche.

Zeigler, E.F. (1980). An evolving Canadian tradition in the new world of physical education and sport. In S.A. Davidson & P. Blackstock (Eds.), *The R. Tait McKenzie Addresses* (pp. 53-62). Ottawa, Canada: Canadian Association for Health, Physical Education and Recreation.

Zeigler, E.F. (1975). Historical perspective on contrasting philosophies of professional preparation for physical education in the United States. In *Personalizing physical education and sport philosophy* (pp. 325-347). Champaign, IL: Stipes.

Zeigler, E.F. (1986). Undergraduate professional preparation in physical education, 1960-1985. *The Physical Educator, 43*(1), 2-6.

A Comparative Study of Induction Programs and Their Implications for Beginning Physical Education Teachers

Ian H. Andrews

This paper summarizes a comparative study that analyzed induction programs in teacher education from five countries (Andrews, 1986) and posits the implications for physical education. First, the paper defines induction and describes the instructional and socialization factors that beginning physical education teachers experience during their induction year. Second, the research findings of the induction study are summarized. Finally, the implications of the study for teacher professional development in physical education are highlighted.

Induction

Induction is the second stage of a teacher's professional development, with pre-service being the first stage, and in-service, the third. Induction has been described as being analogous to trial by fire, a period of fixedness, the joy and pain of giving birth, and the professional bridge. Regardless of the inference that may be generated by each analogy, the importance of induction within the context of a teacher's professional development underlies all perspectives.

Induction programs for beginning teachers are now prevalent in many countries. Legislative and programmatic efforts afforded the beginning professional teacher have become important agenda topics within the reformation of teacher education programs. Consequently, social scientists are beginning to explore pertinent research questions applicable to the program design and implementation of these induction programs. In a recent paper entitled "Teacher Induction: Research Issues," Griffin (1985) identifies numerous research questions that substantiate the important investigative activities that educators must pursue. Common to many of Griffin's questions were the topics of teacher education confluence among pre-service, induction, and in-service programs and the program design implications of formal and/or legislated induction programs. Prior to examining the research findings of the study and its implications for physical education, a description of the instructional and socialization factors of a beginning physical education teacher's induction year is presented.

The Beginning Physical Education Teacher and the Induction Year

It should be remembered that the most traumatic transitions that teachers make during their professional careers begin when they accept their first teaching assignments (Lortie, 1975; Zumwalt, 1984). Not only do beginning teachers for the first time embrace the contractual, legal, and ethical obligations of becoming a professional but they also encounter the sole responsibilities of instructional planning, lesson implementation, pupil assessment, and the myriad of other teaching duties that were assumed previously by the pre-service sponsor teacher.

For the beginning physical education teacher this induction phase of the career becomes a very personally and professionally challenging time. Coaching responsibilities for interscholastic teams; intramural or recreational program planning; gymnasium, playing field, and equipment coordination; and special event programming (e.g., sports day, creative dance festivals, volleyball tournaments) all require immeasurable effort and additional time of the physical education teacher during the induction year. Moreover, many physical educators are responsible for other subject preparations and managing their own homerooms for the first time.

In essence, the beginning physical education teacher becomes immersed in the unique educational environment of the school. Furthermore, the social, professional, and sometimes political ethos of the staff's interactions reflect a powerful influence upon the introductory experiences of the beginning physical educator. Undoubtedly, the process that all beginning teachers experience during this initial year greatly contributes to the reconciliation between the idealism of their professional beliefs and the pragmatic realities of the school as a workplace.

Socialization of the beginning physical education teacher is highly context-specific and dependent in each case upon combinations of the personal characteristics and resources of the individual and the varying encouragements and constraints posed by the situations in which they work (Zeichner, 1983). The socialization process for beginning physical educators can be a process of conformity, an adherence to the conventional wisdom and observed practices of the experienced teachers around them. For some teachers this is a valued measure of professional acceptance. For others it becomes an overwhelming denial of professional autonomy. However, research of induction programming suggests that beginning teachers do attempt to expand and innovate within their instructional practice where supportive supervisory environments and good staff development opportunities prevail. Reaffirmation of personal confidence by beginning teachers in acquiring ownership of their professional development does illustrate that not all beginning teachers succumb to a socialized compliance or are wholly overcome by the professional regulations and expectations of their first year in the profession.

Certainly, one may conclude that not all physical educators lose their idealism or experience transitional shock during their first year of teaching if supportive and respectful teaching environments are present. Consequently, experienced staff members and the principal must support (and thus enhance) the beginning teacher's unique instructional style, emerging curricular orientation, and initial professional development activities. These considerations are all invaluable factors in the positive maturation of the beginning physical education teacher, who is responsible for the cognitive, affective, and psychomotor domains of his or her students' educational programs. In order to investigate the challenge of how induction programs may be developed to promote positive conditions and learning opportunities for beginning teachers, a comparative study of induction programs in five different countries was undertaken.

Overview of the Study

The study was based on the assumption that pre-service and in-service teacher education agencies must work collaboratively to introduce and successfully implement a teacher induction program. This writer posited that teacher education agencies at the legislative, university, teachers' association, school district, and school building levels must contribute appropriately to the governance, academic component, and organization of induction programs. For example, based on experience in Australia, Tisher (1982) has suggested that a collaboration among stakeholders in teacher education leads to more functionally and creatively designed induction programming, resulting in the enhancement of the beginning teacher's ongoing professional development.

Two theoretical frameworks were used in this analysis. The first was Berman's (1981) paradigm for educational change. Berman developed a three-stage process for the implementation of education programs. This analytical framework distinguishes three complex organizational subprocesses that are interconnected, rather than lineally sequenced: initiation, implementation, and institutionalization. Berman has suggested that educational change is a connecting flow of events characterized by choice, rather than a linear process of sequentially planned decisions.

The second framework drawn upon for this study was Conrad's (1978) theoretical framework for curriculum planning in postsecondary education. Conrad's design plan is a three-step process that provides a baseline for analyzing or developing a curriculum plan. The examination of an academic program includes choosing an organizing or conceptual principle, establishing a curricular emphasis, and building a curricular structure. This systematic model emphasizes, however, that the final design of the program is strongly influenced by political, financial, and academic traditions within each planning phase.

Case studies of induction programs in Britain, New Zealand, Australia, the United States, and Canada (Alberta's Initiation To Teaching Project) were examined through the two theoretical frameworks previously described. Policy documents, published reports, fugitive literature, and evaluation documents were the main data sources. This was complemented by visits to three of the countries (England, Canada, and the U.S.) to conduct interviews and meet legislators, program developers, mentor teachers, and beginning teachers involved in the induction programs. Specific program criteria of the induction programs that were acquired and analyzed included the following:

- Academic component: pre-service requirements, goals and objectives, supervision strategies, instructional resources, continuing education options, teacher assessment criteria
- Governance component: legislative act(s), legal status of intern, funding source, certification process, role of collaborating agencies
- Organizational component: management of program, responsibilities of collaborating agencies, beginning teacher placements, selection and training of mentors, stages of implementation

Results

The research data suggested that the establishment of a confluent teacher education process among pre-service, induction, and in-service programs underlies the fundamental perspective that proponents for reforming teacher education in all five countries have proposed. Specifically, enhancement of continuing professional development for teachers is considered a major objective in establishing this confluence. However, such additional educational objectives as (a) establishing sequential pedagogical training for teachers; (b) operationalizing collaborative institutional programming for teacher education agencies; and (c) improving school practice for staff development, teacher assessment, and pupil performance are all perceived as achievable if confluence in teacher education is realized.

In this study, all countries' induction models incorporated one or more of these educational objectives in developing their induction programs. Considering that induction has been considered the weak link within the confluence of teacher education, it was not surprising that educational institutions in the respective countries or states endorsed induction as the vehicle to integrate the three stages of teacher professional development.

In Britain, Australia, and New Zealand, the rationale of induction programs incorporated the theme of continuous professional development and collaborative institutional planning. The curricular organizing principles of these induction programs all emphasized a continuous teacher development theme. Cognitive and affective growth of teachers were inherent in the planning of these programs. In essence, a holistic orientation to professional development was proposed.

In the U.S. and Canada, however, the improvement of teaching performance among beginning teachers was a higher priority within the rationale of establishing induction programs. Selected competency requirements relating to instructional skill and ability represented the curricular organizing principle for these two countries. Regardless of the differing curricular orientation, the establishment of induction programs implies that these factors should be prevalent if confluence is to be incorporated successfully.

In summary, the factors contributing to a pedagogical confluence among the three stages of teacher education must incorporate four programmatic elements. First, there must be a continuous academic framework with a sequential professional syllabus being present. Second, curriculum objectives should reflect an introductory orientation to the profession, a lateral open-ended instructional and curricular focus, and a self-evaluative perspective. Third, theory-practice content within all three stages should be organized so that experiential activities incorporate a theoretical perspective both in the beginning teacher's instructional practice as well as with the complementing supervisory and professional induction activities. Finally, school-based staff development programming must be designed to enhance the continuing professional development of the beginning teacher beyond the induction year.

Implications for Physical Education

The implications for physical education from the study may be summarized within the context of program criteria that must be present if the efficacy of induction programs for beginning physical education teachers is to be realized.

It is hoped that induction programs will become a more intrinsic component of teacher education in the near future. Physical educators responsible for introducing innovation and reform must seriously consider the academic, governance, and organizational challenges that should be addressed within induction if a confluence of pedagogical preparation within the professional development of physical educators is to be realized. To accomplish this task, the new inductees into the profession must receive the best of induction practices, continual instructional and curricular support from all colleagues, and the opportunity to work in a professional environment that enhances and honors their self-directed learning potential.

References

Andrews, I.A. (1986). *Five paradigms of induction programmes in teacher education*. Unpublished doctoral dissertation, Bradford University, England.

Berman, P. (1981). Toward an implementation paradigm of educational change. In R. Lehming & M. Kane (Eds.), *Improving schools: Using what we know*. London.

Conrad, C.F. (1978). *The undergraduate curriculum: A guide to innovation and reform*. Boulder, CO: Westview Press.

Griffin, G.A. (1985). Teacher induction: Research issues. In S.M. Hord, S.F. O'Neil, & M.L. Smith (Eds.), *Beyond the looking glass: Papers from a national symposium on teacher education policies, practices and research*. Austin: University of Texas, Austin Research and Development Center for Teacher Education.

Lortie, D.C. (1975). *School teacher: A sociological study*. Chicago: University of Chicago Press.

Tisher, R.P. (1982). *Teacher induction: An international perspective on research and programs*. Paper presented to the meeting of the American Educational Research Association, New York.

Zeichner, K.M. (1983). Individual and institutional factors related to the socialization of teaching. In G.A. Griffin & H. Hukill (Eds.), *First years of teaching: What are the pertinent issues?* Austin, TX: University of Texas, Austin Research and Development Center for Teacher Education No. 9051.

Zumwalt, K.K. (1984). Teachers and mothers: Facing new beginnings. *Teachers College Record*, **84**, 183-155.

Comparative Research in the Behavior of Physical Education Teachers in Different Types of Schools Concerning Further Training

Klaus Zieschang

The first stage of formal schooling in the Federal Republic of Germany is the Grundschule, or primary school, which the pupils attend for 4 years. After Grundschule there are basically three types of schools, which correspond to three different levels of intellectual ability.

The Hauptschule is the most elementary of the secondary schools. Pupils attending the Hauptschule spend 5 years there before going on to a vocational school, where they will qualify in a manual skill.

The Realschule caters to pupils of somewhat higher intellectual ability. Pupils attending the Realschule spend 6 years there before training for a profession or, if their results are good enough, switching to a Gymnasium.

The Gymnasium is the third and most difficult type of secondary school. The examination (Abitur) that the pupils take after 9 years in the Gymnasium is the prerequisite of entrance to university or college (see Figure 1).

Why Further Training for Teachers?

Since the Second World War, there has been an increasingly rapid succession of changes in technical-scientific and social fields. Representative of this are the many developments in the fields of media, computer technology and microelectronics, as well as genetic technology. As many areas of work and life are affected by these developments, there is constant movement and unrest—nothing remains static. Thus, vocational knowledge and skill must be continuously supplemented and broadened, much more so now than heretofore.

From this outlined situation, two deductions can be made: (a) school and vocational training can only provide a foundation for vocational life—further, lifelong learning is required; and (b) teachers must keep up with current developments in order to fulfill their duties properly—teachers' studies and pedagogical training represent only the foundation for their

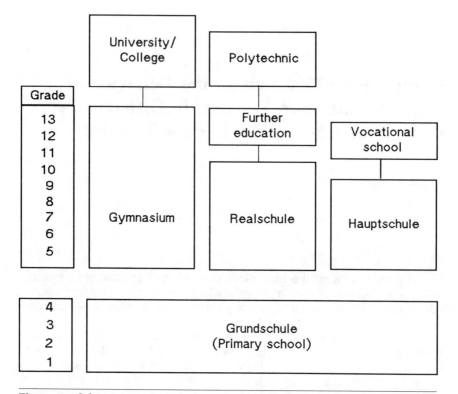

Figure 1.   Schematic structure of the school system in the Federal Republic of Germany.

vocational activity, a foundation that must be continually supplemented, broadened, and deepened.

Teacher training in the Federal Republic of Germany is an integrated system comprising three stages for all types of schools. Stage 1 forms the foundation. It includes scientific educational studies: scientific study of the subject to be taught, teaching methods in that subject, and practical periods of training. Teaching practice in a school follows as Stage 2. Further training, Stage 3, serves to reinforce, broaden, and improve the teaching qualification.

Teacher training can be completed only by further training. This is illustrated by the following arguments:

Technico-Scientific Development

Scientific knowledge is increasing rapidly. The teacher can easily fall into a "modernity backlog" (Engler, 1985). This backlog cannot be made good simply by acquisition of new knowledge. Rather, it often involves, according to Friberg (1981), the difficult processes of restructuring and new conceptions.

Social Changes

Our social structures are now less constant than was the case in earlier times. They often undergo far-reaching changes that do not stop short of the school. Today's school generation is developing at a different rate and rhythm than earlier generations. Their experiences, thoughts, and behavior are characterized by extracurricular effect factors, such as the mass media, noise, stress situations, and peer groups. The teacher is therefore required to adjust to the manifestations and to the thought and behavior structures of today's youth in an unbiased manner and to constructively incorporate social changes in his or her work (Friberg, 1981). The physical education teacher must consider changing events in sports and the changing attitudes of society toward sport. New types of sport and a greater emphasis on leisure time and fitness call for an analysis of traditional roles and require more flexibility on the part of the teacher.

Pedagogic-Didactic Developments

In order to cope with changing school conditions, the teacher requires new pedagogic and teaching qualifications (Boehmer, 1983). Teachers will find adjustment, restructuring, and innovation easier if examples and help are available to them.

Political-Educational Measures

Politico-educational decisions, such as reform of the curriculum, are directed at change and further development of the school system. Yet, this can only be realized with the support of all teachers, which, in turn, can be achieved only by further education (i.e., training courses) for teachers. This also makes sense from an economic point of view. The knowledge and skills imparted in further training courses for teachers directly influence teaching practice, whereas investments in initial teacher training are much slower in showing results (Friberg, 1981).

Reduction in Teacher Training Shortcomings

In addition to the above, further training courses for teachers complete the technical gaps in many areas that result from the shortcomings in initial teacher training. In Bavaria, for example, numerous measures in further training courses in physical education for Hauptschule teachers result directly from this aspect of teacher training, because—even though all the teachers are officially qualified to teach physical education—their qualifications often do not meet the requirements of practical teaching.

These arguments justify the necessity of further training courses for teachers. They are evaluated differently by the interest groups engaged in education policy, and sometimes they overlap or presuppose each other. Working in a teaching capacity without attending further training courses can lead to teaching becoming too routine, stagnated, and stale.

This is especially so when innovation and competition are lacking due to the absence of young teachers (Hecker, 1985).

Further Training Courses for Physical Education Teachers

The general argument for further training courses for teachers also applies specifically for physical education teachers. However, though the requirements demanded of physical education teachers in the different types of schools are the same for each year group, their actual training in the teaching of physical education differs significantly. As a rule, physical education teachers at Gymnasium and Realschulen have all specialized and graduated in physical education. Their training includes the breadth and depth necessary to give them a solid teaching qualification. The situation is somewhat different in Hauptschulen, however, where physical education teachers are far less qualified.

The ministry of education responsible for physical education in schools has for years been offering numerous further training courses. They are supposed to safeguard the qualification of physical education teachers, minimize shortcomings in the initial teacher training, and support new developments. Further training courses have evolved from practical work in the school and are designed for the school. Because the courses are organized by representatives of the school authorities, the extent to which they correspond to the needs and attitudes of the teachers has remained relatively unknown up to now. Our survey aims to help answer this open question and thus provide information that can be used when planning courses in further training that are structured to correspond to actual needs.

Methods

A questionnaire was developed that took into account the position of further training courses for teachers in the Federal Republic of Germany. The following five main points were considered:

1. How and to what extent do physical education teachers further their training?
2. How does the teacher actually find out about training courses, and how satisfactory are they considered to be?
3. How useful does the physical education teacher consider training courses for actual teaching at school?
4. What requests do the teachers have with respect to the organization and subject matter of the training courses?
5. Do the actual and the desired choice of training courses concur?

In a trial run we tested to find if those being surveyed had any problem in answering the questions.

By means of our questionnaire, we hoped to arrive at a universally applicable statement with respect to actual and desired behavior of physical education teachers concerning further training courses. A random sample of physical education teachers employed at Bavarian Hauptschulen, Realschulen, and Gymnasium were surveyed. The Ministry of Education's computer-stored personnel data of teachers being surveyed were used to select candidates by means of an appropriate random number generator. Three hundred teachers per type of school (900 teachers total) received a questionnaire. They remained anonymous. The survey took place in 1983 with the help of the Bavarian Ministry of Education. Seven hundred twenty of the 900 questionnaires (80%) were returned. Only 6 questionnaires could not be evaluated. The questionnaires were analyzed to find the levels of participation in further training courses in physical education and effect of training courses on the teaching of physical education. Physical education teachers at Hauptschulen, Realschulen, and Gymnasium were also viewed comparatively.

Results

The survey results showed that 88.1% of the physical education teachers surveyed attended at least one course in further training during their period of occupation as a teacher. This means, however, that 11.9% never participated in any such course. Results for the different types of schools are shown in Figure 2.

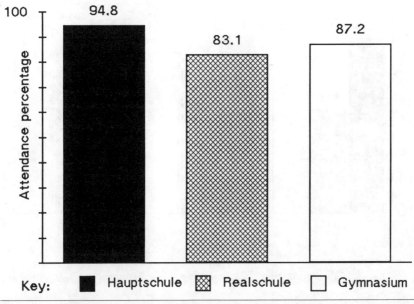

Figure 2. Participation of physical education teachers in further training courses, according to type of school where employed.

Among the physical education teachers who attended further training courses, those at Hauptschulen attended on average 3 courses and teachers at Gymnasium and Realschulen 2.3 courses in the school years 1980/81 to 1982/83. The correlation between the number of years of teaching physical education and participation in further training courses is also interesting. In all three types of schools, the expected tendency of teachers with a long period of service having completed at least one course of further training was confirmed. The extensive course program for teachers at Hauptschulen draws about 90% of young teachers during their first 3 years of teaching, compared to only 65.5% of Gymnasium teachers and 52.6% of Realschule teachers (see Figure 3).

A sex-specific observation does not show any major differences between the different types of schools. Noticeable differences become apparent, however, when sex, marital status, and the location of the training course are considered. In Hauptschulen married male teachers attend training courses, irrespective of location, more frequently than unmarried male teachers. The same tendency can be found among male teachers at Realschulen and Gymnasium. The location of the training course is an important consideration for female teachers, though. The percentage of married and unmarried female teachers who participate in training courses in their hometowns is essentially the same for all types of schools. Attendance is much greater, however, among unmarried female teachers when the courses take place outside the hometown.

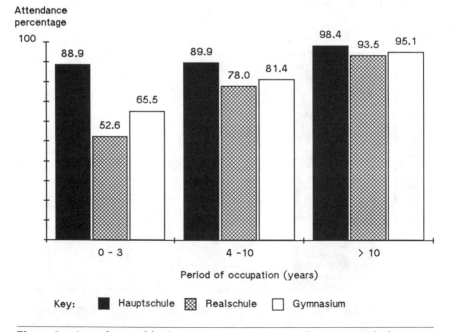

Figure 3.   Attendance of further training course, according to period of occupation as physical education teacher and type of school where employed.

The reasons teachers give for not participating in further training courses are shown in Figure 4.

Despite the fact that the survey remained anonymous, only 2–3% of teachers say they have no interest in training courses. The high frequency of the response "no interest in the theme of the training course" among Realschule teachers (49.7%) indicates that the courses available do not correspond to the needs of this group. The high percentage of "personal reasons" (41.9% for all types of schools) can be explained by the timing of the courses: About half of them take place during free time or during school holidays. An important proportion of married female teachers, namely, 60%, cite personal reasons for nonparticipation. Occupational reasons cited for nonparticipation in training courses appear to be school-specific. Gymnasium teachers cite occupational reasons more often than Realschule and Hauptschule teachers.

The above proportionate relationship of reasons for nonparticipation also applied for teachers who have not attended any further training course. Notable, however, are the 60% of Hauptschule teachers who cite no interest in the theme of the training course. When we consider all Hauptschule teachers—both with and without further training—only 24.1% cite no interest in the theme as the reason.

The effect of further training courses on physical education was ascertained by asking teachers what changes, if any, they introduced after participating in the training course; or why they did not introduce any changes. Figure 5 shows results of these questions.

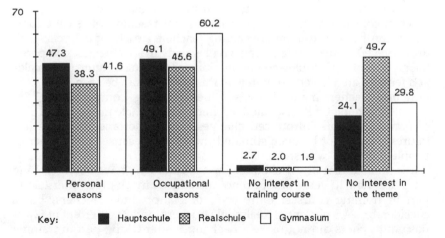

Figure 4. Reasons for nonparticipation in training courses for physical education teachers. *Note.* Those surveyed were allowed to give several reasons.

Change
percentage

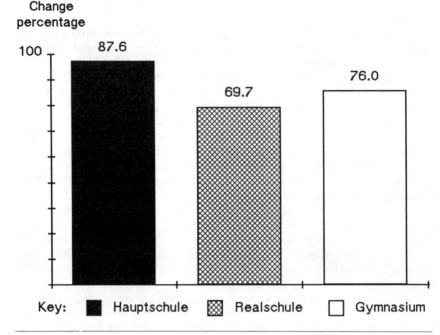

Key: ■ Hauptschule ▩ Realschule □ Gymnasium

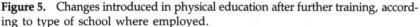

Figure 5. Changes introduced in physical education after further training, according to type of school where employed.

Seen collectively, the 77.6% change among all teacher groups is notable. Hauptschule teachers are particularly open to change, probably because they were not as well trained to teach physical education.

When considering the length of time spent teaching physical education it can be seen that among young teachers (teaching 0-3 years), all the surveyed Hauptschule teachers had already made changes, compared to only half of Realschule and Gymnasium teachers (see Figure 6). If males and females are viewed separately in this group, it can be seen that 63.6% of female teachers made changes in their teaching, compared to 41.7% of male teachers. Of Realschulen teachers, 60% of male teachers and 50% of female teachers introduced changes. The importance of these last figures should not be overestimated, however, because the number of people surveyed was small.

It is notable that physical education teachers who have been teaching for more than 10 years often do not introduce any changes after taking part in training courses. Only 8.1% of Hauptschule teachers, but a considerable 24.3 percent of Realschule teachers, and 23.4 percent of Gymnasium teachers did not make any changes after taking part in training courses. When asking the reasons teachers give for not having made any changes in their teaching of physical education, we gave them two answer categories: "my methods were confirmed" and "I consider my methods more advantageous than those recommended in the training course."

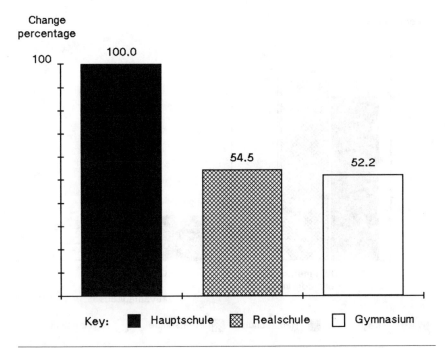

Change
percentage

Key: ■ Hauptschule ▨ Realschule □ Gymnasium

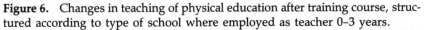

Figure 6.   Changes in teaching of physical education after training course, structured according to type of school where employed as teacher 0–3 years.

In all types of schools, the teachers mainly explain their not having introduced changes with the argument that their own methods were confirmed in the training course (see Figure 7). Only teachers who have been teaching physical education for 4 years or longer say that their own methods are more advantageous than those recommended in the training course. Surprisingly, however, this attitude is far less prevalent among the much more highly qualified Gymnasium teachers (8.3%) than among Hauptschule teachers (21.7%).

Discussion

In the Federal Republic of Germany, the behavior of physical education teachers toward further training courses has until now been ascertained only sporadically by means of surveying teachers who attended such courses. The results derived are therefore unsatisfactory because they are not representative of the whole teaching population. Our survey has avoided this shortcoming and was carried out as a representative survey for all types of schools—Hauptschule, Realschule and Gymnasium—in the federal state of Bavaria.

Even the few results presented here give interesting insights into the behavior of physical education teachers concerning further training:

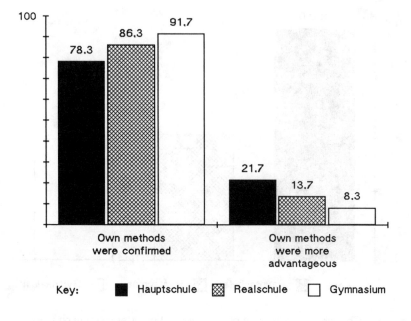

Percentage

Figure 7. Reasons for not making changes in teaching of physical education after training course. *Note.* The figure refers to teachers who have never introduced changes.

- They provide information about participation and nonparticipation.
- They show at which stages of time teachers participate in training courses.
- They demonstrate how quickly young teachers are drawn into further training courses.
- They give insight into the behavior of different groups of teachers toward training courses.
- They show what effect further training has on actual teaching.
- They illuminate the persistence with which some teachers cling to their own methods.

We can thus draw conclusions with respect to how further training for physical education teachers has been viewed by teachers in general, and to where and how further training can be improved. The differences in behavior toward further training among teachers in the various types of schools must also be considered.

The results presented here are limited to the comparison of behavior of teachers concerning further training in different types of schools in one country. This symposium could provide us with an opportunity to gain information on further training in physical education in different countries. It could be the starting point for international comparison in this field.

References

Bauer, H. (1983). *Zur Lehrerfortbildung im Fach Sport* [In-service teacher training in physical education]. Unpublished thesis, University of Bayreuth, Bayreuth, West Germany.

Boehmer, M. (1983). *Zentrale und dezentrale Lehrerfortbildung* [Centralized and decentralized in-service teacher training]. Weinheim & Basel: Beltz.

Engler, H.-J. (1985). Problemfelder in der Lehrerfortbildung [Problematic areas in in-service teacher training]. Sportunterricht, **34**, 125-135.

Friberg, D. (1981). *Lehrerfortbildung und Lehrerweiterbildung unter dem Anspruch auf Mitwirkung und Mitbestimmung der Lehrer* [In-service teacher training and further training with special respect to teachers' contribution and active participation]. Doctoral dissertation, University of Essen, Essen, West Germany.

Hecker, G. (1985). Zu diesem Heft [Introduction]. *Sportunterricht*, **34**, 125.

Widmer, K. (1979). Fortbildung als Beitrag zu einer umfassenden Handlungskompetenz des Lehrers. In W. Weibel (Ed.), *Lehrerfortbildung: Variante CH* (pp. 7-28). Zürich, Köln.

Zieschang, K., Algayer, H., & Buchmeier, W. (in press). *Zum Fortbildungsverhalten von Lehrern im Fach Sport* [On the behavior of physical education teachers concerning in-service training]. Schorndorf: Hofmann.

Education for Leisure: A Comparison of Current Physical Education and Recreation Approaches in Selected English and Canadian High Schools

Joy Standeven
G. Barry Thompson

"The significance of leisure in decisions regarding patterns of work, retirement, education, residential growth, health, and family and social group behavior supports the observation that it is an increasingly important element of the social structure of contemporary industrial societies" (Innes, 1983). The school systems in these societies appear to be seen as one of the major sources of preparation for the use of such time (Cardinal Principles, 1918; Munn Committee, 1977; Newsom Report, 1963; Report of Minister's Study, 1970).

In spite of the frequent claims on both sides of the Atlantic that substantial changes have been made in school curriculum in recent years toward appropriate and relevant programs of leisure education, numerous authorities provide evidence that schools continue to concentrate their resources on attempting to satisfy short-term aims in the provision of recreational activities, rather than tackling a more long-term process of education for leisure. Hendry (1985) believes that radical changes need to be made if schools are to increase their effectiveness.

Originating from these concerns, a concurrent cross-national pilot study was devised to assess leisure education in two representative English and Canadian high school physical education and recreation programs. This will be followed by an investigation of the extent to which selected physical education teacher preparation programs in the two countries are providing for leisure education.

This paper is a progress report on the first phase of that study, which attempts to examine and compare (a) current conceptions of education for leisure in high schools in Eastbourne, England, and Fredericton, Canada; and (b) the manner and extent to which these sample English and Canadian high schools in general, and their physical education and recreation programs in particular, match stated or implicit leisure education objectives with programs and practices. Leisure perceptions and practices of high school students in the two settings and their opinions of their schools' leisure education programs were considered subproblems.

From its inception the project has been a collaborative one, developed with a view to establishing a model for future cooperative cross-cultural investigations of this nature. It is essentially descriptive, combining some basic quantitative comparisons from the survey data with qualitative treatment of information from structured interviews designed to address cultural subtleties.

The locations of Eastbourne, England, and Fredericton, Canada, were considered sufficiently similar to render a comparative study valid. Both communities have a predominantly service, rather than an industrial, economic base; have the lowest unemployment rate in their respective regions; and generally share a number of physical similarities. On the other hand, the British and Canadian economies and educational systems are seen to be sufficiently different to warrant contextualizing the case studies.

Literature Review

Leisure is a generic term likely to be distorted if pressed into a simple "definitional corset." Though some writers use other classifications (Godbey, 1981; Kaplan, 1975), from a review of the literature, Bernard (1983) has proposed leisure as (a) a concept, in terms of its purpose and function to (b) the individual and (c) society, in relation to (d) time and to (e) work, and as (f) an activity.

Time is the most commonly accepted context in which the term is used today—time free from work (Murphy, 1974; Parker, 1976), unoccupied time, spare time, time that is not obligated (Bernard, 1983; Brightbill, 1961; Roberts, 1970). However, for the institutionalized, unemployed, and handicapped who may have ample free time but little freedom, Robinson (1985) has suggested that "time is not necessarily the precursor to a leisure experience" (p. 7).

Kaplan (1978) and Dumazedier (1967) have developed an activity concept of leisure, but, as Kelly (1978) has pointed out, consensus is lacking over which activities are, or are not, leisure. Other writers perceive leisure as a state of mind (DeGrazia, 1962; Geba, 1985; Godbey, 1981; Pieper, 1965). Harper (1981) has emphasized that there is no single or common leisure experience, and that to answer the question "What is leisure?" requires reflective description by the participant.

If there is a problem with leisure, Jelfs (1970/71) has considered it to do with man's knowledge of himself. Education, he concludes, must concentrate on developing capacities to externalize private inner states in creative activities in which men and women can make meaning for themselves.

Dewey (1916) proposed that education had no more serious responsibility than to "make adequate provision for the enjoyment of recreational leisure" (p. 205), a view gaining support from contemporary writers, such as Hargreaves (1982). Rutter's study (1979) clearly demonstrated the lasting effects of, and therefore the opportunities open to, schools to influence postschool life. Research by Longland (1969), Leigh (1971), and Hendry (1978), and studies in both Ontario (1970) and New Brunswick (1974) found that what was done in schools bore little relation to what pupils chose to do in their leisure activities out of school.

Differential effects between subjects, schools, and pupils have shown the school favoring the academic, middle class, sport-loving youth (Hendry, 1978; Ryrie, 1981). Further, Boothby (1981) and Leaman and Carrington (1985) have demonstrated the way the school curriculum constructs attitudes that contribute to women's marginality in sport as leisure. Schools have a responsibility to develop in all pupils the ability to make effective and significant choices. Education for leisure can increase the range of those choices, according to Leigh (1971).

Mere provision of facilities or recreational skills training is inadequate; educational policies need to be more concerned with "enabling strategies," in order that young people may derive fulfillment and meaning from and in their leisure (Hendry, 1983, 1985; Mundy & Odum, 1979). The emphasis should be on the facilitation of independent decision making. Thus, Mundy and Odum's "enabling strategies" may be seen as closely related to metacognition. Hendry (1985) has recommended the adopting of "enabling strategies," rather than the prevailing recreational provision model. Such a perspective would, Hendry believes, "require learning strategies akin to the metacognitive skills proposed by Nisbet and Shucksmith (1984)" (p. 36).

Methods

Concurrent data collection from the two settings involved documentary analysis and the use of identical questionnaires and interview formats. Emphasis was placed on detailed preplanning, a carefully coordinated research schedule, and weekly contact between researchers.

Relevant school documents were examined, where available, for leisure education content, curriculum objectives, and design relating to physical education and recreation.

Teachers and local supervisors involved in each program were interviewed using the Yauss Perception of Leisure Education questionnaire (1974), combined with open-ended questions, to determine their commitment and approaches to leisure education.

A 58-item questionnaire was developed to assess the effectiveness of current leisure education by surveying leisure perceptions, attitudes, and practices of students along with their opinions of their school's leisure education provision. It was subjected to expert opinion, pretested in both settings, modified, and administered concurrently in both settings during regular school periods. The 218 Fredericton high school students (112 girls and 106 boys) and 181 of their counterparts (75 boys and 106 girls) from a comprehensive high school and a sixth-form college in Eastbourne were considered to be representative samples.

Results

Education for Leisure and High School Physical Education

Education in Canada is a provincial matter. In 1985 the high school adopted the compulsory credit course of five 50-minute periods per week called "Lifetime Fitness and Physical Recreation Activities." This follows set curricula of motor skill development in grades 1 to 6, and fitness, gymnastics, traditional team games, dance, and health education in grades 7 to 9; is coeducational; and may be taken in any one of the three final high school years. The course's purpose is "to provide students with the opportunity of acquiring knowledge about the relationship between their own personal health and physical activity and to introduce them to a number of physical recreation activities which they may be able to pursue beyond their high school years" (New Brunswick Department of Education, 1975, p. 7). Evaluation is based on skill learning (50%), knowledge (40%), and attitude (10%). Canada's national policy and vigorous promotion of sport and fitness (i.e., "Participaction") has a strong local influence.

Leisure provision has become accepted as a major element of social policy in England; numerous policy papers indicate that sport and recreation have wide political support. Department of Education documents illustrate the historic role for physical education of forming the groundwork of healthy exercise and habits of recreation for the future. However, physical education is an individual school matter within national guidelines. The comprehensive school offers elective physical education courses for all levels. Students may attend three or four 35-minute periods per week, depending on course loads. Students in lower grades are offered gymnastics and games; those in upper grades may choose one or more individual activities from a wide variety available. Teachers aim to make students think about what they should do in their leisure time. Sixth-form college students may elect a five-period-per-week optional recreational activities course offering a broad range of individual activities.

Physical Education Teachers and Leisure Education

Six Canadian and four English teachers all demonstrated a strong positive attitude toward leisure as an important part of their lives, reported leisure experiences at least two to three times per week, felt that leisure education can have a profound effect on adjustment to one's entire life, and agreed that one function of the school is to provide leisure skills and attitudes.

The six Canadians said leisure education is basically skill teaching. Only one English teacher agreed. Three English and four Canadian teachers thought it should be mandatory, and all teachers but two (English) felt present leisure education in their schools involved physical education and recreation. All wanted teacher preparation programs to include provision for leisure education.

Student Opinions and Leisure Behaviors as Indicators of School Leisure Education Effectiveness

Results of the student questionnaire showed a surprising number of similarities between the two sample groups in broad terms, and often in particulars, suggesting differences in emphasis more than anything else. A brief summary of selected results follows.

Leisure Perceptions. Students in both countries generally identified the same activities as leisure and nonleisure. The major exception was training and practice for a sports team. Considered a leisure activity by more than 60% of the English students, it was ranked as leisure by only 36% of the Canadians.

Leisure Attitudes. All students shared a number of similarities in the way they viewed leisure. A majority of both sample groups felt they "had plenty of interesting things to do" in their spare time, were satisfied about the way they used it, said that their leisure activities were more satisfying than their schoolwork, and believed that it was more important to be good at their homework than at their leisure.

Current Leisure Behavior. Student responses to "the *main ways* you are *actually* using your spare time" and "the amount of time you spend on each activity per week" were combined and recorded in rank order. Table 1 demonstrates some interesting similarities and differences between the two groups.

Perceived Leisure Education Relevance of School PE and Recreation. Figure 1 compares student responses to four "relevance indicator" questions.

Students' Perception of the School's Influence on Their Leisure Behavior. Only 46% of the Canadian students (40% of boys, 50% of girls) and 39% of the English students (40% of boys, 37% of girls) felt that their school helped them learn about things to do in their spare time. A number of Canadian students who were interviewed indicated they were not told why they were doing the particular activities selected for them by their teachers. The students in both samples that felt they had learned spare-time activities at school cited team, individual, and dual sports more often than all of the other listed activities combined.

Conclusions

A preliminary analysis suggests that (a) education for leisure occurs in both physical education settings, but is given significantly more formal recognition, emphasis, and time in Canada; (b) both programs employ the traditional recreation provision model; (c) the Canadian student sample is considerably more involved in sport and fitness and is made more conscious of the link between activity and health; and (d) although

Table 1 Rank Order of Main Ways Student Sample Reported Using Current Spare Time

	Canadians (n = 210)				English (n = 160)		
Rank	Activity	Responses	Total hr/wk	Rank	Activity	Responses	Total hr/wk
1	Other[a]	138	998	1	Other[a]	102	812
2	TV	132	979	2	TV	86	793
3	Team sports	94	667	3	Music listening	72	636
4	Music listening	78	559	4	Hanging around chatting	59	237
5	Fitness activities	68	459	5	Reading	49	235
6	Talking on phone	74	371	6	Individual sports	46	209
7	Dating	50	344	8	Visiting friends	25	172
8	Individual sports	52	339	9	Drinking	20	159
9	Parties	43	335	11	Parties	24	115
10	Hanging around chatting	28	219	12	Team sports	24	96
11	Reading	49	195	13	Dual sports	27	56
12	Visiting friends	36	193	14	Dancing	14	42
13	Dual sports	15	92	19	Talking on phone	10	30
				23	Fitness activities	3	7

[a]Homework, music lessons, and so on.

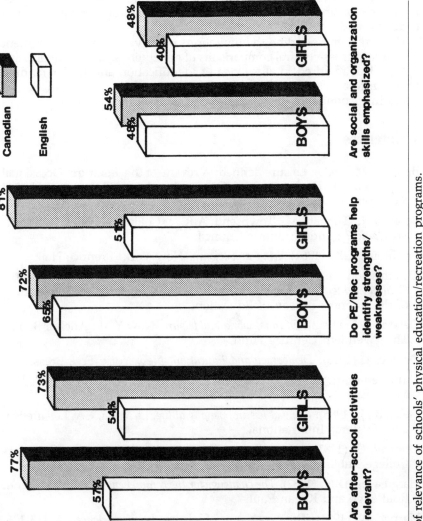

Figure 1. Student perceptions of relevance of schools' physical education/recreation programs.

there are many differences between the two student samples, a surprising degree of similarity exists regarding leisure attitudes, activities, perceptions, and opinions.

These results underline the limitations of survey data that document and permit cross-cultural comparisons of generalities. A more qualitative approach is required to allow clearer identification and understanding of the differences in meaning of a leisure experience and of subtle nuances in respondents' terminology that are culturally specific.

References

Bernard, M. (1983). Leisure defined: A review of the literature. Occasional Paper No. 3, Department of Geography, Keele University, United Kingdom.

Boothby, J., Tungatt, M., Townsend, A.R., & Collins, M.F. (1981). *A sporting chance?* London: Sports Council.

Brightbill, C.K. (1961). *Man and leisure.* New York: Prentice-Hall.

Commission on the Reorganization of Secondary Education. (1981). *Cardinal principles of secondary education.* Washington, DC: Department of the Interior, Bureau of Education.

DeGrazia, S. (1962). *Of time, work, and leisure.* New York: Anchor Books, The Twentieth Century Fund.

Dewey, J. (1916). *Democracy and Education.* New York: Free Press.

Dumazedier, J. (1967). *Toward a society of leisure.* London: Collier-Macmillan.

Geba, B.H. (1985). *Being at leisure, playing at life.* La Mesa, CA: Leisure Science Systems International.

Godbey, G. (1981). *Leisure in your life: An exploration.* Toronto: Saunders College Publishing.

Hargreaves, D.H. (1982). *The challenge for the comprehensive school.* London: Routledge and Kegan Paul.

Harper, W. (1981). The experience of leisure. *Leisure Sciences,* 4, 113-126.

Hendry, L.B. (1978). *School, sport, and leisure.* London: Lepus.

Hendry, L.B. (1983). *Growing up and going out.* Aberdeen, Scotland: Aberdeen University Press.

Hendry, L.B. (1985, April). Young people, school, and leisure: Developing metacognitive skills? Paper presented at the Conference of the Leisure Studies Association. Yorkshire, England.

Innes, M. (1983). Leisure education and the transition from school to work. In T. Burton & J. Taylor (Eds.), *Proceedings of the Third Canadian Congress on Leisure Research* (pp. 235-245). Edmonton, Alberta: Canadian Association for Leisure Studies.

Jelfs, B. (1971). *The concept of leisure*. The philosophy of physical education. Conference Reports 1970/71 Association of Teachers in Colleges and Departments of Higher Education Physical Education Section. Derby, UK: Bishop Lonsdale College of Education.

Kaplan, M. (1975). *Leisure theory and policy*. New York: J. Wiley & Sons.

Kaplan, M. (1978). *Leisure: Perspectives on education and policy*. Washington, DC: National Education Association.

Kelly, J.R. (1978). A revised paradigm of leisure choices. *Leisure Sciences*, 1(4), 345-363.

Leaman, O., & Carrington, B. (1985). Athleticism and the reproduction of gender and ethnic marginality. *Leisure Studies*, 4(20), 205-217.

Leigh, J. (1971). *Young people and leisure*. London: Routledge and Kegan Paul.

Mundy, J., & Odum, L. (1979). *Leisure education: Theory and practice*. New York: Wiley.

Munn Committee. (1977). *Munn Report: The structure of the curriculum in the third and fourth years of the Scottish secondary school*. Edinburgh: Her Majesty's Stationary Office.

Murphy, J.F. (1974). *Concepts of Leisure*. Englewood Cliffs, NJ: Prentice-Hall.

New Brunswick Department of Education. (1975). *Lifetime fitness and physical recreation activities*. Fredericton, NB: Author.

Newsom report. (1963). *Half our future*, London: Her Majesty's Stationary Office.

Nisbet, J., & Shucksmith, J. (1984). The seventh sense. *Scottish Educational Review*, 16(2), 75-87.

Parker, S. (1976). *The sociology of leisure*. London: Allen & Unwin.

Pieper, J. (1965). *Leisure: The basis of culture*. London: Faber & Faber.

Report of Minister's Study Committee on Recreational Services in Ontario. (1970). Toronto: Ontario Department of Education.

Roberts, K. (1978). *Contemporary society and the growth of leisure*. London: Longman.

Robinson, A. (1985). Editorial. *Recreation Canada*, 43(3), 7.

Rutter, M., Maughan, B., Mortimer, P., & Ouston, J. (1979). *Fifteen thousand hours: Secondary schools and their effect on school children*. London: Open Books.

Yauss, J.E. (1974). *The perceptions of selected department of education personnel toward the concept of leisure education in the province of New Brunswick*. Unpublished master's dissertation, Florida State University, Tallahassee.

Autonomy Versus Centralism: A Comparative Study of Physical Education in England and France

Anthony Mallalieu
Ken Hardman

Studies of education systems have revealed fundamentally different approaches developed by countries in the control and organization of their educational services. Such approaches range from *autonomy*, where teachers at school level have the freedom to engage in educational decision making, to *centralism*, where the central government determines educational policy and implements it through legislation.

In England, tradition is a significant feature of present-day curricula and is seen as the major criterion for the present system. The teacher, according to Wiseman and Pidgeon (1970), has more "freedom in the choice of what to teach" than "anywhere else in the world." This is a view that is supported by Hoyle (1970), who has suggested that within his or her own classroom, the teacher enjoys a high degree of privacy and autonomy. Although such autonomy is sometimes exaggerated, there is little doubt that it is real and, "in comparison with that of any other major educational system, emphatically unique" (Featherstone et al., 1972).

This unique system has its roots firmly in the prevailing laissez-faire philosophy of the 19th century, though seeds of the spirit of freedom within the evolving governmental constitution can be discerned in the *Magna Carta* (1215). This spirit of freedom persisted into the 20th century, when the complexities of state and church interaction, together with local authorities (especially after the 1944 Education Act), led to a special partnership in providing an educational service that "is a national system, locally administered" (Department of Education and Science, 1985).

Recently, however, this partnership and coveted freedom extending from local authorities to schools have been under strain, and the Conservative Party Secretary of State has been seen to take a more central role in controlling the education system. This central involvement is not simply party politics, for it was a Labour government that opened the "Great Debate" into standards in the education service. Since 1979, the Conservative government, in its rigorous pursuit of controlling public spending and obtaining "value for money," has established the need for greater accountability within education. To this end, the Department of Education and Science (DES) is involved in reforms designed to raise national standards while controlling financial resources.

This centralist approach proffers a challenge to the traditional autonomy of the other "prominent partners." Local authorities have vociferously condemned "the growing centralism of the education service" and have argued that "power (is) moving from the local authorities to the center." Indeed, it has been suggested that "the government no longer (believes) in the traditional partnership with local authorities. It (is seeking) to dominate" and that "the essential autonomy of the teaching profession is being undermined" (Evan, 1985). Despite these recent maneuvers, however, the English education system still facilitates school and teacher autonomy.

Since the French Revolution, France has "laboured under the Napoleonic and Jacobin Heritage of an excessive centralisation" (Ardagh, 1982). Napoleon established a centralized system of education in which "national subjects" would dominate the course of study. Such ideas were strongly evident in early post-World War II days, when the Ministry of Education controlled approval of textbooks, courses of study, standards of examinations, and training and certification of teachers (Van Dalen et al., 1953). Even more recently, Elvin (1981) has asserted that "content of various subjects taught, the numbers of hours allocated weekly to each of them, are based on provision laid down at national level."

When Giscard d'Estaing became president of France in 1974, he proclaimed that education was part of his blueprint for an "advanced liberal society." His education minister, Halby, presented a hurried master plan for education in 1975, with a basic aim of ensuring all children up to the age of 16 years would follow identical courses and receive equal opportunities, thus echoing de Gaulle's 1963 reform attempt to democratize the Lycees.

Since the ousting of the Center-Right Party by the Socialists under Mitterand in 1981, a number of reforms have been introduced, which essentially aim at "setting up a unified secular public education system" and "devolution in local affairs and cutting back the power of the state," with "the granting of more autonomy to the regions and other local units" (Ardagh, 1982).

This paper is drawn from a study that examined the themes of autonomy and centralism in the English and French systems of physical education and related aspects of the secondary school curriculum. Although the themes of autonomy and centralism have been identified within the respective systems, it has also become apparent that the admixture of deeply rooted and more recent causal factors may have led to a "blurring of the edges."

Purposes of the Investigation

The primary aim of the investigation was to discover the extent to which the concepts of autonomy and centralism can be identified at school level.

This paper's introduction highlighted the approaches of England and France in "controlling" education and suggested that they are undergoing changes that ultimately would lead to convergence. On this basis it was hypothesized that the systems would show their respective traditional characteristics, but with a "blurring of the edges." The investigation used a micro case study technique to sample data from the twinned towns of Bury, England and Angoulême, France. The following areas related to the hypothesis were addressed: (a) attitudes of physical education teachers to autonomy/centralism, (b) objectives of physical education in the schools, (c) curriculum content, (d) time allocated to physical education, and (e) compulsory/voluntary physical education.

This investigation's secondary aims were to establish the size of the school pupil rolls, the sex distributions, and the size of classes for physical education, and to establish facilities and staffing for physical education. These aims relate to the primary aim but are subsidiary to it. They provide additional information that can also be utilized as a basis for future comparisons.

Methods

A literature search and survey assisted in the formulation of aims and structure of a questionnaire. A structured questionnaire was designed with appropriate modifications to allow for problems of language, definition, and terminology in the French version. Quantitative data were sought on school size, sex distribution of pupils, facilities and staffing, time allocation and curriculum content, objectives in physical education, and teachers' views on curriculum control in relation to autonomy/centralism. A variety of statistical techniques were used to analyze the data collected.

A representative sample of six Bury schools and five Angoulême colleges were selected for the investigation. To provide a common base for comparative purposes, it was decided to sample classes with pupils in the age range 11-14, that is, years 1-4 in Bury and grades 6-3 in Angoulême.

Results

Attitudes to Autonomy and Centralism

The attitudes of the staff to autonomy and centralism in the schools was determined. The Mann-Whitney U Test indicated a significant difference at the .01 level (p .01) in teachers' responses. A subsequent t test confirmed the difference between the two samples, thus lending support to the notion of identification of differences in approach to control in education.

Physical Education Objectives

Ojectives of physical education in the schools were analyzed. With the use of the Mann-Whitney U Test, it was established that objectives related to self-realization and motor skills (top category), social competence (middle category), and aesthetic appreciation (bottom category) were similarly placed; only the objective related to leisure time activity preparation was significantly different at the .01 level. Analysis using Spearman's rank order correlation *within* each group was also inconclusive, though correlations for the Angoulême sample had a closer clustering than those for Bury.

Curriculum Content

In all schools, all pupils participated in games, gymnastics, and athletics (track and field). Cross-country running was engaged in by all Bury schools and 60% of Angoulême schools. Only female pupils in both samples participated in dance. Outdoor pursuits were featured in Angoulême schools only. Swimming was undertaken by 50% of Bury schools and 80% of Angoulême schools.

The proportion of curriculum time spent on each activity in Angoulême schools was consistently similar with relatively small differences between male and female activity. In Bury schools, activities were more disproportionately presented in allocation of time to different activities and between males and females in the same school sample. Three notable features of the Bury sample were the much greater amount of time devoted to games, the large proportion of time taken up by "other activities," and the inconsistent pattern of activities on the curriculum. For example, "other activities" accounted for over 30% of physical education curriculum time in two schools, about 10% in two other schools, and did not feature at all in the remaining two. In summary, the Angoulême sample showed greater uniformity, whereas the Bury sample showed greater inconsistency. (However, the Bury sample may not be representative, because many English school physical education programs *do* include outdoor pursuits.)

Physical Education Time

Time allocated to physical education was compared. Overall, Bury schools had a lower time allocation, but a greater range between schools, than Angoulême: Bury, 264–364 hours; Angoulême, 396–432 hours. The Angoulême sample had little variation between schools and over class years, i.e., 100 hours per year (grades 6–4) and 120 hours (grade 3); whereas the Bury sample again had inconsistencies, for example, one school had 30 hours (years 3 and 4) and 90 hours (years 1 and 2).

Compulsory/Voluntary Physical Education

The compulsory/voluntary status of physical education was studied. In one Bury school, 40% of the pupils did not have compulsory physical education, whereas the other schools had compulsory physical education for 90–100% of the pupils. In two Angoulême schools, 40% had no compulsory physical education, one had 90%; the others, 60%. In voluntary physical education, Angoulême had 30% of pupils involved, with one school an exception at 10%. In Bury schools, on the other hand, there was greater variability in pattern: three at 50%, two at 30%, one at 10%.

Student, Facility, and Staffing Characteristics

Eight of the 11 schools had pupil rolls of about 1,000; the rest (two in Angoulême) had rolls of about 500. Genders were equally distributed in all schools. Hence, there was uniformity in both size of school and distribution of the sexes. Approximately 50% of all physical education classes had 25 pupils, 12% had classes of 30 pupils and 7% had classes of 20 pupils (all the same as classes in other subjects). 30% of classes had differences in class size between physical education and other subjects; Angoulême had only one school where this was the case and, thus, had a higher degree of standardization.

Bury schools showed a greater range of on-site facilities, specifically gymnasia, sports halls, playing fields, and track and field areas. Only two schools did not have a gymnasium (they did, however, have sports halls that contained gymnasium apparatus, etc.), and only one school did not have an athletics track. The main "off-site" facility was a local swimming pool, which was used by four schools. No Angoulême college had a sports hall, four had gymnasia, only two had playing fields, and only one had track and field facilities. Much greater use was made of off-site facilities.

There was no real distinction between the two samples in the pattern of head of physical education department staffing: one per school (with one Bury school as an exception having two, a male and a female). On average, Bury schools had four full-time physical education staff, Angoulême three. A notable difference in staffing was in teacher assistance. Bury had an average of four assistant teachers per school; Angoulême, only one.

Conclusions

It is perhaps reasonable to suggest that in a system oriented toward autonomy, analysis of data will reveal inconsistency and variety of pattern. Conversely, in a centralist-oriented system, data analysis might be expected to show a higher degree of similarity or conformity. From a similar common base of school pupil rolls and sex distribution, differences between Bury and Angoulême schools can be discerned in responses to questions on compulsory and voluntary physical education. The Angoulême sample was more uniform, with Bury showing greater variation, especially in the time devoted to—and proportion of pupils involved in—"voluntary" activities. Likewise, class sizes in Angoulême schools were more standardized, and there was overall less difference in the sizes of class groups for physical education and other subjects.

Both samples indicated well-qualified physical education teachers, with many having further and higher degree qualifications. Differences in teacher preparation render any comparative comment difficult; more information on the nature and scope of teacher training is necessary to justify any valid comparison. One significant feature was the greater number of assistant teachers involved in physical education in Bury schools. This probably reflects historical traditions and associated employment expectations.

There were significant differences in the availability and provision of facilities. Bury schools predominantly utilized a range of on-site facilities, whereas Angoulême schools relied heavily on off-site provision. Rather than attributing such differences directly to issues of autonomy and centralism, causation is possibly best sought in reviewing the historical antecedents of the development of physical education (in its generic sense) in England and France and the differing importance attached to sport in clubs (a feature that distinguishes many European systems from that of England), as well as government legislation introducing statutory requirements for local education authorities to provide facilities.

In time allocated to physical education, Angoulême schools generally had both a greater number of hours per year in all class year groups and greater consistency of time across the age groups. Where centralism is the norm, this is to be expected. In Bury schools, on the other hand, greater variation was indicated and may reflect the tendency within more autonomous systems for schools to utilize the timetable in a variety of ways.

Comparison of curriculum contents revealed similarities, but analysis of activity proportions demonstrated that Angoulême had greater uniformity both in distribution of allocated time and gender participation. Bury showed disproportionate characteristics in both aspects; moreover, it had a greater proportion of time allocated to "other activities." This may imply evidence of more individual school planning and give support to the general hypothesis. Statistical analysis of teachers' objectives in physical education suggested no significant differences between English and French teachers' responses. However, within-sample analysis showed a higher correlation among the French teachers than their Bury counterparts. The results were far from conclusive, and only a tentative inference can be drawn that points to greater convergence among French teachers in objectives of physical education.

Responses to the issues related to autonomy and centralism in curriculum control clearly indicated significant statistical differences between Bury and Angoulême teachers. They lend support to the hypothesis that English physical education teachers enjoy a high degree of autonomy in their sphere of the curriculum, whereas French teachers are subject to centralized control at the national level.

It would be wrong to draw firm and fast conclusions from the evidence of the data analyzed. In some instances, there were similarities and the "edges" somewhat "blurred." Nonetheless, it is noticeable that responses from Angoulême teachers did show a greater tendency than Bury teachers to uniformity and standardization. Hence, overall, there is a suggestion from this investigation that English teachers do indeed have a higher degree of autonomy in curriculum control and organization than their French counterparts, who suffer the consequences of state centralism.

References

Ardagh, J. (1982). *France in the 1980s.* London: Secker & Warburg.

Department of Education and Science. (1985). *The educational system of England and Wales.* London: Her Majesty's Stationary Office.

Elvin, L. (Ed.) (1982). *The educational systems in the European community: A guide.* National Foundation for Educational Research.

Evan, D. (1985). Increase in government interference condemned. *Times Educational Supplement.*

Featherstone, J. et al., (1972). *British primary schools today.* New York: Schools Council Publications, Macmillan.

Hoyle, E. (1969). *The role of the teacher.* New York: Humanities Press.

Van Dalen, D.N., et al. (1953). *A world history of physical education.* Englewood Cliffs, NJ: Prentice-Hall.

Wiseman, S., & Pidgeon, D.A. (1970). *Curriculum evaluation.* National Foundation for Educational Research.

A Comparative Study of Physical Education in South Rio Grande, Brazil, and Iowa, United States of America

Janice A. Beran
João C.J. Piccoli

In 1975, a National Plan of Physical Education and Sports aimed at the improvement of physical education in the schools of Brazil was established by law. This legislation formed the basis for the implementation and betterment of first-level (grades 1–8) physical education in the state of South Rio Grande. Prior to that time, there had been little physical education for pupils in grades 1–4, and the program in grades 5–8 was generally sport instruction.

In 1981, the Department of Physical Education in South Rio Grande implemented a plan to provide physical education instruction for all first-level students. This landmark plan included training 3,000 physical education teachers and providing a wide distribution of physical education and sport equipment, designed to provide children in grades 1–4 (7–10 years of age) a movement education program appropriate to the children's growth and developmental characteristics. The physical education instruction in grades 5–8 (ages 10–14) was oriented to sport, with the final goal of participation in the State Student Games. These competitive games are held every year. Competitors are grouped by age. The games offer competition in rhythmic gymnastics, Olympic gymnastics, swimming, judo, chess, track and field, basketball, handball, soccer, and volleyball.

Since the 1950s, physical education has been required by state law in Iowa. The Iowa Code of Education (Section 257.25) stipulates that every elementary school must offer physical education. Each school district determines the time allotment in elementary physical education. The Iowa Code of Education does not state objectives for the program, illustrating the fact that the principle of home rule has been strongly upheld in Iowa. In contrast to South Rio Grande, where teachers generally follow and adapt the directives issued by the Secretariat of Physical Education at the Ministry of Education and Sport, Iowa teachers are given considerable latitude in developing objectives and designing curricula. In 1985, a tool for assessing and designing a K-12 physical education program was developed under the direction of the State Consultant of Health and Physical Education. This was intended to give some direction to physical education teachers and school administrators in planning and evaluating school physical educators.

The purpose of this research was to compare physical education programs in the two states of South Rio Grande and Iowa. Although these programs are distant in geographic location, they are close in purpose, and it was projected that such a study would bring forth information that would strengthen programs in each state.

Methods

A mail survey was used to collect the data in both states. The 38 regional Offices of Education, represented by physical education supervisors of 3,211 state-controlled first-level schools in South Rio Grande, were surveyed to determine objectives, curriculum offerings, physical education teacher professional preparation, and facilities and equipment available in first-level (1-8) schools in the 244-city state-controlled education system. In Iowa, a random sample of 250 physical educators in the 435 school districts at the 1-4 and 5-8 levels were surveyed to obtain the same information as in South Rio Grande.

The components and items were selected as a result of prior literature review. The original instrument was written and administered in Portuguese in Brazil. It was translated into English and adjusted for use in Iowa. The selection dealing with objectives was adapted in Iowa to more closely follow the verbiage set forth in the Iowa Curriculum Assessment Tool.

All 38 supervisors of South Rio Grande completed the instrument. In Iowa there was a 46% response. The data were analyzed and compared.

Results and Discussion

Class Size

The data analysis yielded information showing similarities and differences. In Brazil the aforementioned federal law stipulated that each class be composed of 50 students. Sixty-three of the respondents indicated that in their regions, classes ranged in size from 18-35 students, and 29% reported 36-50 students per class. Sixty-three percent of the classes at the 1-4 level, and 26% at the 5-8 level were coeducational.

In Iowa, 72% had from 20-29 students per class at all levels, whereas just 3% had more than 40 students per class. All 1-4 classes were coeducational; at the 5-8 level, all were coeducational, except in a few schools where students were separated for particular activities such as wrestling.

Physical Education Teachers

In South Rio Grande, 92% of the respondents reported that classroom teachers taught the physical education classes, whereas in Iowa 94% of the classes were taught by physical educators. Forty-one of the Iowa respondents indicated there had been a decrease in the number of specialists employed in their district, with 14% reporting a decrease of three positions. Twenty percent reported an increase of at least one position.

Although the Brazilians reported a great shortage of specialists teaching physical education, it was noted that there was a concentrated effort to prepare teachers. In 1983, 3,000 teachers had been trained by Regional Offices of Education and the State Physical Education Professional Preparation Institutions. In addition, 1,018 classroom teachers teaching physical education have been supervised by Regional Offices of Education, physical education institutions, and physical education specialists.

In Iowa between 1970 and 1980, physical education was taught by specialists. Due to economic factors, schools in some districts faced with declining budgets consolidated schools and enlarged classes in order to minimize costs. This permitted classes to be taught by specialists but resulted in a general decrease in the number of physical education teachers employed and, thus, an oversupply of professionals.

The diametric differences in who teaches physical education point up an interesting fact. Whereas South Rio Grande considers that it has made definite progress over the last 5 years toward professionalizing physical education teaching, Iowans consider they have "lost ground," in that 6% of the physical education classes are not taught by specialists.

Time Allotment

Federal law in Brazil decreed that physical education classes be held three times weekly at both the 1-4 level and the 5-8 level. The respondents in the study reported that as students advanced in grade levels, the time allotted to the physical education classes tended to increase to 50 minutes three times a week. Ninety-five percent reported that classes were generally scheduled within the school classroom periods, but, 38% of the same respondents indicated that some classes were also scheduled at other times.

All 1-8 physical education classes in Iowa were held within the regular class periods. Iowa law decrees that 1-6 students be offered physical education, but does not stipulate a specific number of minutes. Forty-four percent of the respondents reported that the average amount of time in 1-4 physical education class was between 50 and 70 minutes. The amount of time ranged from 20 to 29 minutes (2%) to more than 90 minutes (29%) per week. At the 5-8 level, 53% indicated more than 90 minutes per week; 23%, less than 60 minutes.

Both the Brazilian and Iowan physical educators perceive the time allotment for physical education as inadequate. Philosophically, and by law, the Brazilians are committed to thrice-weekly physical education classes but, due to lack of teachers and equipment, are only working toward that goal, rather than having accomplished it. Iowans, through their Iowa Association for Health, Physical Education, Recreation, and Dance, are working toward the requirement of 5 days a week physical education. Because currently there is only the requirement that physical education be offered, it seems unlikely that in the near future there would be a 5-day-a-week requirement or, for that matter, a 3-day-a-week requirement.

Objectives

Table 1 shows the relative ranking of objectives by physical educators in the two states. The respondents indicated the foremost objective was to develop an awareness of the position and involvement of one's body or parts in space and time, coordinating one's perceptions and motor abilities. Closely following that was the cultivation of positive social behavior and interpersonal relations, and the fostering of creative expression. Although the stated primary objective of Brazilian physical education was development of perceptual and motor control and abilities, this was ranked fifth in importance by the respondents. The Iowans considered it to be of primary importance, with coordination second and the cultivation of positive social behavior and interpersonal relations ranking a rather distant third.

Table 1   Ranking of Physical Education Objectives for Grades 1–4

	Rank	
Objective	South Rio Grande	Iowa
Develop an awareness of the position and involvement of the body and its parts in space and time	1	6
Cultivate pattern of positive social behavior and interpersonal relations	2	3
Develop positive attitudes toward the participation in physical activities during leisure time	6	5
Develop motor, perceptual, and mental abilities	5	1
Develop the ability to coordinate fundamental basic movements	4	2
Foster creativity and encourage the students to express themselves	3	4

Table 2 shows that in Brazil the development of sport skills was of primary importance. This was a clear reflection of centrally planned goals for this level. The Iowans identified the development of positive attitudes toward participation in leisure time physical activities as being of first importance. This, too, reflects a contemporary societal emphasis upon the need for active lifestyle and wellness. Improvement by organic development was important for all respondents, but at the 5-8 level, the development of the ability to communicate expressively and creatively declined in importance.

The movement education approach deemed so appropriate for young students in both South Rio Grande and Iowa was absorbed in the development of sports skills. In Brazil the goal of developing skilled athletes through physical education was more implicit than in Iowa and, no doubt, was strongly emphasized in physical education training.

Curricula

The curricula in each state were determined by objectives, available equipment and facilities, and, in Brazil, the availability of teacher training. Although a movement education program was ranked first in importance, it was included in only 29% of the programs (Table 3). This was not due to lack of equipment. However, it did reflect a lack of training in movement education teaching styles. Recreational activities constituted the largest percentage (71%) of the curriculum. Most of these could be done

Table 2 Ranking of Physical Education Objectives for Grades 5-8

| | Rank | |
Objective	South Rio Grande	Iowa
Develop sport skills, preparing students to live in a society and be successful in sport activities through their own efforts and technical performance	1	4
Develop positive attitudes toward participation in leisure-time physical activities	6	1
Develop leadership skills	3	2
Develop the ability to critically analyze performance and physical potentialities	4	5
Develop the ability to communicate expressively and creatively	5	5
Improve organic development through physical exercise	2	3

outdoors on the unpaved schoolyards common to most schools. Also, these activities did not require equipment or particular teaching styles. Although not specified as such, these activities likely included indigenous Brazilian games and dances, and were thus popular with the children and perceived by the teachers as appropriate.

The fostering of creative activity and expression was ranked as the third most important objective by the Brazilians, but only 29% of them taught dance or rhythmic activities. This, coupled with the few teaching movement education activities, leads to the conclusion that there was little opportunity for creative expression.

Although the Iowans indicated that the development of motor and perceptual abilities was of first importance, they evidently perceived that this could take place in sports as well as movement education activities at the 1–4 grade level. The majority of the teachers taught sports at the 1–4 level, with basketball (91%) being the most frequently taught. As shown in Table 3, 89% included soccer; 81%, volleyball; and 63%, football.

A major difference emerges at the 5–8 grades in curriculum. As prescribed by the Brazilian physical education decree, the curriculum is almost totally devoted to sports. As shown in Table 4, team handball is taught by 78% of the teachers, with volleyball (73%), track and field (63%), soccer (53%), and basketball (50%) following closely behind. There is minimal attention given to dance or rhythmic activities and lifetime or leisure

Table 3   Physical Education Curriculum for Grades 1–4

Activity	South Rio Grande (%)	Iowa (%)
Movement education activities	29	95
Tumbling	12	95
Games	26	100
Soccer	13	89
Dance-rhythmic activities	29	75
Recreational activities with or without equipment	71	—
Physical fitness activities	—	96
Presport games	50	—
Basketball skills	—	91
Football skills	—	63
Volleyball skills	—	81
Physical exercise aimed at the improvement of posture and body awareness	26	—

Note.   Data given in percentage of schools reporting specific curriculum activity.

activities. The sports most commonly taught do not require a hard surface court or a great deal of equipment. The fact that handball, volleyball, and basketball are taught reflects the European and North American influence on the curriculum.

The Iowans place great value on the development of physical fitness, as well as leisure activities. The activities most frequently taught were volleyball and basketball (99%), with soccer (95%), gymnastics (94%), track and field (93%), and football (91%) close behind. Three fourths of the teachers taught dance and rhythmic activities, whereas only 28% offered swimming. Iowa schools generally provided adequate facilities for all activities except swimming. Only 30% had swimming pools available either at the school or in the community. The Iowa curriculum showed a wider variety of activities at the 5–8 level than did the Brazilian; however, it did not include team handball. This sport, from the European tradition, was one in which the teachers had no personal experience and knowledge; so, as in Brazil, curriculum activities reflected teacher preparation and availability of facilities and equipment.

Table 4   Physical Education Curriculum for Grades 5–8

Activity	South Rio Grande (%)	Iowa (%)
Tumbling-gymnastics	.05	94
Dance-rhythmic activities	13	72
Physical fitness activities	—	99
Games	15	96
Aquatics	—	28
Leisure/lifetime activities	5	91
Adaptives	—	58
Basketball	50	99
Football	—	91
Golf	—	38
Racquetball	—	15
Soccer	53	95
Tennis	—	50
Volleyball	73	99
Track and field	63	93
Team handball	78	—
Physical activity aimed at the improvement of posture and body mechanics	—	7

Note. Data given in percentage of schools reporting specific curriculum activity.

Summary

This study revealed that both states perceive physical education to be an integral part of education at the first level (1–8). In Brazil this philosophy is implemented through a centralized education system operated through individual states. In the United States, there is no centralized plan; each state is autonomous. In Iowa, the decentralized American plan is further implemented in that the state law dictates that physical education is to be offered but does not specify time requirements, objectives, or curricula. The long-standing principle of home rule by individual school districts permits great latitude in curricular offerings, development of facilities and equipment, and objectives and outcomes. The contrast between the centralized administration and local option regarding physical education instruction is reflected in the other findings in this study.

The amount of time allotted for physical education in Iowa varied greatly. In South Rio Grande, also, this was true. However, in Iowa it was a reflection of local district philosophy; whereas in South Rio Grande, the variation was due to lack of professional teachers, facilities, and equipment. The latter factor was also a contributing reason for the inability to offer some activities.

Objectives are nationally determined in Brazil; the curriculum activities offered in South Rio Grande did not seem to completely reflect those objectives but, rather, the availability or lack of professional preparation in the activities that would most likely result in implementation of the objectives. In Iowa, where the teachers determined their own objectives using guides and assessment tools, the curricular offerings seemed to be those that would serve to implement the objectives.

Recommendations

As a result of this study, the following are recommended:

1. The programs in South Rio Grande should include more rhythmic activities and dance at the 1–4 level, and, particularly, at the 5–8 level. This activity requires minimal expense, serves the stated objectives, and could assist in preserving traditional Brazilian movement forms.
2. At the 5–8 level in South Rio Grande, although the emphasis in sport skills is understandable, there should be an increased emphasis upon the development of physical fitness and lifetime leisure activities.
3. It is suggested that the Brazilians continue to work toward the full implementation of their commendable goals of weekly physical education with professionally prepared teachers.
4. The unevenness of time allotment to physical education in the Iowa schools suggests that professional physical educators should make

use of recent research findings to bring before the public the necessity of 5-day-a-week physical education for the development of physical skills and fitness.

5. The Iowa programs should be expanded to include activities such as team handball and rhythmic gymnastics, because these are international sports in which there is increasing participation.

6. The Iowa physical educators should use the K–12 Assessment Tool to evaluate and improve their programs.

7. The availability of adapted programs needs to be increased in both states.

Physical Culture in the Consciousness and Attitudes of Young People From Selected Milieus

Zofia Zukowska

The purpose of this research was to determine the influence that physical culture exerts on youth culture in Poland. About 1,500 Polish youth were interviewed using a questionnaire. The youth were categorized into peasant, working class, and student groups. Questionnaire results are organized by respondent characteristics and attitudes about, and participation in, physical culture.

Respondent Characteristics

Men comprised a majority of those surveyed. They made up 53.80% of the peasant category and 64.20% of the students. The majority (62.56%) of the respondents were unmarried, 34.95% were married, and 2.53% were divorced. Married respondents comprised 51.0% of the peasant class, 43.0% of the working class, and 10.8% of the students.

The majority of the respondents (66.9%) had no children, 16.27% had one child, 10.47% had two children, and 6.4% had three or more children. Respondents from the peasant class were most likely to have children, because 46.0% were parents.

Of those surveyed, 37.92% were students, 6.74% were intellectuals, and 56.09% were physical workers. In terms of family background, 39.55% of the respondents were of peasant origin, 38.95% of working class origin, and 19.4% of intellectual origin. The educational background of those polled consisted of the following: vocational education, 27.74%; secondary vocational education, 23.21%; high school, 19.14%; primary school, 15.01%; and general secondary education, 12.47%.

The largest group of respondents ranged in age from 20 to 23 years (47.82%); the smallest was between 18 and 19 (9.87%).

The daily working hours ranged from 5 to 8 hours for 71.5% of the respondents. Only 14.67% of the people in the surveyed group were working 10 or more hours a day; 95% of these were peasant youth, female as well as male.

Physical Culture Attitudes and Participation

More than half of those surveyed (52.3%) considered themselves to be of good health; 29.81%, very good, and only 1% mentioned bad health.

Thus, we are dealing here with a group of young and healthy people, who, from this point of view, are well prepared for participation in physical culture. Peasant youth evaluated their state of health as very good; the lowest marks in this respect were given by the working class youth.

Nearly half (48.96%) of the respondents have never practiced sport. Of those who did, the largest number went in for team games (23.61%) as well as track and field events (10.81%). Only a slightly larger number of men practiced sport than women.

Fully 85.90% of the respondents properly understand the significance of physical culture. However, responses differed: Some spoke about a person's attitude toward his or her own body, physical efficiency, and health, whereas others understood it as the entire aspect of a person's efforts to preserve his or her health and to achieve physical development, motor efficiency, and high performance. Peasant youth revealed the highest percentage of lack of awareness in this respect (21%).

Physical culture was placed by 73.64% of the surveyed youth on the same level as other spheres of culture. Awareness in this respect was highest in student youth, whereas most individuals who could not make up their minds were in the peasant youth group (23.2%). The educational influence exerted by the school in a positive sense toward physical culture was confirmed by 37.87% of the surveyed youth (only 2.73% express a negative opinion).

Especially emphasized was the role of physical education and school sports in a rising interest in sport—especially in urban and student youth—and the development of efficiency. In evaluating the role of physical culture, the respondents pointed to its dominant position in school sport (58.02%) and in peer groups (42.54%). There was differentiation in the role physical culture played in the consciousness of the family (22.21% described it as very significant, but 19.27% maintained that it was without any significance). In the workplace, 22% felt it was very significant, whereas 30.48% felt it had no significance. It is interesting to note the high percentage of respondents who do not perceive any role of physical culture in these milieus.

However, the respondents were aware of the role that motor activity plays in health (94.85%). Of the surveyed youth 84.9% confirmed the influence that physical exercise exerts on the character of human beings.

The interviewed youth are also aware of the need of participating in physical culture by their own children (87.98%). Only 11.53% of the surveyed young people revealed a negative attitude toward the practice of sport by their own children. The largest percentage (25.42) left the choice of the specific sport participated in to the child, but showed preference for the following sports in descending order: team games, track and field events, and swimming.

The respondents saw in physical activity, above all, the value of health (47.75%), followed by the concept of skill perfection (24.08%) attaching perfectionist ideas to it; and educational values (9.8%). The influence competitive sport exerts on a young person was positive to 69.63%; negative, 16.6%; and no influence at all, 13.8%.

Student youth were the dominant group participating in the following elements of physical culture: recreation, 58.8%; tourism, 54.4%; and competitive sport, 25.6%. This order was the same in all milieus. Lack of participation was highest among peasant youth (51.4%) and working class youth (29.8%). The determinants for participation were quite interesting: 61.24% justified it by maintaining that their bodies needed it, 12.59% stressed the desire to maintain contact with a certain group of people, 6.53% maintained that they did it for health reasons (such as following a doctor's recommendations), and 4.06% stressed the wish to become more proficient at skills. Peasant youth felt little need for organic development, probably due to their active physical lifestyle.

Factors inspiring the development of interests in physical culture were led by the school (24.21%); which was stressed, above all, by working class youth, followed by the influence of teachers (27.19%) and the family (13.14%). Of the surveyed youth, 9.2% mentioned their own initiative, and 6.4% stressed the inspiring role of the mass media. Alarming was the low percentage of youth pointing to inspiration on the part of sport clubs (1.47%) and youth organizations (0.6%).

As regards favorite leisure pursuits, 49.09% of the respondents mentioned active rest, participation in recreation and tourism, physical exercises, and sport. This, however, was not identical with real participation in physical culture. Of all the forms of motor activities, the respondents most liked walking and excursions, and, to a lesser extent, exercises and sports.

Active forms of rest took place much more on free Saturdays (36.62%) than on normal workdays (10.01%). On workdays, such forms of leisure pursuits were strongly differentiated, depending on the given milieu.

An average of 35.88% of young people practice physical exercise systematically, but this includes only 17% of the peasant youth. 28.48% of the surveyed young people devote more than 7 hours a week to participation in various forms of culture; 14.27%, 1–2 hours; 11.6%, 3–4; 7.93%, 5–6 to 6; and 4.7%, 6–7 hours. It should be noted that the student milieu markedly contributes to an increase in the data.

A very insignificant percentage of active leisure pursuits is found during holidays—fluctuating between 4% for sport camps, and 5.74% for tourism—is very strongly differentiated, depending on the given milieu.

Forms of passive rest predominate. Tourist and recreational events on a mass scale do not seem to be popular in the surveyed group—only 22.78% participated in them. This phenomenon holds true for all the various milieus.

When it comes to ownership of certain types of sport and tourist equipment, students predominate. On the average, half of the surveyed young people possess the basic equipment, a smaller percentage own skis (16.94%), dumbbells, spring expanders (26.48%), and tennis rackets (25.48%). More than half possess a bicycle (79.1%); 66.8%, a ball; 62.63%, overalls; and 75.23%, trainers.

Although the respondents rarely thought about championship titles (4.4%), they devoted much time to listening to and viewing reports about sports events (59.16%), reading the sports press (37.88%), and collecting sports souvenirs (10%). When asked which they preferred—participation in, or watching of, sports events—52.63% were in favor of active participation in physical culture; 39.29% favored watching competitions. Factors responsible for lack of active participation were cited as lack of space (22.01%) and equipment for exercises (22.88%), reluctance to make an effort after work (14.21%), lack of proper company (13.41%), lack of interest displayed in sport at home (18.74%), and bad organization of time (6.14%).

PART IV

Fitness

A Comparative Analysis of Youth Physical Fitness Programs in the United States, Canada, and the People's Republic of China

Ren Hai

The national youth physical fitness test battery (though it may have different names in different countries) has become a significant social phenomenon in many nations. This study analyzes how test programs reflect their social backgrounds in three selected countries: the United States, Canada, and the People's Republic of China (P.R.C.).

In the United States, the program evolved from the AAHPERD Youth Fitness Test (YFT) in 1958, was modified in 1965 and 1976, became the Health Related Physical Fitness Test (HRPFT) in 1980 and the National Children and Youth Fitness Study (NCYFS) in 1984 (see Table 1; American Alliance for Health, Physical Education, Recreation and Dance, 1958, 1965, 1976, 1980; Ross, Dotson, Gilbert, & Katz, 1984).

Table 1   United States Physical Fitness Tests

Youth Fitness Test Battery (1976)	Health-Related Physical Fitness Test Battery (1980)	Test Battery of the National Children and Youth Fitness Study (1984)
Pull-ups (boys)	Distance runs	One-mile walk/run
Flexed arm hang (girls)	Measure of sum of skinfold fat	Timed bent-knee sit-ups
Sit-ups	Modified sit-ups	Chin-ups
Shuttle run	Sit and reach	Sit and reach
Standing long jump		Measure of sum of skinfold fat
50-yard dash		
600-yard run (options: 1-mile or 9-minute run for 10–12 years; 1.5-mile or 12-minute run for 13 years and above)		

Note. Adapted from American Alliance for Health, Physical Education, Recreation and Dance, 1976, 1980; Ross et al., 1985.

The Canada Fitness Award (CFA), based on the CAHPER Fitness-Performance Test, appeared in the 1960s. The test currently used is a 1980 revision of this (Canadian Association for Health, Physical Education and Recreation, 1966, 1976; see Table 2).

Table 2   CAHPER Fitness-Performance Test

1966	1976
One-minute speed sit-ups	One-minute speed sit-ups
Standing broad jump	Flexed arm hang
Shuttle run	Standing long jump
Flexed arm hang	Shuttle run
50-yard run	50-meter run
300-yard run	Endurance run

Note. Adapted from Canadian Association of Health, Physical Education and Recreation, 1966, 1976.

The Chinese program appeared in the early 1950s. The current one is the National Standard of Physical Fitness Training, issued in 1981 (see Table 3).

Table 3   Test Battery of Chinese Program Standards of National Physical Fitness Training

Category	Test	Age group
I	50-meter run	All
	Shuttle run	Children and youth
	100-meter run	Youth and adult
	One-minute rope-jump	Children
II	400-meter run	Children
	1500- or 1000-meter run	Male youth and adult
	800-meter run	Female youth and adult
	100-meter swim	Children
	200-meter swim	Youth and adult
	500-meter ice skating	Children
	1000-meter ice skating	Youth and adult
III	High jump	All
	Long jump	All
	Standing long jump	All
	Softball or sandbag throw	Children

(Cont.)

Table 3   (Cont.)

Category	Test	Age group
IV	Medicine ball throw	Youth and adult
	Shot put	Youth and adult
	Stick climbing	Children
V	Sit-ups	All
	Chin-ups	Male youth and adult
	Weight lifting	
	15 Kg	Male youth and adult
	10 Kg	Female youth and adult

Note. Adapted from *The Handbook of the Standards of the National Physical Fitness Training* by The Branch of Mass Sport of the National Sport Committee of People's Republic of China, 1982, Bejing: People's Sport.

There are many similarities among the three programs: They all were initiated by concern for fitness, are fully supported by governments, have national norms, have mainly student participants, and are the largest fitness programs (in terms of the number of participants) in these countries.

Physical fitness is not an abstract concept; it always closely relates to certain time periods and circumstances. In general, to be fit means that one can survive well in the particular surroundings in which he or she is living; thus, people in different countries often face fitness problems caused by unique physical and social environments. Because influencing factors often vary from country to country, fitness problems vary, too. The youth physical fitness program of each country is intended to improve the national fitness level by solving the country's specific major fitness problems; thus, they reflect their social context. By comparing the programs we can gain some insight into their social contexts, and by observing the social backgrounds, we can further understand the natures of the programs.

Social Context of the Fitness Test Programs

United States

In the past 3 decades, lifestyle in the United States society changed rapidly and dramatically. Automation freed Americans from most heavy labor; sedentary work is common and lack of physical activity is endemic.

Automation also provides Americans more leisure time. However, the traditional idea that leisure time should mainly be used for relaxation, in order to allow the body to recover from heavy labor, has not changed concomitant with development of the highly automated society. In addition, television induces millions of people to spend many hours sitting and watching (see Table 4).

Table 4   Distribution of American Leisure Time

Activity	Percent
Watching television	45.0
Listening to radio	36.0
Reading newspapers	6.0
Listening to records	5.7
Reading magazines	4.0
Reading novels	2.1
Playing computer games	1.0

Note. From *Broadcasting Magazine* (1982).

High calorie and fat diets and a lack of physical activity have resulted in 30–40% of the adult American population being overweight. Coronary heart disease, largely diet related, is the major cause of death, accounting for half a million American deaths annually. The cost of cardiovascular disease in the United States is about $35 billion annually; the loss of manpower, 62,000,000 man-days per year (Wilson, Fardey, & Froelicher, 1981). The result of sedentary lifestyle is that an estimated 16% of the population have suffered classical low back pain syndrome; 80% have had "simple," but significant, backache. Low back injuries may well account for more lost man-hours than any other occupational injury (Plowman & Falls, 1978).

It is evident that the major problem threatening American physical fitness is the so-called hypokinetic disease, particularly coronary heart disease, obesity, and low back pain, which are related to a highly automated society. Moreover, these health problems, or their precursors, are found in alarming percentages at early ages (American Alliance for Health, Physical Education, Recreation and Dance, 1980). Prevention of these three influential diseases is urgently needed. The early YFT, based on the theory that physical fitness can be determined by measuring athletic ability, did not fully meet the social need. The reformation of the theory, by differentiating physical fitness related to functional health from physical performance related to athletic ability, made the youth physical fitness program closely connected with the national concerns, namely, cardiorespiratory function, body composition, and abdominal and low back musculoskeletal function. Thus, the HRPFT, with the purpose of testing these functions of health, appeared.

Canada

Canadians face the same fitness problems with the same causes as do the Americans. Seventy-six percent of the population over age 13 devote less than one hour a week to participation in sports; 79% had less than one hour of other physical activity. This is coupled with 4–15 hours of watching television each week.

The Nutrition Canada Society revealed that 50% of the whole population is overweight and that 65–87% of women 40 years of age or older fall into this category (Wearring, 1977). According to Marc Lalonde, the Minister of National Health and Welfare, in 1974 disease of the cardiovascular system was by far the principal cause of hospitalization; at age 35, coronary-artery disease first appears as a significant (> 5%) cause of death. By age 40 it becomes the principal cause and holds this position in increasing ascendancy through all subsequent age groups.

Because the youth fitness programs in both Canada and the U.S. are intended to measure physical fitness, and because both countries have the same physical fitness problems, the programs in both countries should be similar. However, though the American program shifted to the dimension of health-related fitness, the Canadian program still followed its original format. Its revision in 1980 did not change the direction, though a long-distance run was substituted for the 300-yard run, which reflected the increasing concern about cardiorespiratory problems.

Why the Canadian program continues in the same way may be explained by two factors. First, because physical fitness is a multidimensional concept, no general definition of the exact nature of physical fitness has been universally accepted. Shephard (1977) has pointed out that many authors conceive of physical fitness in terms of athletic performance. For example, physical performance and fitness are the same thing in the opinions of Astrand and Rodahl (1970). Based on this theory, the Canadian CFA and American YFT were designed to test fitness with athletic performance. Even in the reformed American program, the HRPFT or the NCYFS, the test battery still includes such components of physical performance as speed sit-ups, distance run, and chin-ups. Thus, the different understanding of the concept of physical fitness and the different means to measure it result in the continuance of the Canadian CFA.

The second factor for the CFA's continuance may be even more important. Since the 1960s, competitive sports at the national and, especially, international levels have become a major concern of the federal government. It may not be true that the 1961 Fitness and Amateur Sport Act was passed largely because Canada's performance at the 1960 Rome Olympics was a low point in the history of her participation in international sport (Zeigler, 1976). Yet, the first object of the Act is, indeed, to provide assistance for the promotion and development of Canadian participation in national and international amateur sport (Government of Canada, 1961). H.J. Munro, Minister of National Health and Welfare, stated in 1968 that it was essential to build Canadian excellence in international amateur athletics. Eleven years later, I. Campagnolo (1979),

Minister of State Fitness and Amateur Sport, also pointed out that the controlling consideration, from the federal point of view, is the pursuit of excellence nationally and internationally.

Thus, the Canadian youth physical fitness program, a major national project sponsored by the federal government, reflects the objective of the government, as does its name, "Fitness-Performance Test," rather than just "Fitness Test," the Americans' term. Thus, the current test battery is better suited to the CFA program than functional health items would be (MacIntosh & Greenhorn, 1979). Actually, the current Canadian program is quite relevant in dealing with Canada's fitness problems. With the exception of the measure of body composition, almost all the aspects of the American program can be identified in it. Therefore, the program is quite suitable to its social context, and there is no strong motivation to shift it to another dimension.

People's Republic of China

Most of the population of China lives in rural areas (see Table 5), and manual labor still plays an important role in production. There are six working days a week. In addition, Chinese daily life to a large extent relies on physical ability, rather than automatic devices. In terms of nutrition, calorie and fat intake is much lower than in the United States and Canada (see Table 6).

Moreover, television is not a serious problem, because there are fewer sets in Chinese households. In 1980, the total number of televisions per 1,000 persons was 27 in the P.R.C., compared to 624 in the United States and 471 in Canada (Summary of international, 1984).

Hypokinetic disease is still rare in China. However, improvement of living conditions and development of medicine and hygiene, the leading causes of death in China have changed their order. Infectious diseases dropped from the greatest cause in the 1950s to the seventh in 1983, while heart disease jumped to the top, causing 17.20% of the total deaths from 1973 to 1975 (Zhou, 1984). However, by contrast, coronary heart disease is the major North American killer, causing 31.1% of all disease-related death in Canada (Lalonde, 1974) and two-thirds of the heart disease in the United States (Wilson, Fardey, & Froelicher, 1981). In China it causes only 8.33% of all heart disease deaths; pulmonary heart disease accounts for 61.08% (Zhou, 1984).

Because hypokinetic disease is not prevalent, and because lifestyle in China more frequently demands the routine use of such physical abilities as strength, endurance, agility, and coordination, these qualities should already be enhanced. Thus, the Chinese fitness program is used to prevent disease and to prepare citizens to easily cope with their working and living conditions. In addition, the concept of physical fitness, in the view of Chinese scholars, has a broad context, including improvement of the physical structure of human body, motor ability, and capability of adapting oneself to circumstances by various physical exercises

Table 5   Rural Population Percentage by Country

Country	1970	1975	1982
P.R.C.	82.6	82.7	79.2
U.S.	3.7	2.8	2.0
Canada	8.2	6.5	4.6

Note. Adapted from *The Summary of International Economic and Social Statistical Data*, 1984, Bejing: Chinese Statistics.

Table 6   Daily Caloric and Fat Intake per Person

| Country | 1975–1977 | | 1978–1980 | |
	Vegetable	Animal	Vegetable	Animal
Calories				
P.R.C.	2,169	142	2,564	215
U.S.	2,256	1,296	2,322	1,331
Canada	1,931	1,421	1,961	1,397
Fat (in grams)				
P.R.C.	16.0	13.9	23.3	21.1
U.S.	62.5	99.0	66.0	103.2
Canada	33.7	116.1	36.0	114.9

Note. Adapted from *The Summary of International Economic and Social Statistical Data*, 1984, Bejing: Chinese Statistics.

(Wang et al., 1981). It should also be noted that competitive sport is highly valued in China, and that improvement of athletic performance is declared as one of the objectives of physical culture. The national youth fitness program therefore reflects social demand. A motor ability aspect of physical fitness is emphasized. Consequently, the Chinese program contains five categories of items dealing with the basic traits of physical fitness.

Conclusions

The particular form of the youth physical fitness program in each of the three countries is mainly determined by two broad factors: The first considers interpretation of the concept of physical fitness—which provides a theoretical basis for programs—and social conditions, such as lifestyle, shaped by political, economic, and technological conditions; the main concerns of the fitness problem; and the government policy on sport. The second aspect provides the practical demand to the program. Because both aspects are different in the three nations, their programs differ from one another. In the United States, the program shows increasing concern for the health problems caused by a highly automated society. In Canada, it reflects the concern for competitive sports by the federal government. In China, the program is not only used to measure physical fitness levels but also as a means of physical training.

References

Åstrand, P.O., & Rodahl, K. (1970). *A textbook of work physiology*. New York: McGraw-Hill.

American Alliance for Health, Physical Education, Recreation and Dance. (1958, 1965, 1976). *Youth fitness test manual*. Washington, DC: Author.

American Alliance for Health, Physical Education, Recreation and Dance. (1980). *Health-related physical fitness test manual*. Washington, DC: Author.

The Branch of Mass Sport of the National Sport Committee of People's Republic of China. (1982). *The handbook of the standards of the national physical fitness training*. Bejing: People's Sport.

Canadian Association for Health, Physical Education, Recreation, and Dance. (1966). *The CAHPER fitness-performance test manual*.

Canadian Association for Health, Physical Education, Recreation, and Dance (1980). *The CAHPER fitness-performance II test manual*.

Campagnolo, I. (1979). *Partners in pursuit of excellence: A national policy on amateur sport*. Ottawa: Government of Canada.

Government of Canada. (1961). *Bill C-131: Fitness and Amateur Sport Act*. Ottawa: Author.

Government of Canada. (1982). *Canada fitness awards manual*. Ottawa: Author.

Kraus, H., & Raab, W. (1961). *Hypokinetic disease*. Springfield, IL: Charles C Thomas.

Lalonde, M. (1974). *A new perspective on the health of Canadians: A working document*. Ottawa: Government of Canada.

MacIntosh, D., & Greenhorn, D. (1979). Another visit with the CAHPER fitness test. *Journal of the Canadian Association for Health, Physical Education, Recreation and Dance, 45*, 30–37.

Munro, J. (1968-69). Canadian sports potential. *Journal of the Canadian Association of Health, Physical Education, Recreation and Dance, 35*, 5–11.

Plowman, S.A., & Falls, H.B. (1978). AAHPERD youth fitness test revision. *Journal of Physical Education, Recreation and Dance, 49*(9), 22–24.

Shephard, R.J. (1977). *Endurance fitness* (4th ed.). Toronto: University of Toronto Press.

The summary of international economic and social statistical data. (1984). Beijing: Chinese Statistics.

Wang, Z., Guo, J., Niu, X., & Qian, Y. (1981). *A textbook of the theory of physical culture.* Beijing: People's Sport.

Wearring, A. (1977). Where the health are we going? *Journal of the Canadian Association of Health, Physical Education, Recreation and Dance, 44*, 6.

Wilson, P.K., Fardey, P.A., & Froelicher, V.F. (1981). *Cardiac rehabilitation, adult fitness, and exercise testing.* Philadelphia: Lea & Febiger.

Zeigler, E.F. (1976). Canada at the crossroads in international sport. In P. Graham & H. Uberhorst (Eds.), *The modern Olympics.* Champaign, IL: Leisure Press.

Zhou, Y.S. (1984). The causes of death of Chinese residents. In Y.L. Cui (Ed.), *The Chinese hygiene year book 1984* (pp. 46-52). Beijing: People's Hygiene.

International Perspectives of Aerobic Dance

Richard S. Baka

The so-called fitness boom of recent decades has been international in its scope and has been characterized by a series of exercise crazes—running or jogging, aerobic dance classes, and, most recently, ultra sports (e.g., triathlons). The function of this paper is to explore a number of key issues related to the area of aerobic dance. A difficulty in this relatively new realm of physical activity called *aerobic dance* is one of terminology. Due to the lack of a consistent international label, *dance exercise, exercise-to-music,* and *aerobic fitness/exercise classes* are meant to be synonomous with aerobic dance.

The international appeal of this form of physical activity is analyzed from various sociocultural perspectives, with comparative data primarily delimited to Australia, Canada, and the United States. Major issues examined in this paper are the increases in participation rates, growth of specialized classes, instructor training and certification, legal issues, and research trends (see Table 1).

Growth Patterns: Fad or Genuine Exercise Option?

There is abundant documentation attesting to the growth in popularity of aerobic classes in a variety of countries. For example, the American publication *Sports Illustrated* reported there were 22.7 million aerobic dancers in the United States in June, 1984 (McCallum, 1984). The Australian Department of Sport, Recreation, and Tourism reported in its *Survey of Physical Activity of Australians* (1985) that 13% of respondents engaged in calisthenics or aerobics during the summer of 1985; this figure was slightly higher (14.9%) during the winter months of the same year. The very detailed Canada Fitness Survey (Highlights, 1981) concluded that over 650,000 Canadians want to join an exercise class. Other Western countries have experienced similar increases in participation in this activity.

Despite such a widespread and dramatic growth in popularity, much of the contemporary writing in the last few years discusses these increases in participation levels in terms of it being a recent "fad." The fad label

Table 1 Comparative Information on Aerobic Dance

Factor	Australia	Canada	United States
Aerobic dance participants[a] (in millions)	1.95	2.30	22.70
Instructor certification programs	National scheme	National scheme	Variety of private schemes (over 50)
Professional agencies with services for instructors	Australian Fitness Leaders Association	Canadian Association of Sports Sciences Provincial (e.g., Ontario Fitness Council)	American College of Sports Medicine International Dance Exercise Association Aerobics & Fitness Association of America Others
Legislation pertaining to qualifications of staff	Union wage guidelines: no firm legislation, but a voluntary code of practices in Victoria	Discussion of legislation, (e.g., in Ontario)	Proposed legislation in California (Senate Bill 14 Health Studios Act)

[a]Estimated.

may be correct. Recent literature reports that the boom period has ended. For instance, a report in the United Kingdom concluded that "the 'craze' for aerobics has passed and people are turning now towards more individual programmes" (Health Clubs, 1985, p. 32).

However, though the growth curve has possibly leveled off, there is increasing sophistication as a more specialized structure emerges. No longer are classes simply for young females, the very fit, or yuppies. Participants now have access to a variety of class styles: water aerobics; pre- and postnatal, low-impact, elderly, stretch, circuit, and weight aerobics; dance-oriented classes, and others (Baka, 1985).

Moreover, this once traditionally female domain is attracting more men. The Canada Fitness Survey reported one third of those who attend exercise classes are men, a 13% increase (Highlights, 1984). Classes that do not place as much emphasis on the dance component or those using light weights or a circuit style tend to attract men (Baka, 1985).

Similarly, the emphasis on specialization has seen an upsurge in interest in classes for older people and for such specific target populations as people with lower back pain or pre- and postnatal mothers. The fact that many schools use aerobics within their physical education curricula or as recreational activities indicates the broad appeal of this form of exercise. The increasing diversification and sophistication of class styles is a trend that is helping to entrench aerobic dance as a viable exercise option, as opposed to a soon-to-be-forgotten fad.

Instructor Training and Certification: A Quest for Quality

"The most important question is the selection of a director and instructors."

With the growing interest in aerobic exercise classes has come a corresponding need for trained personnel. During the initial stages in the growth of this field, instructors tended to be self-taught, usually with backgrounds and/or interests in dance, gymnastics, sport, physical education, or combinations thereof. Often instructors were simply former class participants who followed limited guidelines from previous instructors.

Eventually, various professionals, such as physical educators, dance specialists, sportsmedicine practitioners, physiotherapists, and other health professionals, began lobbying for improved instructor certification through training courses. At first, private agencies, professional associations, and government bodies in some nations began operating a variety of short training courses of a few hours duration. Over the last few years, this has generally expanded to include more sophisticated training schemes, several with government-backed accreditation status or certification approval from reputable professional associations.

There are some important cross-national differences in fitness leadership. A recent issue of an Australian publication noted the effect of Australia's new "Fitness Leadership" courses:

This puts Australia in line with Canada as the two countries most advanced in acknowledging nationally minimally trained community Fitness Leaders. Fractionalisation in the U.S. and an apparent lack of interest in the U.K. has so far prevented a national approach from those countries. (In brief, 1986, p. 8)

A survey found that in the United States, 50 different dance exercise training programs claim to have produced 66,000 certified instructors in programs ranging from a questionable standard to excellent. The American College of Sports Medicine, the International Dance Exercise Association, and the Aerobics and Fitness Association of America seem to be the largest organizations involved in this certification issue. Recent attempts by some of these agencies to work cooperatively may lead to a more unified approach in the near future (Morgan, 1985).

The American setting is in contrast to both Canada and Australia, which have national schemes administered at the provincial and state levels, respectively. Both of these national programs are undergoing fine-tuning in their administration, with the Canadians at a more advanced level. In both countries, training courses have been well received, with academic curricula designed cooperatively by professional bodies, government agencies, tertiary institutions, commercial fitness operators, and others.

Legal Issues: Law and Order in a Dynamic Field

There are three major legal issues examined at this juncture: government legislation, music copyrights, and litigation involving instructor negligence. The first of these addresses government intervention through legislation in the field of health and fitness clubs or studios. Due to the large number of dubious consumer-related practices in the health and fitness area, more stringent legislation may soon govern the field in all three of the countries examined in this study.

Already the state of California has initiated action to pass Senate Bill 14, the Health Studios Act, which will establish a vehicle for the standardization and certification of persons teaching in health/fitness programs. If this bill is passed, other states in the U.S. are likely to follow the Californian lead (Morgan, 1985).

In Australia, union interest in gymnasium workers has resulted in recommended wage and other guidelines as set out by the Victorian Health and Sports (Centre) Employees Conciliation and Arbitration Board. Several Australian states—led by Victoria, which has a voluntary code of practices pertaining to the health and fitness industry—are examining legislative options in an industry that has witnessed numerous gym closures and associated consumer problems. In Canada, as well, there are rumblings of legislation being passed in several provinces, due to dubious business practices in the fitness area (Business Journal, 1986).

Another legal issue involves the question of music copyrights. Because most instructors use music in a "public performance" in their classes, this vast and complex issue has come into play. Until recently, music companies and other music-associated bodies have not prosecuted fitness centers or individuals for music and copyright infringement. Attempts have been made through instructor training programs and publications to educate individuals of the need to obtain the various and relevant music licenses that apply in all countries. Whereas in the United States there would appear to be a trend toward legal action in this area, neither Canada nor Australia have yet had to deal with this issue.

A positive development in this area is the emergence of such organizations as the American-based Music in Motion company. For an annual fee based on amount of use, subscribers can legally obtain music copyright clearance through a compliance program. Moves are already underway in Australia and in Canada to have similar agencies established.

A final legal concern is the growing incidence of litigation against instructors citing negligence (e.g., use of dangerous exercises, hazardous routines, etc.). These claims are emerging in Canada as well as Australia and are not limited to the U.S., with its history of being more litigation-conscious.

This problem may grow; although it may never reach the magnitude of doctor malpractice suits, there is a twofold lesson for instructors: guarantee a sound training program and obtain some type of professional indemnity or liability insurance. Group liability insurance for fitness leaders is available in all three countries.

Research: Catching Up With the Public Interest

Until quite recently, there has been a dearth of high-quality research on aerobic dance. Research into this field began in the United States in the early to mid-1970s, with most studies centering around the worth of aerobic dance as an effective form of cardiovascular fitness training. Early studies were not conclusive, but further investigations have generally given this mode of exercise an acceptable rating, provided classes are well designed (Legwold, 1982; Milburn & Butts, 1983; Watterson, 1984).

More recent studies (again, primarily American) have concentrated on injuries associated with this form of physical activity. For example, *Physician and Sports Medicine* published a three-article series on aerobic dance injuries in February, 1985. A wide array of other research covers such diverse topics as class design (Fein, 1980), music (Brown, 1982), grading of exercise classes (Baka, 1984), footwear (Rosenberg, 1986), and legal aspects (Caffray, 1986).

Although most research still tends to come from the United States, there have been examples of some research efforts from Canada (e.g., MacIntyre, 1985), Australia (e.g., James, 1984; Lowdon & Ross, 1985; Baka & Cera, 1981), and other nations. With aerobic dance gaining such a popular following in a relatively short period of time, it would seem that the research is finally catching up to the widespread public interest.

In the future, more sophisticated research will likely emerge covering such areas as biomechanics, potentially inadvisable exercises, class design, and social and psychological factors. This will assist in the development of a much-needed body of knowledge of aerobic dance, a field still characterized as being in its embryonic stages regarding research.

Summary and Conclusions

Within the space of 15 years, aerobic dance has gained an enormous following of active participants spanning a diverse population base. With this quick growth has come a host of difficulties often associated with a boom activity. However, moves toward better instructor training, the solving of legal issues, and more sophisticated research are all helping to shape the future direction of this very popular mode of physical activity, which is so well advanced now that it can shed any fad labeling.

Although this study was primarily delimited to analyzing aerobic dance within Western democratic nations, many socialist nations have had similar types of mass aerobic-style exercise schemes around for decades. Whether these nations will embrace more characteristics of the "capitalist" style of aerobic dance (loud rock music, attention to fashionable fitness wear, etc.) remains to be seen. Already several third world countries and nations in Southeast Asia and South America have experienced the aerobic dance phenomenon.

References

Aerobic Dance Injuries Symposium. (1985). *The Physician and Sports Medicine, 13*, 105–140.

Baka, R. (1984). Exercise class grading versus the "one size fits all" approach. *Exercise Science and Community Fitness.* Australian Council for Health, Physical Education and Recreation Biennial Conference, pp. 1–5.

Baka, R., & Cera, M. (1981). An historical overview of exercise to music. *Proceedings of 51st ANZAAS Congress,* (pp. 131–144).

Baka, R., & MacLeod, M. (1983, Oct. 28). Aerobics: Exercise your discretion. *Age Newspaper (Weekender Supplement),* p. 9.

Brown, P. (1982, May–June). The use of music in a fitness program. *Canadian Association Health, Physical Education and Recreation Journal,* pp. 39–43.

Caffray, D.B. (1986). Legal considerations in the dance for fitness environment. In Shell, C., (Ed.), *The dancer as athlete: 1984 Olympic Scientific Congress proceedings* (Vol. 8, pp. 145–148). Champaign, IL: Human Kinetics.

Cote, K., & Milmo, S. (1983, July 18). Europe catches a dance bug. *Advertising Age (Fitness Marketing),* p. 20.

Fein, M. (1980). Fitness dancing: Not for dancers only! *Fitness Motivation* (pp. 51–53). Toronto: Oreol.

Griffin, J. (1985, November–December). National guidelines for the training and recognition of fitness leaders in Canada. *Canadian Association for Health, Physical Education and Recreation Journal*, p. 44.

Hammond, K. (1986). Aerobics U.K.-style: Survive it or not. *Australian Accredited Fitness Leaders Association Newsletter*, **1**(3), 4–5.

Health clubs doing well in U.K. (1985, October). *Sportslink*, p. 32.

Highlights. (1984). *Canada Fitness Survey*. No. 34.

Highlights. (1985). Department of Sport, Recreation, and Tourism. *Survey of Physical Activity of Australians*. No. 2.

In brief. (1986). *The Fitness Reader*, **4**, 8.

James, B. (1985). The potential and importance of aerobic dance classes for general conditioning, and the structure of programmes from a scientific basis. *Sport Health*, **3**, 33.

Legwold, G. (1982). Does aerobic dance offer more fun than fitness? *The Physician and Sports Medicine*, **10**, 147–151.

Lowdon, B., & Ross, K.N. (1985, June). Are beginners in aerobic classes being overstressed? *Australian Council for Health, Physical Education and Recreation Journal*, pp. 22–25.

MacIntyre, J.C., Taunton, J.F., Clement, D.B., McKenzie, D.C., Lloyd-Smith, D.R., & Matheson, D.O. (1985). A comparison of fitness class injuries to participants and instructors. *Canadian Journal of Applied Sport Sciences*, **110**, 198.

McCallum, J. (1984, December 3). Everybody's doin' it. *Sports Illustrated*, pp. 72–86.

Milburn, S., & Butts, N.K. (1983). Comparison of the training responses to aerobic dance and jogging in college females. *Medicine and Science in Sports and Exercise*, **15**, 510–513.

Morgan, S. (1985, October–November). A crusade for quality. *Corporate Fitness & Recreation*, pp. 20–23.

Rosenberg, S.L. (1986). Proper footwear for dance for fitness. In Shell, C., (Ed.), *The dancer as athlete: 1984 Olympic Scientific Congress proceedings* (Vol. 8, pp. 139–143). Champaign, IL: Human Kinetics.

Watterson, C.V. (1984). The effects of aerobic dance on cardiovascular fitness. *The Physician and Sports Medicine*, **12**, 138–145.

The year fitness shaped up. (1986, January-February). *Business Journal*, p. 22.

Cross-National Comparisons of Motivation for Participation in Physical Activity of Australian and American Adolescents

Barry Watkin
Lois Youngen

The development of lifelong patterns of participation in sport, dance, and exercise activities is assumed to be a major goal of physical education, recreation, and youth sports programs. Fundamental to achieving this goal is the identification of people's perceived reasons or motives for participating in physical activities. In the past those responsible for the leadership of physical activity programs have had to rely on intuition in determining why some individuals/youths begin and continue to participate, whereas others become activity dropouts. Investigations with this focus are strongly supported by youth sport researchers and sport psychologists in the United States (Gould, Feltz, Weiss, & Petlichkoff, 1981).

Despite such expressions of participation motivation as a high-priority research area, little has been done. Passer (1982) reviewed the work of Alderman and Wood (1976); Gould, Feltz, Weiss, and Petlichkoff (1981); and Gill, Gross, and Huddleston (1983). Synthesizing the theoretical models and research findings of these authors, Passer suggested that children's participation motives can be grouped into six main categories:

1. Affiliation, which may be further divided into factors reflecting team atmosphere—to be on a team or experience team spirit or friendship—to be with, and to make new, friends
2. Skill development—to improve skills or learn new skills, to become good at something
3. Excitement—to experience action, challenge, and interesting, novel activities
4. Success or status—to win, feel important, gain recognition, obtain rewards
5. Fitness—to get exercise, stay in shape
6. Energy release—to get rid of tension (p. 232)

Although the literature suggests some common dimensions of participation motivation, these dimensions have been identified only for young athletes actively participating in specified sports. The present paper reports on the investigation of motives for participation in a broad and general sample from the state of Washington, United States, and Australian grade 10 secondary school adolescents. Twenty motivator variables were used for comparisons by country and by gender, between-factor structures from factor analyses, and factor scores generated from an all-subjects factor analysis.

Methods

Questionnaire responses were obtained from grade 10 students in 11 Australian secondary schools, 5 in New South Wales and 6 in Victoria, prior to the end of the 1984 school year. Similar responses were obtained from grade 10 students in 3 secondary schools in the state of Washington prior to the end of the 1984 school year. The Australian sample comprised 687 females and 666 males, a total of 1,353 subjects. The Washington sample comprised 261 females and 330 males, a total of 591 subjects.

A questionnaire developed by Watkin (1977) was used. Responses to the general question "to what extent do each of the following motivate you to participate in physical activity" were requested for each of 20 motivator variables (MVs). The 20 MVs are identified in Table 1 and Table 2.

Results

Intensity of Motivator Variables

Respondents were asked to indicate the degree to which each MV motivated them to participate in physical activity using a 5-point scale: not at all (1), a little (2), a fair amount (3), a lot (4), and a great deal (5). The initial analysis was undertaken to determine intensity ratings for each of the MVs and to make comparisons by gender between the Australian and Washington samples. The mean scores and importance of rankings for females are reported in Table 1 and for males in Table 2.

For females, intensity ratings were strikingly similar. Both Australian and Washington subjects were most highly motivated to participate in physical activity "as an opportunity to develop or improve physical skills." Additional high ratings were given to participating for "the pleasure of doing something well," "to improve your physical appearance," "to improve your level of health and physical fitness," and "because it provides you with a challenge." Females from both samples rated the same three variables ("as a form of beautiful and graceful movement," "for the responsibility of leadership," and "because it provides an opportunity to achieve prestige and/or social status") as least important.

For males, the comparison between Australian and Washington samples indicated less agreement in intensity ratings. Washington males were most

Table 1   Mean Comparisons of Motivator Variables for Females

Motivator variables	Australia Mean	Australia Rank	Washington Mean	Washington Rank
Improving fitness/health	3.53	3	3.47	4
Opportunities to socialize	3.02	10	3.10	16
Vertigo	2.47	16	2.87	14
Testing skill versus opponent	2.97	11	3.18	10
Beautiful/graceful movement	2.20	20	2.41	20
Doing something well	3.58	2	3.67	3
Testing skill versus nature	2.44	17	2.84	15
Responsibility of leadership	2.22	19	2.65	18
Improving/developing physical skills	3.66	1	3.77	1
Liking to win	2.51	15	3.14	11
Feeling a need for movement	3.14	8	3.26	9
Prestige/social status	2.26	18	2.54	19
Liking a challenge	3.41	5	3.42	5
Struggling or contesting	2.74	13	3.07	13
Feeling of well-being	3.10	9	3.32	7
Escaping boredom	3.20	6	3.20	6
Hard and strenuous training	2.53	16	2.72	17
Playing fairly	3.16	7	3.27	8
Relaxation	2.95	12	2.80	16
Improving physical appearance	3.53	3	3.76	2

highly motivated because they "like to win" and "for the pleasure of doing something well," whereas Australian males were most highly motivated, as were their female counterparts, for "the opportunity to develop or improve physical skills" and "because it provides you with a challenge." Males in both samples were least motivated to participate "as a form of beautiful movement." The same five variables were noted for both male groups as the next least motivating, although with minor differences in rankings: "for the responsibility of leadership," "for achieving prestige and/or social status," "for relaxation," "for engaging in hard and strenuous training," and "for the opportunity to socialize." The only extreme difference in motivator rankings was for "liking to win," ranked equal first in the Washington sample and eighth by the Australian males.

Table 2 Mean Comparisons of Motivator Variables for Males

Motivator variables	Australia Mean	Rank	Washington Mean	Rank
Improving fitness/health	3.31	6	3.47	8
Opportunities to socialize	2.97	15	3.08	16
Vertigo	3.18	9	3.38	10
Testing skill versus opponent	3.62	4	3.68	3
Beautiful/graceful movement	1.55	20	1.97	20
Doing something well	3.67	2	3.72	1
Testing skill versus nature	2.98	14	3.32	12
Responsibility of leadership	2.55	19	2.95	17
Improving/developing physical skills	3.71	1	3.68	3
Liking to win	3.25	8	3.72	1
Feeling a need for movement	3.15	11	3.22	14
Prestige/social status	2.67	18	2.91	19
Liking a challenge	3.71	1	3.63	5
Struggling or contesting	3.53	5	3.49	7
Feeling of well-being	3.08	12	3.41	9
Escaping boredom	3.26	7	3.34	11
Hard and strenuous training	2.79	17	3.15	15
Playing fairly	3.06	13	3.26	13
Relaxation	2.95	16	2.92	18
Improving physical appearance	3.17	10	3.57	6

Factor Analyses

In order to identify underlying dimensions for participation in physical activity and to compare these dimensions for the Washington and Australian samples, factor analyses were undertaken. Principal component analyses with orthogonal varimax rotations and Kaiser normalization procedures were performed for groups of Australian and Washington subjects. For these analyses, Kaiser-Meyer-Olkin measures of sampling adequacy ranging from .89 to .93 were obtained. Only factors with eigenvalues of greater than one were retained for consideration.

Australian Sample. The factor analysis yielded four identifiable factors. The total variance accounted for by these four factors was 51.0%. These results are presented in Table 3. Variables with high factor loadings on

Factor 1 appeared to fall into two groups. The first group ("liking to win," "to achieve prestige or social status," and "for responsibility of leadership") were considered to be related to "success and status," as defined by Passer (1982). The second group of variables ("as an opportunity to try your skill against an opponent," "because you like to engage in a struggle or contest," "vertigo," "because it provides you with a challenge," and "as an opportunity to try your skill against nature") reflected a component identified by Passer (1982) as "excitement." Passer described excitement incentives as being "to experience action," "challenge," and "interesting and novel situations." Factor 1 accounted for 31.2% of the variance and was labeled as a *Success and Status/Excitement* factor.

Factor 2, accounting for a further 9.2% of the variance, was less complex. Three variables ("to improve your level of physical fitness and health," "as an opportunity to develop or improve your physical skills," and "to improve your physical appearance") clearly reflected a dimension of "personal development." The fourth variable loading on this factor was "to provide opportunities for social participation." Alderman and Wood (1976) described "affiliation" incentives as revolving around opportunities for social intercourse, being socially reassured that one is

Table 3   Factor Analysis for Australian Adolescents

| Motivator variables | Rotated factor loadings | | | |
	1	2	3	4
Testing skill versus opponent	.72	—	—	—
Struggling or contesting	.70	—	—	—
Vertigo	.65	—	—	—
Liking a challenge	.55	—	—	—
Testing skill versus nature	.54	—	—	—
Liking to win	.68	—	—	—
Responsibility of leadership	.64	—	—	—
Prestige/social status	.61	—	—	—
Improving fitness/health	—	.82	—	—
Improving/developing physical skills	—	.73	—	—
Improving physical appearance	—	.57	—	—
Opportunities to socialize	—	.54	—	—
Escaping boredom	—	—	.78	—
Relaxation	—	—	.59	—
Beautiful/graceful movement	—	—	—	.72

Note. Only factor loadings of greater than .5 were retained for consideration.

acceptable or worthwhile by making friends, or the maintaining of already existing friendships. Factor 2 was labeled as a *Personal Development/Affiliation* factor.

Two variables ("for something to do to escape boredom," and "for relaxation") had the highest loadings on Factor 3. This factor accounted for 5.4% of the variance. The variables for this factor indicated an activity substitution to modify or change a current state and was seen as being more than energy release, as defined by Passer (1982). As a result, this factor was labeled *Diversion*.

Factor 4 accounted for a further 5.2% of the variance. Only one variable, "as a form of beautiful and graceful movement," loaded on this factor, and it was labeled as an *Aesthetics* factor.

Washington Sample. As with the Australian sample, this factor analysis identified four factors. The results of this analysis, accounting for 55% of the total variance, are presented in Table 4. The factor structure obtained was very similar to that produced for the equivalent group of Australian subjects.

Factor 1 accounted for 38.7% of the variance and contained five variables with high loadings. This factor reflected the similar dimensions of

Table 4 Factor Analysis for Washington Adolescents

Motivator variables	Rotated factor loadings			
	1	2	3	4
Testing skill versus opponent	.71	—	—	—
Struggling or contesting	.67	—	—	—
Vertigo	.64	—	—	—
Liking a challenge	.61	—	—	—
Liking to win	.68	—	—	—
Improving fitness/health	—	.80	—	—
Improving/developing physical skills	—	.73	—	—
Improving physical appearance	—	.64	—	—
Doing something well	—	.57	—	—
Feeling a need for movement	—	.54	—	—
Relaxation	—	—	.72	—
Escaping boredom	—	—	.50	—
Playing fairly	—	—	.59	—
Beautiful/graceful movement	—	—	—	.80
Responsibility of leadership	—	—	—	.53

Note. Only factor loadings of greater than .5 were retained for consideration.

success and status, and excitement as found in the Australian group of all subjects.

Factor 2 was also similar to the Australian sample, with a personal development dimension; however, the Affiliation dimension was not identified for this group. Two additional variables ("doing something well" and "need for movement") were found to load highly here. Factor 2 added 6.8% to the variance accounted for.

Both of the variables "for relaxation" and "to escape boredom" loaded highly on Factor 3, as they did for the Australian sample. Factor 3 accounted for a further 5.3% of the variance and contained the additional variable "to play fairly."

"Aesthetics" was again the dimension for Factor 4, which accounted for a further 5.0% of the variance. For this sample, it contained the additional variable of "responsibility of leadership," which loaded on Factor 1 for the Australian sample.

The factor dimensions of Success and Status, Excitement, Personal Development, Diversion, and Aesthetics were found to be common to the Australian and Washington samples.

Comparison of Motivational Levels

The next step in the analysis was to make comparisons of motivational levels for males and females between countries. A factor analysis was undertaken with a combined sample of all subjects. Factor scores for each factor identified in the above analysis were generated. Z scores from each factor were summed with a constant of 10 (to remove negative values) to provide a composite motivational score. A one-way analysis of variance was conducted by category of subjects. It was observed that both Washington males and females had significantly higher mean scores ($p < .01$) than their Australian counterparts.

With the above differences observed, one-way analyses of variance were conducted to investigate differences between means for each factor by category of subjects. The difference in overall motivational level between Washington and Australian subjects was noted for two of the four factors (see Table 5). Both Washington males and females were more highly motivated on the Success and Status/Excitement and Aesthetics factors. No significant differences were observed for the Personal Development/ Affiliation or Diversion factors.

Discussion

The cross-national findings from this study, using a large sample of secondary school adolescents, not necessarily interested in developing a high level of skill in one sport, supports the existing youth sports literature by confirming the improvement of skill levels as a high priority motive for participation in physical activity. Gill et al. (1983) have made the comment that program organizers should not lose sight of this objective. With

Table 5   Factor Intensity Mean Score Comparisons

| | Australia | | Washington | |
Factors	Females	Males	Females	Males
Excitement/success and status[a]	13.23	16.13	14.97	17.14
Personal development/affiliation	11.05	10.73	11.29	11.14
Diversion	5.74	5.73	5.82	5.86
Aesthetics[b]	1.81	1.27	1.98	1.62

[a]All between-group comparisons of differences between means were significant ($p < .01$). [b]Between-group mean differences were significant ($p < .01$) between males and females from both Australia and Washington, and between Washington and Australian males.

the compatible finding from this study, this comment can be reiterated. High-ranking variables for both Australian and Washington females were associated with the need for development of skills, fitness and health, and appearance; whereas for males, high-ranking variables were related to the need for success and status, and the experiences of excitement. Program organizers should also note these sex-based differences of expectations for physical activity.

Factor analyses from this study produced remarkably similar results for Australian and Washington samples. Three of the six categories identified by Passer were retained: Success and Status, Excitement, and Affiliation. This study combined Passer's classifications of Fitness and Skill Development into one dimension of Personal Development, and redefined Energy Release as Diversion to cater for a broader modification of state. The additional dimension of Aesthetics was identified. The classifications as defined in this study represent a further step in the process of understanding participation motivation. Some guidelines are provided for those interested in promoting ongoing participation in physical activity. Further research is needed to investigate the relationships between dimensions identified and actual levels of participation. Such research would provide clearer indications and directions for teachers and program organizers in structuring physical activity programs.

References

Alderman, R.B., & Wood, N.L. (1976). An analysis of incentive motivation in young Canadian athletes. *Canadian Journal of Applied Sports Sciences*, **1**, 169–175.

Gill, D.L., Gross, J.B., & Huddleston, S. (1983). Participation motivation in youth sports. *International Journal of Sport Psychology*, **14**, 1–14.

Gould, D., Feltz, D., Weiss, M., & Petlichkoff, L. (1981, June). *Participation motives in competitive youth swimmers*. Paper presented at the Fifth World Congress of Sport Psychology, Ottawa, Ontario.

Passer, M.W. (1982). Children in sport: Participation motives and psychological stress. *Quest, 33*(2), 231–244.

Watkin, B.C. (1977, August). *Measurement of motivation for participation in physical activity*. Paper presented at the International Symposium on Psychological Assessment in Sport, Israel.

Watkin, B.C., & Wright, M.F. (1985, July). *Why participate? Factors motivating for participation in physical activity of Australian youth*. Paper presented at the Sixth World Congress of Sport Psychology, Copenhagen.

An Analysis of the Inhibitors to Participation in Sport in Two Capitalist Countries

Patrick J. Duffy

Mass participation in sport is a phenomenon that is often assumed to exist in Western capitalist societies. Democracy in society has been linked to the democratization of sport (Sleap & Duffy, 1982), with the supposition that in a "free society" it is at least theoretically possible for everyone to have equal opportunities to participate. The European Sport for All Charter (1976) is an example of how this notion has become ingrained within the political thought on that continent, while popular writings in North America indicate that "everybody is doing it" (Pollock, 1983). In Ireland, a prolonged Sport for All campaign attests to the desire to achieve widespread participation in physical activity.

Despite obvious differences in the manner in which sport is organized cross-nationally, the establishment of reliable figures relating to participation is a difficulty experienced in all countries. Frequency and intensity of participation, nature of the activity, and the unreliability associated with using membership figures make the study of participation and nonparticipation particularly problematic. Numerous empirical studies, however, have pointed to a considerably lower level of participation than is often assumed (Robinson, 1969; Sillitoe, 1967; Sleap & Duffy, 1982). Work reported by Kirshenbaum and Sullivan (1983) and Thomas (1985) suggests that the publicity associated with the fitness boom is a weighty contributor to the conception that the major proportion of the population participates in sport. Given these difficulties and the need identified by Dickinson (1977) to investigate problems of nonparticipation, there is a clear need to establish patterns within and between countries. By so doing, it becomes possible to identify key influences on participation and the extent to which they are tied to the organizational structure of sport in a given country. Alternatively, common trends between countries may indicate that there are inherent elements of sport that result in occurrences that span national boundaries.

In an effort to identify situational inhibitors to participation in sport, this study attempted problem solving at the applied level, as identified by Gruneau (1978). It is clear, though, that a comparative study such as this also deals with the political and social implications of sport (Gruneau,

1978), ultimately leading to a consideration of the nature of sport and its place in capitalist society.

The current study chose two societies in which markedly different sports structures have evolved. The United States of America relies heavily on schools, colleges, and professional teams to promote involvement in sport. Commercial interests and concerns play a major role in the promotion of activities, reflecting the industrial and consumer basis of the society. Sport in American society has become both professionalized and commercialized. A particularly strong feature of the American sports structure is the organization of high-level sport through the college system.

By contrast, Ireland uses voluntary involvement of committed individuals to promote sport in the amateur tradition. Three of the country's most prominent activities—Gaelic football, hurling, and rugby—have resisted efforts to introduce high levels of remuneration for involvement. The predominant competitive structure is formed around clubs that primarily rely on voluntary effort. Hence, club officers, managers, coaches, and players make their services available free of charge. This high input of voluntary labor in Ireland has resulted in reduced priority being accorded to the promotion of sport and physical activity through "professional" channels. Hence, there are few professional teams, and highly paid coaches and physical educators are viewed as being nonessential within the second-level school system.

Despite these obvious differences, Irish sportsmen and -women bear a strong affinity toward American sports—manifested in the emigration of hopeful Irish athletes and the increasing coverage of American sporting events on Irish television. However, it was the intention of this study to focus on nonparticipants, not participants. This was done principally because of (a) the need for applied research at the micro level relating to why individuals do not become involved in sport; (b) the need to establish the extent to which inhibitors to participation in sport span international boundaries, thereby leading to (c) a determination of the nature of sport and its place within capitalist societies.

Methods

The results of two separate, yet similar, investigations were compared for the purposes of this study. The first, carried out in Ireland, was a study of a random sample of 561 nonparticipants in sport from 18 different towns and cities. The second, conducted in Springfield, Massachusetts, involved 117 interviews with residents of the city in their homes. Both studies attempted to draw the sample population from lower socioeconomic groupings, although this was not entirely successful (Duffy, 1986).

The Irish study concentrated on establishing the level of participation among the sample, as well as the factors affecting participation in sport. These factors were ranked on a priority basis from one to five.

The American study, which took place in 1983, 3 years after the Irish investigation, used a more structured schedule, in which respondents were asked to rate 13 inhibitors on a Likert-type scale of 1 to 7. Again, the participation rate among the sample was a focus of study, with a criterion for a regular participation level being set at once per week. Table 1 summarizes the main procedures used in each study.

Despite obvious differences between the studies, the general orientations of both research efforts were strikingly similar, because both were directed by the same researcher. Many features of the American study were a direct result of the experiences gained during the earlier series of interviews in Ireland. Both studies used face-to-face interviews, which yielded a high proportion of consenting subjects (in both cases, greater than 80% of those approached). It could be suggested, therefore, that a truer picture of participation patterns and inhibitors to participation was obtained in both cases than might have been attained through the use of, for example, a postal questionnaire. Indeed, in both cases, many subjects were encountered who may not have had the capacity to return such a questionnaire. The approach adopted, therefore, was regarded as most conducive to an applied level of research.

Results

Rates of participation in sport at a level of once per week were 10.9% (61 of 561 respondents) in Ireland and 12.8% (15 of 117 respondents) in the United States. The situational inhibitors to participation in sport were ranked by raw score and compared. The results are presented in Table 2.

Discussion

The strikingly low levels of participation in both samples appear to undermine the claims that sports involvement in both countries has reached

Table 1 Comparison of the Irish and American Studies

Study variable	Ireland	United States
Location	18 urban areas	5 areas within one city
Year	1980	1983
Number of subjects	556	117
Scale	Ranking 1–5	Rating 1–7
Identification of subjects	Random sample from place of residence	Random sample from place of residence
Number of interviewers	5	3
Study duration	3 months	2 months

Table 2   Comparative Ranking of Situational Inhibitors to Participation in Sport

Factor	Ireland		United States	
	Raw score	Rank	Raw score	Rank
Facilities unavailable	865	1	179	11
Lack of time (family commitment)	794	2	365	3
Lack of time (work commitment)	706	3	368	2
Not interested	649	4	375	1
Age	541	5	275	6
Friends do not participate	533	6	216	8
Too tired due to work	407	7	305	5
Never taught skills	375	8	216	8
Health	316	9	309	4
Cost	165	10	222	7
Competitiveness	80	11	214	10

Note.   Spearman rank order rho = .29.

high levels. Despite the stringent definition of a participant in this study, the results indicate that some measures used to monitor levels of participation need reexamination. Common assumptions relating to mass involvement in sport may owe their origins to the tendency of the sportsperson to mix within the network of sportspersons, weaving a web of acquaintances who have similar interests and orientations. Given that students and scholars of the sociology of sport are likely to be at least associated with such networks, it is reasonable to suggest that the question of nonparticipation is one that has been overlooked.

This, however, might be an overly simplistic and sympathetic view. In both Ireland and the United States, it appears that working class persons are more disinclined to participate than anything else. It might be suggested that sport, and perhaps the study of sport, fits neatly into a capitalist hegemony, as described by Gruneau (1983):

Hegemony is a concept developed out of the Italian Marxist theorist Antonio Gramsci. It reflects to all of those processes by means of which a dominant class extends its influence in such a way that "it can transform and refashion its way of life, its moves and conceptualisation, its very form and level of culture and civilisation in a direction which, while not directly paying immediate profit to the narrow interests of any particular class, favours the development and expansion of the dominant and social productive system of life as a whole." (p. 170) (Quote from Williams, 1957)

This hegemony has a clear influence on the ability of an individual to participate in sport. Traditionally, mainly due to Marxist thought, hegemony was largely perceived to be a function of class relations. The work of Edwards (1981), Hall (1985), and White and Brackenridge (1985) has served to associate the hegemonic relationship with the sphere of gender and race relations, also.

Relating to this, three of the first four inhibitors in both the Ireland and the United States studies are similar ("not interested"; "no time, due to work"; "no time due to family"). The salience of time as a factor here is particularly relevant and highlights the importance of "critical passages" (Sheehy, 1976) in analyzing participation patterns. Likewise, Witt and Goodale (1981) have indicated that different stages in the life cycle are associated with varying degrees of involvement in leisure activity outside the home.

Clearly, the notion of time is crucial, but it involves much more than the study of the number of hours in a day. Perceived lack of time relates directly to the perception of worth of the proposed activity, as well as to the ability of the individual to overcome barriers to involvement, given that sufficient interest exists. In many cases, however, this is patently not the case, with "not interested in sport" coming out first in the United States and fourth in Ireland. This lack of interest appears to relate to upbringing and social milieu (see Duffy, 1980), which in turn leads to a crucial knowledge of, and interest in, resources, as was neatly stated by Witt and Goodale (1981):

There seems to be some advantage in having knowledge of resources, knowing how to use resources, and having contact with people with whom to participate as a function of either training, job related opportunities. (p. 37)

This idea is interestingly related to the concept of "resourcefulness," developed by Rapoport and Rapoport (1975), which "means knowing and being able to make a meaningful life for oneself within the realities of one's existence as well as how to change these realities" (p. 26). It follows then, that given even a vague interest in sport, one's participation depends very much on this capability to order and change the "realities of one's own existence." Clearly, this ability is intricately bound to the social, educational, and economic background of the person, thus linking the important notion of market capacity (Giddens, 1973) to the propensity to participate. The implications of such a link in capitalist society conclusively lead to a stratification not only of the economic order but also of the sporting order.

The apparent lack of interest in sport found in this study is intriguing. In both the United States and Ireland, extensive coverage of sports events takes place in national and local media. Clearly, though, in both societies the perception of sport is not altogether favorable, and this may well relate to the competitive connotations associated with the word *sport*. Chaney (1978) has alluded to the desire of many Western European countries to move away from the use of *sport* as a term. Interestingly, Ireland has not followed suit, and *sport* is ever prominent in the promotion of physical activity in the United States. The studies of Thomas (1985), Ostrow, Jones, and Spiker (1981), and Duffy (1983) have clearly indicated that many sectors of the population are not attracted to the competitive male model of sport. The old, the unskilled, and the noncompetitive find it difficult to identify with the cut and thrust of winning and losing.

Two striking differences between the Irish and United States sample did emerge from the study. In Ireland, lack of facilities was perceived to be the most significant barrier to participation; whereas in the United States, it was the least important of the inhibitors. Levels of disposable income, stage of economic development, and access or mobility considerations seem to have an influence here. Average incomes in Ireland are considerably lower than in the United States, and the involvement of private enterprise in the provision of facilities boosts the range of options available in the United States. Bierstedt (1985) has suggested that improved economic conditions lead to higher levels of participation in Socialist countries. This may relate to the earlier discussion on resourcefulness and market capacity, but, equally, it seems that higher levels of provision associated with economic prosperity may be a factor.

Secondly, concern for health as a factor inhibiting participation was rated fourth in the United States but only ninth in Ireland. This may well be a reflection of the respective stages of development within each society. The urban United States is an automated, sedentary, and industrialized society. Ireland, on the other hand, is still a developing nation, with less automation and a greater reliance on more natural forms of calorie intake—with consequent implications for health.

Conclusions

To conclude, it has been noted that differences and similarities with respect to situational inhibitors to participation in sport were found between the United States and Ireland. Lack of time and family and work commitments were important inhibitors in both countries. Lack of interest in sport was also identified among the top four inhibitors in both countries. These inhibitors may relate to the lack of appeal of the competitive model of sport or to deeper influences within a capitalist hegemony.

Differences found in relation to facilities and health may well relate to the separate economic and social circumstances existing in both countries. These differences did not preclude, however, the finding that the democratization of sport in the two capitalist nations studied is far from complete. Given the nature of both sport and capitalism, it is unlikely to reach such an idealized state.

References

Bierstedt, H. (1985). The athletic activities of citizens of the G.D.R.: Some sociological aspects of their structure and social conditions. *International Review for the Sociology of Sport*, **20**, 39–53.

Chaney, K. (1978). A review of selected international "Fitness and health" and "Sport for All" campaigns. *Research Papers in Physical Education*, **3**(4), 22–29.

Dickinson, J. (1977). *A behavioural analysis of sport*. Princeton: Princeton Book.

Duffy, P.J. (1980). *Factors affecting active participation in sport by the working class*. Unpublished undergraduate dissertation, Thomond College, Limerick, Ireland.

Duffy, P.J. (1983). *Gender differences in situational inhibitors to participation in sport*. Unpublished master's thesis, Springfield College, Massachusetts.

Duffy, P.J. (1986). Inhibitors to participation in sport: Gender differences. Unpublished manuscript.

Edwards, H. (1981). Authority, power, and intergroup stratification by race and sex. In G. Luschen & G. Sage (Eds.), *Handbook of the Social Science of Sport*. Champaign, IL: Stipes.

European Sport for All Charter. (1976). Brussels: Council of Ministers.

Giddens, A. (1973). *The class structure of the advanced societies*. London: Hutchinson.

Gruneau, R.S. (1978). Conflicting standards and problems of personal action in the sociology of sport. *Quest*, **30**, 80–90.

Gruneau, R.S. (1983). *Class, sports, and social development*. Amherst: University of Massachusetts Press.

Hall, M.A. (1985). How should we theorise sport in a capitalist patriarchy? *International Review for the Sociology of Sport*, **20**, 109–115.

Kirshenbaum, J., & Sullivan, R. (1983, May). Hold on there, America. *Sports Illustrated*, pp. 60–75.

Ostrow, A.C., Jones, D.C., & Spiker, D.D. (1981). Age role expectations and sex role expectations for selected sport activities. *Research Quarterly for Exercise and Sport*, **52**, 216–227.

Pollock, C. (1983, March 20). America's love of sports: How strong the feeling. *New York Times*, p. 2.

Rapoport, R., & Rapoport, N. (1975). *Leisure and the family life cycle*. London: RKP.

Robinson, J.P. (1970). Daily participation in sport across twelve countries. In G. Luschen (Ed.), *The cross-cultural analysis of sport and games*. Champaign, IL: Stipes.

Sheehy, G. (1976). *Passages: Predictable crises of adult life.* New York: E.P. Dutton.

Sillitoe, K.K. (1969). *Planning for leisure.* London: Her Majesty's Stationary Office.

Sleap, M., & Duffy, P.J. (1982). Factors affecting active participation in sport by the working class. *International Review of Sport Sociology,* 17, 5–21.

Thomas, J. (1985). Why doesn't Mum go out to play? *Physical Education Review,* 6, 7–13.

White, A., & Brackenridge, C. (1985). Who rules sport? Gender divisions in the power structure of British sports organisations from 1960. *International Review for the Sociology of Sport,* 20, 95–109.

Williams, P. (1957). *Marxism and literature.* Oxford: Oxford University Press.

Witt, P.A., & Goodale, T.L. (1981). The relationship between barriers to leisure enjoyment and family stages. *Leisure Sciences,* 4, 29–49.

Sport, Fitness, and Recreation in the Japanese Workplace

Gordon L. Opel
Mark W. Clark

Two prominent influences upon American society during the 1980s have been the success of the Japanese in business and the increased awareness of the benefits of regular physical exercise. Every day, one encounters one of these two topics in the headlines. *Quality control circles* and *aerobics* have become part of the American lexicon. Moreover, there is a relationship between these two seemingly unrelated topics.

In a 1983 address to the Health Insurance Association of America on the role of physical fitness in the workplace, President Reagan said, ''We are all aware of the fitness programs in Japanese companies'' (Freudenheim, 1984, p. 29). Indeed, the popular press has frequently published photographs of Japanese workers lined up row upon row performing calisthenics. To some, this image has fostered an association of physical fitness with the high productivity capabilities of the Japanese work force and Japanese corporations' paternalistic attitude toward worker health and welfare (Lee & Schwendiman, 1982).

Despite this image that Westerners have of the Japanese performing calisthenics at work, the role of physical fitness and health promotion in the Japanese company is an enigma. Further, little is known about the availability and function of these programs in Japanese companies located in the United States, where American workers are employed. Thus, this study was developed as an investigation of the cultural orientation to, and relative extent of, physical fitness and health promotion programs provided by the Japanese companies both in the United States and Japan. Additionally, this study attempted to determine whether differences in these programs exist between American production sites and those in Japan. Lastly, an informal outcome would be the comparison between the Japanese and American orientation to fitness and health promotion in the workplace.

285

Methods

A self-assessment survey was developed and pilot-tested on local Japanese business personnel. Then, 62 Japanese companies with United States production sites were surveyed concerning the availability of fitness and health promotion programs here and abroad. Companies were randomly selected from the *Directory of Foreign Business in the United States* and the *Standard and Poor's Index*. A follow-up mailing was conducted. Of the 62 questionnaires mailed, 9 were considered undeliverable, and 12 were returned. This produced a 23% (12 of 53) rate of return. The low return may be attributed to the general reluctance of the Japanese to divulge company information to outsiders (DeMente, 1981). However, this return was deemed adequate, given the exploratory and descriptive nature of this study.

Fitness and Health Promotion in the Japanese Company

Despite a lack of a long-standing tradition toward fitness, sport, and health promotion in the workplace, Japanese business seems to be embracing this idea in a big way. In Japan, 95% of all large firms (5,000 or more employees) and 46% of all small firms (30-99 employees) offer sport and fitness facilities and programs to their employees (Yakabe, 1974). Many larger firms share facilities with smaller suppliers and trading partners. Eighty percent of the sport and fitness facilities in all of Japan are company owned and operated (Patrick, 1976). This same kind of involvement is currently displayed with health promotion, in which 96% of all large, and 52% of all small, companies offer preventive measures (Yakabe, 1974).

Although many Japanese fitness and health promotion programs in the workplace resemble those in operation in the United States, others have evolved with a unique Japanese flavor. For example, the Minolta Camera Company provides meditation rooms where workers can relax while trying to solve production problems (''Orchestrated efforts,'' 1984). Japan Air Lines offers its employees cultural courses in the arts, horticulture, and cooking that are aimed at helping workers relax as well as at improving communication between various job classifications. Honda of Japan provides natural dirt trails where workers can unwind while riding off-road motorcycles (Sakiya, 1982).

Employees in many Japanese organizations often participate in fitness and health promotion programs, knowing that this behavior is in the company's best interest. Therefore, participation in these programs tends to be extremely high without the use of supplemental incentives, which are frequently used in American programs. According to a National Poll on Sport conducted by the Prime Minister's Office (1976), 71% of employees who have access to sport and fitness facilities in their workplace participate. In many companies, like Osaka Gas, participation is mandatory. Osaka employees are expected to use the company facilities for 1 hour per day. This exercise period is provided to workers in addition to their regular meal breaks ("Osaka Gas," 1984).

Where exercise is not mandatory, Marsh and Mannari (1976) found that company facilities are principally used by unmarried male workers who aspire for promotion. By making use of these services, an employee expresses his appreciation to, and commitment toward, the firm for making these facilities and benefits available. This arrangement contrasts with many Western companies, where fitness facilities and health promotion programs are offered but may not be used, because the employees may feel little moral obligation to use what has been provided.

Still another explanation for the high use of programs and facilities in Japan is demonstrated at Sumitomo Metal, where employees' chances for promotion within the firm are dependent upon their physical condition. The motivation here is obvious.

Fitness and Health Promotion in the American Operations of Japanese Companies

Since the 1950s, the Japanese have developed United States–based production sites at which American workers are employed. By 1973 the Japanese had invested $152 million in the United States, with projected growth to $4.2 billion by 1980 (Sethi, Namiki, & Swanson, 1984).

Doing business in the United States has meant that for some enterprises, traditional Japanese business practices would have to be amended to accommodate a nonhomogenous and more individually oriented American labor force. Further, the reluctance of some companies to extend the full Japanese benefit system overseas is attributed to their belief that the paternalistic orientation is culturally unique and, therefore, may not be workable in the West. For example, Sony of America dropped a Japanese-style calisthenic program when it became apparent that employees did not wish to participate.

Of the Japanese companies responding to this survey, 63% are engaged in some type of manufacturing in which blue-collar workers are predominantly employed. In general, North American blue-collar workers do not regularly participate in physical training or activity. Studies indicate that the persons most likely to exercise tend to be younger, more highly educated, more affluent, and employed as professional or white-collar workers (Harris and Associates, 1979; Government of Canada, 1978). Despite these findings, Japanese companies are making a commitment to encourage production workers, as well as managers, to exercise. This is especially true of large manufacturing operations. Fifty percent of the firms responding indicated that they provide some means of physical exercise for their employees within the context of the company. This figure seems higher than what may be expected in a similar sample of American-owned companies. Facilities provided by companies ranged from a changing room and shower to a multimillion dollar fitness center.

The availability of company-sponsored fitness programs seems related to company size. The two largest organizations responding in this study provided the most extensive facilities and programming. It should be noted that the majority of Japanese companies in the United States employ less than 100 people (Sethi, Namiki, & Swanson, 1984). However, company size alone does not appear to predict these services. Sony and Sharp (both over 4,000 employees) do not provide their workers with any physical fitness programs or facilities. Unlike Japan, where smaller companies share facilities with their larger trading partners, there is no indication of such cooperation in the United States. This seems best attributed to the way companies are geographically dispersed and to their relative self-sufficiency.

The Fitness Company: A Profile

Two companies that best represent Japanese paternalism by offering extensive employee benefits are Honda of America and Nissan. By producing in the United States, Honda and Nissan avoid paying large tariffs on their products. Money made available from this savings and production efficiency is returned to workers. Both companies plan to construct the most extensive, state-of-the-art fitness facilities in North America. Company paternalism carries beyond fitness and health promotion at Honda, where workers receive benefits equaling 35–40% of their regular wages ("Quality is top priority," 1984).

Honda and Nissan encourage production workers to use company facilities by integrating the health or wellness concept into the organization's management philosophy. For example, the concept of wellness resembles the Japanese quality control circle concept, which is based on preventing—not merely detecting—defects (Schonberger, 1982). In this manner, fitness and health promotion are consistent with the rest of the company's values.

Another important ingredient that helps firms like Honda and Nissan incorporate physical fitness into the workplace is doing so only when the employees are ready for it. This has allowed workers to first gain trust in the organization and become familiar with company values. This orientation process is very indicative of Japanese management style.

Many American companies that provide fitness programs use incentives such as cash and additional free time to encourage employees to initiate or adhere to preventative health measures. None of the Japanese companies responding to this survey used incentives to encourage participation. Instead, companies like Nissan rely on changing values through education and behavior modification.

The Health Promotion Company: A Profile

It appears that smaller Japanese firms in the United States find more cost-effective health promotion measures to be better suited to their needs.

This correlates with Japan, where large firms spend more on health facilities and programs, whereas small firms pay more attention to preventative health and hygiene (Yakabe, 1974). Of the companies responding, 58% said they provide health promotion programs to their employees. Again, this figure seems higher than what might be expected from a similar sample of American businesses.

By far, the most popular health promotion measure is the physical exam, which is offered by 58% of the companies responding. In some of the American-based Japanese companies, exams were offered to all employees, whereas in others this service was offered only to management. This division between management and other employees in service regarding physical examinations is the only program cited that distinguishes between the two job classifications. This is considered unusual because the sharing of all facilities and programs between management and labor is a common characteristic of the Japanese management system. A speculative explanation for this division may be attributed to the high costs of these tests, especially as it concerns a smaller operation.

Although facilities and programs are commonly shared between management and labor, employee family members are generally not welcome to participate. Only 25% of the companies offering fitness and health promotion facilities and programs extend invitations to employee family members. Only in the largest firms is there an indication that family members of employees are welcome to use company facilities and programs. In these cases, companies are located in rural areas, and the worksites have become focal points for nonwork activities for employees. This use pattern is similar to what is often found in Japan, where company programs and facilities are frequently utilized by employee family members or retirees, especially during weekends or nonpeak hours.

Program Initiation

A common feature of Japanese management is a bottom-up communication system in which employee input is highly valued. Also, many decisions in the Japanese organization are made by consensus. However, when it comes to determining which fitness facilities and health promotion programs will be provided, 90% of the firms said these benefits are initiated at the request of management. Only at Honda of America is there evidence of strong employee input to program development. Using an employee advisory board to help determine programs, Honda offers a unique variety of employee services, which range from women's bodybuilding to a company-sponsored water ski club.

Program Expansion and Costs

Many Japanese companies in the United States have established their operations recently; these firms may also develop facilities and programs in the near future. However, citing financial limitations, a majority of respondents indicated that they had no plans for expansion.

Table 1 Comparisons of Major Company Fitness and Health Promotion Program Variables

Program variables	Japan[a]	Japan/American[b]	American[c]
Participation	Often mandatory	Voluntary	Voluntary
Gender use	Primarily male	Coed	Coed
Competing facilities outside the company	Few	Some in rural locations	Many
Popularity	Health promotion more popular than physical fitness	Health promotion more popular than physical fitness	Health promotion more popular than physical fitness
Use of individual incentives	Seldom	Seldom	Often
Family use of facilities	Generally open to employee family members, retirees, and, in some cases, the general public	Primarily for employees only; however, some larger firms are open to family members on weekends	Primarily for employees only
Influence of company size on availability	Related to company size; larger firms provide the most	Related to company size; larger firms provide the most	Related to company size; larger firms provide the most
Cost	None to employees	None to employees	Some cost sharing

[a]Review of available literature. [b]Results of this survey. [c]O'Donnell and Ainsworth (1984).

Although capital appears to be tight for these programs, especially in smaller Japanese firms operating in the United States, 90% of the companies that provide some type of fitness and health promotion program do so at no direct cost to the employee. This figure compares favorably with policy in Japan.

Summary

The purpose of this study was to examine and compare the cultural orientations to, and relative extent of, physical fitness and health promotion programs that are provided by the Japanese company, both in the United States and Japan. Further, an informal outcome was the comparison between the Japanese and American orientation to fitness and health promotion in the workplace (see Table 1).

The presence of extensive benefits such as fitness and health promotion programs in the Japanese company stems from its paternalistic management style. Whereas employee fitness programs in the United States companies are primarily intended for the improvement of physiological function, company programs in Japan have traditionally placed a special emphasis on improving human relations and as a means to refresh or warm up workers.

The paternalistic nature of Japanese management alone does not appear to predict the availability of employee fitness and health promotion programs in the United States. It does seem, however, that programs in Japanese companies based in the United States exceed those services provided by American companies. The size of the Japanese company in the United States appears to be an indicator as to whether programs might be offered. Cost-effective health promotion programs are more popular than physical fitness programs, especially to smaller firms.

References

DeMente, B. (1981). *The Japanese way of doing business*. Englewood Cliffs, NJ: Prentice-Hall.

Freudenheim, M. (1984, October 14). Millions spent in efforts to keep employees well. *New York Times*, p. 29.

Government of Canada. (1978). Canada's fitness. Ottawa, Ontario: Fitness Canada.

Harris, L., and Associates Inc. (1979). *The Perrier Study: Fitness in America*. Perrier-Great Waters of France.

Lee, S.M., & Schwendiman, G. (Eds.) (1982). *Management by Japanese systems*. New York: Praeger.

Marsh, R.M., & Mannari, H. (1976). *Modernization and the Japanese factory*. Princeton, NJ: Princeton University Press.

O'Donnell, M., & Ainsworth, T. (Eds.) (1984). *Health promotion in the work-place*. Salt Lake City: Wiley.

Orchestrated efforts worked out for company-wide fitness programs. (1984, July 17). *Japan Economic Journal*, p. 7.

Osaka Gas company pursues fitness with vigor. (1984). *Athletic Business*, 8(7), 70–72.

Patrick, H. (1976). *Japanese industrialization and its social consequences*. Berkeley: University of California Press.

Prime Minister's Office of Japan. (1976). *A national poll on sport*. Tokyo: Prime Minister's Office.

Quality is top priority at U.S. plants of Japanese automobile manufac-turers. (1984, January 17). *Japan Economic Journal*, p. 11.

Sakiya, T. (1982). *Honda motor: The men, the management, the machines*. Tokyo: Kodansha International.

Schonberger, R. (1982). Production workers bear major quality responsi-bility in Japanese industry. *Industrial Engineering*, **14**(12), 34–40.

Sethi, S., Namiki, N., & Swanson, C. (1984). *The false promise of the Japanese miracle*. Boston: Pitman.

Yakabe, K. (1974). *Labor relations in Japan*. Japan: International Society for Educational Information.